ADOLESCENT USE OF NEW MEDIA AND INTERNET TECHNOLOGIES

This book engages with contemporary, and often polarizing, debates surrounding the risks of adolescent use of digital media and internet technologies.

By drawing on multiple research studies, the text synthesizes current understandings of the impacts of social network use, online gaming, pornography, and phenomena, including cyberbullying, cyberstalking, and internet addiction, to develop recommendations for the effective identification of at-risk youth, as well as strategies for informed communication about online risks and opportunities. It shows how media discussion of risks to children and teenagers from new technology is highly emotive and often exaggerated, rooted in the "moral panic" surrounding new cultural practices that young people engage in, but which adults do not understand. Online risks are thus conceptualized as centering on three areas, specific to adolescence, which have undergone radical changes due to new internet technology. These include young people's identity, the types of content that are accessed, and social relationships. The author shows how these matters stem from the potential of new technology to establish new interpersonal connections, emphasizing how it brings opportunities, as much as risks. As such, he provides a uniquely balanced discussion of potential dangers, while also emphasizing the opportunities for social, academic, and personal growth which new technologies afford young people.

It will be indispensable for researchers and clinicians interested in assessing levels of online risk, as well as scholars and educators with interests in cyberpsychology, social psychology, cyber culture, social aspects of computing and media, and adolescent development.

Gordon P. D. Ingram is Associate Professor of Psychology at Universidad de los Andes, Colombia.

ADOLESCENT USE OF NEW MEDIA AND INTERNET TECHNOLOGIES

Debating Risks and Opportunities in the Digital Age

Gordon P. D. Ingram

Routledge
Taylor & Francis Group
NEW YORK AND LONDON

Designed cover image: © Getty Images

First published 2023
by Routledge
605 Third Avenue, New York, NY 10158

and by Routledge
4 Park Square, Milton Park, Abingdon, Oxon, OX14 4RN

Routledge is an imprint of the Taylor & Francis Group, an informa business

ISBN: 978-0-367-89482-5 (hbk)
ISBN: 978-1-032-43851-1 (pbk)
ISBN: 978-1-003-01945-9 (ebk)

DOI: 10.4324/9781003019459

Typeset in Bembo
by SPi Technologies India Pvt Ltd (Straive)

CONTENTS

ILLUSTRATIONS

Figures

Tables

ACKNOWLEDGMENTS

As far back as I can remember I have dreamed of writing a book. I therefore start this, my first one, by thanking my parents, Kathleen and Peter Ingram, for raising me in house and a childhood surrounded by books, for frequently reading to me and for helping me with my own early reading and writing. My love of books was rekindled by reading regularly to my own sons, Faolán and Comghall, when they were small. Although they have now almost finished being teenagers, I miss them dearly and thought of them all through writing this book, especially while we were unexpectedly separated for almost a year by the COVID-19 pandemic. On the subject of COVID-19, I would like to thank all the friends who reached out to me during that dark and difficult time, and who helped me stay sane off to finish the writing process. Most especially, I remember the anchor to reality formed by regular Zoom calls for film quizzes with Chand, Dave, Kath, Neil, and Philippa. I may have scored terribly, but I enjoyed those interactions thoroughly.

In terms of the actual writing, my thanks go to all the staff at Routledge who patiently stayed with me and guided me through the process, along with the three anonymous reviewers who helped me improve the original proposal. Special thanks go to Linda Kaye, Chris Ferguson, and Masa Popovac, who respectively read each of Chapters 2–4 and made incredibly insightful and useful comments on them; and to my former PhD supervisor, Jesse Bering, who incredibly read the whole thing.

Finishing by going back to a personal note, I would like to thank my wife, Alma De Castro, most of all for her patience, forbearance, and emotional support during a writing process that turned out to be much longer and more difficult than we had expected. Hopefully you can now see that it all *valió la pena*!

1

INTRODUCTION

"Moral Panics" and the Debates over Online Risks

1.1 Introduction: How Online Risks Are Portrayed in the Media

These days we are all exposed to a constant stream of news stories about the perils of new technology. From young men in Taiwan or South Korea who suffer heart attacks after playing video games for 24 hours straight, to a young woman in New Zealand murdered by a man she met on Tinder, to vulnerable adolescents in America or Russia who take their own lives as a result of cyberbullying or sinister online "challenges", to the voters in many different countries targeted by "fake news" stories on Facebook, it seems that almost anyone can be a victim and that online social networks are solely a force for evil. Yet how realistic is this picture? The odd thing is that when new internet technologies (especially the World Wide Web) were developed in the 1990s and early 2000s, they were accompanied by a wave of optimism about their potential to revolutionize communication, encourage collaboration, spread knowledge, and break down barriers between social groups. Is it really the case that all they have achieved is to withdraw individuals into their shells, increase competition and envy, indulge the ignorant, and reinforce boundaries between nations, social classes, and political ideologies?

In this book, I examine both sides of the argument, analyzing how we can classify the risks to young people that are associated with their online activities, how severe each kind of risk is, and how to mitigate them. I also look at the corresponding opportunities to young people of internet use, whether there is still potential for still-unseen benefits to arise, and why such benefits may be currently underemphasized. I focus on adolescents because they are a common target for fears about online risks, whether one is looking at addiction to new technology, exposure to extreme content, exploitation by unscrupulous adults

DOI: 10.4324/9781003019459-1

online, or the effects of conflict and bullying. And since young people tend to be more open to new social connections, they have arguably the most to gain from the benefits of internet use.

My argument centers on the premise that concerns about online risks represent a form of "moral panic". This term refers to the widespread fear of some new or unknown activity within a society, a fear that nowadays is often stoked by sensational media reports and influence-seeking politicians. The oldest examples of moral panics include the persecution of heretics or religious minorities, such as Christians in the early Roman Empire, and witch hunts like the Salem Witch Trials. Much more recently, in the 1980s, youth culture activities such as Dungeons & Dragons, rap and heavy metal music, and "video nasties" were all targets of moral panics, before attention turned to the internet in the following decade. Common denominators are that the targeted activity is obscure or mysterious to "mainstream" adults, who fear that it could end up "corrupting" the youth of their society in some way. Unlike some other authors, however, I do not raise the idea of "moral panic" in order simply to dismiss worries about new technology as spurious concerns. Rather, in the current chapter I seek to explain what causes moral panics, why they are associated with some activities more than others, and why they tend to focus on young people in particular. I will show that some concerns about risks may be partly legitimate, in that moral panics are associated with cultural change, which can be problematic for certain groups, activities, and individuals.

A huge range of online activities have become targets of recent internet-related moral panics. One way of classifying them is to analyze whether they directly involve a malevolent third party, or entail purely internal risks for the victims. In the former category may be included, among other things, the sexual "grooming" of minors by adults who solicit personal details, explicit material or a real-life meeting; risks associated with breaches of cybersecurity, such as identity theft, hacking or "phishing"; and the radicalization of youngsters in online communities such as those linked to Islamic terrorism or far-right nationalism. In the latter category are concerns about addiction to video games or other online activities, including worries about "screen time": the idea that kids are spending too much time staring at tablets, smartphones, and other devices, and hence may end up with problems including obesity, sleep disorders, social deficits, academic underachievement, depression, or loneliness. To this category could be added concerns about specific risks of extreme content for young people, for example the idea that violent video games encourage violent behavior, or that viewing online pornography from an early age could lead to higher rates of sexual assault. Another worry centers on the negative effects of cyberbullying, especially in terms of susceptibility to suicide. Nor is bullying the only online activity perceived to cause suicide or self-harm: specialized online communities and fora have been accused of actively promoting eating disorders, self-cutting, and suicide. In the most extreme examples, classic moral panics have arisen around the (largely uncorroborated) encouragement of suicide by online "challenge" games, such as the "Blue Whale game" or the "Momo challenge".

In the next section I offer an explanation for why moral panics are particularly associated with young people and new technology. The moral panic around the "Blue Whale" suicide game is a good case study for this purpose. According to the urban legend of the Blue Whale, a player starts by being sent several anonymous, but innocuous, messages asking them to perform certain challenges. They are instructed to complete one challenge a day for 40 days in order to "win" the game. These challenges, however, gradually get more extreme and dangerous, culminating in the last few days with severe self-harm and, finally, suicide. The Blue Whale has several interesting properties that help explain why it sparked a moral panic and attracted attention from media organizations. First, it targeted young people, taking the form of a game – a cultural activity especially attractive to youngsters, with the "Blue Whale" moniker recalling children's fondness of animals. Second, it involved new technology, being distributed over a messaging system by anonymous authors whose identity could not be established. And third, young people were supposedly surrendering their agency to follow this game, losing their will to the point of taking their own lives for no reason. In the next section I explain why all three elements are important for understanding the power of moral panics in public discourse.

1.2 Why Moral Panics Tend to Focus on Young People and New Aspects of Culture

The concept of moral panics is almost 50 years old and has been subject to a vast amount of theoretical debate, mainly in sociology. The term was introduced by Cohen (1972) in his famous study of Mods and Rockers on the south coast of England. Cohen argued that while some violence certainly did break out at the time between the young people who belonged to these two rival British subcultures, it differed little from the sort of alcohol-fueled high jinks that were (and are) seen after closing time at weekends in towns up and down the country in the years before and since. What was different was the media's framing of these rough and rowdy ways as something new: an epochal conflict driven by two groups of demonized youths (the "folk devils" of the book's title). Cohen observed that media reports of disorderly incidents tended to follow set tropes, molding the facts to an idealized picture of how the conflict was assumed to work. They usually exaggerated the violence, emphasized the different cultural labels of each group (particularly the use of motorbikes by Rockers and scooters by Mods) and the opposition between them, and editorialized the need for "something to be done" about the situation. In Cohen's words, a moral panic occurs when "a condition, episode, person or group of persons emerges to become a threat to societal values and interests; its nature is presented in a stylised and stereotypical fashion by the mass media" (Cohen, 1972).

The term "moral panic" caught on almost immediately (as Garland, 2008, pointed out much later, it has such a ring to it that if Cohen hadn't invented it, someone else probably would have soon afterward). Sociologists quickly realized that it could be applied to a great number of other situations of the same type. In the decades since, they have described "moral panics" that centered on phenomena as diverse as AIDS, child abuse, drugs, immigration, media violence, street crime, and youth deviance (Critcher, 2008). What do all these things, and the responses to them, have in common? In an influential analysis, Goode and Ben-Yehuda (1994/2010) argued that moral panics tend to be marked by five separate characteristics. First, they cause concern (but not necessarily uncontrolled panic as such) in many people who hear about the social problem to which the panic relates, regardless of whether the problem is real, exaggerated or wholly invented. Second, they are marked by hostility toward a group of people believed to be responsible for the social problem that has triggered the panic (the "folk devils" of Cohen's book). Third, there is consensus across a large section (though not necessarily the majority) of society that the problem is real and something needs to be done to address it. Fourth, whether or not the problem is real, there is a level of concern about it in society that is disproportionate to the actual scale of the problem: the risks are exaggerated by those who believe in them, and the resources put into fighting the problem – or at least, the media attention it receives – are much greater than those received by certain other problems that are objectively more of a threat (e.g., road accidents, which rarely seem to cause panic in any society). And finally, moral panics are volatile: they have much in common with fads or fashions, since they may blow over as suddenly as they appeared, and the social movements dedicated to fighting them may sink into obscurity just as quickly.

We can see from this list of characteristics that the sociological perspective of Goode and Ben-Yehuda is more concerned with general characteristics of moral panic as a shared reaction within a society than with the reasons why particular behaviors are selected as targets of specific panics. In their own words,

> … the behavior that ignites [moral panics] can be "about" almost anyone and anything … moral panics are not "about" specific activities – real or imagined – or social categories so much as they are "about" the fear and concern about, and the perceived threat from, those activities and categories.
>
> *(2010, p. 17)*

While accepting that moral panics can arise in response to a vast range of social phenomena, in this book I want to dig a little deeper and try to explain why they are so often associated with certain kinds of activities and categories: specifically, those having to do with new technologies (or new cultural practices in general) and with young people. To explain these tendencies, I will use a relatively new theory, known as cultural group selection, that arose within the evolutionary study of human behavior.

The basic idea of cultural group selection is that environmental pressures on human evolution are almost completely mediated by accumulations of cultural knowledge that are passed on within societies (Henrich, 2015). Humans are thus adapted primarily to learn from the other humans around them and respond to the actions and concerns of their social groups, creating a "conformity bias" that can also contribute to ethnic differentiation between groups. This is particularly important given that competition with other groups has probably been one of the primary selective pressures – for example, through war and other forms of intergroup conflict – throughout much of human history and prehistory (Alexander, 1987).

Conformity bias may be due to simple cultural learning (we are biased to learn practices that are socially accepted, as well as ones that are objectively useful, since the former is an easier heuristic to deploy and, over time, useful practices will tend to survive disproportionately within the group) and to processes of intergroup competition. Henrich (2015) identified three such processes: groups may be overwhelmed demographically (if another group's cultural strategies allow them to either out-survive or out-reproduce the first group), defeated by direct competition (whether by war or by plundering resources), or converted by preferential spread of another group's cultural practices that are seen as more prestigious (whether by immigration into the group or by prestige-biased diffusion of their practices). In all of these types of intergroup competition, the importance of not ending up on the "losing" side is clear.

It is this final type of intergroup competition, what Henrich calls "prestige-biased group transmission", that is most important for my argument. He argues that, "Because of our cultural learning abilities, individuals will be inclined to preferentially attend to and learn from individuals in more successful groups, including those with social norms that lead to greater economic success or better health" (2015, p. 168). This creates a problem for other, relatively successful individuals in the less successful group, who are well accustomed to other social norms and cultural practices. In effect, we can see here the evolutionary origins of social conservatism: if people are adapted to learn new cultural practices when they are young, they should also be adapted to try to conserve those cultural practices when they are older, aiming to preserve a social environment in which their particular skills, habits, and preferences (which they tend to pass on to their children and other younger members of their community) will flourish. These conservative attitudes could potentially generate support for moral panics in relation to new social norms or cultural practices, for example, those surrounding new technologies. But how often do moral panics center on such norms and practices?

Returning to Critcher's (2008) list of the seven main areas of moral panics in recent years (AIDS, child abuse, drugs, immigration, media violence, street crime, and youth deviance), three of them relate directly to novel cultural practices. The various drug panics of the 1960s–1990s did not center on the traditionally accepted recreational "drugs" within Western society – alcohol, caffeine, nicotine, and sugar – but on unfamiliar chemical substances, like cocaine, ecstasy, heroin, and LSD, that had originated either in scientific laboratories or in other parts of the world. Immigrants, too, are frightening largely because they bring unfamiliar cultural practices with them: many of the concerns that natives of a host country express about immigration center on the idea that their own way of life may be replaced or "overwhelmed" by that of the immigrants. And the moral panics around media violence (clearly, the most connected to the themes of this book) often focus on the fear that new forms of media may encourage people to behave in new and disturbing ways.

Three of the other areas relate more tangentially to new cultural practices. The panic about AIDS (while similar in some respects to non-moral panics about diseases such as SARS, swine flu, and COVID-19) drew much of its strength from the idea that previously suppressed homosexual practices had become more accepted. Panics about street crime and youth deviance relate to generalized concerns about a breakdown in law and order, and an informal social control that supposedly led to more conformity and "community spirit" in local neighborhoods in the past, thus arguably reflecting more fears about the loss of "old" cultural practices than about the adoption of "new" ones. Perhaps the only broad type of moral panic that has little to do with the replacement of old practices by new ones is that which centers on child abuse, since unfortunately such abuse is, probably, as old as the institution of the family itself.

This cultural group selectionist account of moral panics explains well why they tend to focus on young people, since this group is more open to new cultural ideas (due to the very evolutionary instincts that promote cultural learning) and thus more vulnerable to "conversion" to a prestigious set of ideas from outside the group. Indeed, panics about child abuse, media violence, and youth deviance all center very explicitly on children and young people: in the former two cases as passive victims, in the latter case as "folk demons" who are held responsible for causing the panic. In the cases of AIDS, drugs, and street crime, the association seems more implicit, but it is there all the same: few people are concerned about pensioners mugging people at knifepoint, getting off their heads on E and meth at illegal raves, or contracting AIDS through unprotected anal sex or unsanitized needles.

Only with moral panics about immigration does concern about young people seem rather peripheral. Perhaps this is because, from the perspective of cultural group selection, concern about immigration may more reflect a fear of being directly replaced by another population, rather than of one's way of life disappearing because other lifestyles are seen as more prestigious by young people. In fact, however, the two fears are often connected, and fears about immigration frequently merge with other moral panics, dating back to 19th- and early 20th-century concerns about Chinese opium dens and abductions of young women.

Immigrants are easily vilified as "bad influences" who encourage deviance and delinquency in white youth, as street criminals or drug-dealers, as spreaders of disease (as in the COVID-19 pandemic), and even as child abusers. Perhaps even media violence can be related to immigration, if one includes fears about the "radicalization" of young white Europeans or North Americans by immigrant preachers who sympathize with Islamic terrorism, since such radicalization has been linked to closed, politicized online communities.

If concerns about both young people and new cultural practices (including new technologies) are a common, though not a necessary, part of moral panics, the question remains of whether the two tend to be linked together in a way that cultural group selectionists would predict. The "original" moral panic identified by Cohen – the mid-1960s conflict between Mods and Rockers on the south coast of England – provides a nice case study of this linkage.[1] These two rival subcultures were marked by subtly different sets of cultural practices (both novel, though one slightly more so) which they used like badges of identity. The Mods listened to very new British bands like The Beatles, The Kinks, and The Who; wore more colorful, "smarter" clothes inspired by the stylings of continental European countries like France and Italy; and rode motor scooters that were also usually Italian.[2] The Rockers preferred 1950s American rock'n'roll (particularly Elvis Presley, Eddie Cochran, and Gene Vincent); dressed mainly in denim and leather that harked back to James Dean films and the American biker culture of the same decade (still relatively new and alien to older Britons at this time); and rode motorbikes, usually British ones. The Rockers were often seen as scruffier and more working-class than the Mods, though both subcultures transcended social class to some extent.

Since Cohen's original analysis of the moral panic that the two subcultures' conflict caused, many sociologists and social commentators have reanalyzed what happened, often centering their analyses – following Cohen – on the "demonization" of the young people involved. Surprisingly, less attention seems to have been paid to the importance of new technologies in constructing these labels, both from the point of view of the young people looking for badges of identity and from that of older folks who saw them as a new threat. For example, the Mods' and Rockers' expression of rival identities through music was clearly due to the widespread availability of automatic record players and vinyl LPs, which were cheaper and more portable than gramophones and shellac discs, and had a very different sound (including stereo, applied to mass-released music only from 1957) that was unfamiliar to older generations. Even more important was the identification of each group with either scooters or motorcycles, which was frequently emphasized in contemporary media accounts. Like vinyl LPs, the Lambretta and Vespa scooters of the Mods (and, to a lesser extent, the Norton and Triumph bikes of the Rockers) were newly available and newly affordable. They allowed young people more mobility, permitting them not only to go on impromptu excursions to the beach on holiday weekends (two for the price of one) but also to quickly evade capture by police or attacks by rival gang members. Thus we can see how the combination of youth culture and new technology must have contributed to a moral panic in this case: what frightened older generations was the newfound freedom of younger people to travel far from parental control, and form new associations with novel cultural rules.

An aspect of the Mods and Rockers moral panic emphasized by Cohen was of course the folk-demonization of these new associations. But are such "folk devils" a necessary element of moral panics? Cohen certainly thought so, and subsequent commentators such as Goode and Ben-Yehuda have largely agreed with him. However, many psychologists today have turned away from the idea that social phenomena can be defined by necessary and sufficient conditions, preferring prototype-based accounts in which phenomena are commonly associated with certain typical features, but do not have to possess all of them. According to this type of account, some types of moral panic could be "prototypical" and involve all of the five features identified by Goode and Ben-Yehuda (including folk demons), while others lack one or more of them. It is my contention in this book that moral panics about new technology often lack folk demons (although tech billionaires such as Mark Zuckerberg, Jeff Bezos, and Elon Musk may take on something of that role). It is unclear why this would be: perhaps new technology is seen as sufficiently complex to be something of a demon itself; or perhaps it is seen as somehow taking away agency from its users – something that was already hinted at in the 1980s, in panics over media violence and drug use. These ideas will be further explored in the next section, which looks at how psychologists and other academics have deployed the concept of "moral panic" in relation to new technology use.

1.3 The Scientific Response to Moral Panics about New Technologies

Before looking specifically at moral panics about new technology, it is worth spending a little time considering the sociological debate over what causes moral panics. There have been three main types of theories about how moral panics are generated (Goode & Ben-Yehuda, 2010, ch. 3). The grassroots model sees concern about the target of the panic as welling up from ordinary people, to then be exploited (or, more positively, addressed) by political elites. The elite-engineered model, in contrast, posits that members of these elites themselves deliberately generate panics, in order to jostle for power, increase social control once they have gained power, or distract from criticism once their power has begun to wane. Finally, the interest-group model combines elements of the other two and is arguably the most sophisticated. It argues that since modern society is made up of diverse groups with widely varying interests, only some of these groups will be particularly concerned about a given moral panic. One or more mid-level interest groups that represent certain sections of society (e.g., trade unions, chambers of commerce, industry lobby groups, charitable foundations, activist groups, churches, academic associations, medical trusts, the police, the judiciary, and so on) will fuel a moral panic out of genuine concern, but also with the intentional side effect of gaining advantages in political debate for the social grouping that they represent. Seeking a policy response to the panic, they will thus tend to exert political pressure both upward, on members of the elites, and downward, seeking to recruit electoral, financial, and mass-protest support from the grassroots by fueling the panic.

The interest-groups model is the theory of moral panic origins that has most in common with the cultural group selectionist approach that I outlined above. Interest groups are constantly competing within a given society to spread "their" ideas about what a society should be, in terms of the social norms and cultural practices that they think the society ought to value. The cultural group selectionist approach is also quite compatible with the grassroots model, however, if one focuses on the majority and ignores the fact that not everyone in a society follows the same cultural practices or has the same social interests. On the other hand, cultural group selectionists would predict that elite-engineered moral panics will only succeed when they tap into grassroots' or interest groups' deeper fears about the direction a society is going in.

In the rest of this section, I will cite a few examples of how academics have deployed the term "moral panic" in four recent debates about new technology: those centering on violent video games, internet gaming addiction, online pornography, and "screen time". I will argue that the dominant scientific reactions to these panics are based on a misguided rejection of moral panics as "irrational", and that a cultural group selectionist approach can help provide a much more nuanced understanding of why the moral panic has taken hold. In each case, the role of diminished agency is very important in understanding why the target activity of the panic is seen as dangerous to young people. I conclude with some reflections on why the idea of diminished agency may be so powerful and attractive, and what we can do to counteract it.

The debate about the effects of violent video games has been long and acrimonious, drawing as it does on earlier moral panics about violent comics, films, and TV cartoons, and dividing researchers largely into two rival camps, arguing for and against an effect of violent video games on violent behavior such as school shootings. Two prominent figures who have argued that there is no such effect are Patrick Markey and Chris Ferguson, who have published numerous articles (separately and together) as well as a joint-authored book (2017) expressing skepticism about the link. In one chapter of the book, the authors define the term "moral panic" and explain the typical circumstances in which they tend to arise. They draw much the same links with youth culture and new technology that I set out earlier in this chapter:

> Very often when a new form of media or technology is released, society goes through a period of overblown fear in which this media or technology is blamed for any number of social ills, whether real or merely

> perceived. These panics can be explained in large part by generation gaps in adopting new technology or media. The young are far more proficient at adapting to innovation than are the old. This can create a perception among older adults that they are losing control of the culture they helped shape—which, of course, they inevitably will—to the very youth they fear and view as morally bankrupt.
>
> *(Markey & Ferguson, 2017, p. 101)*

They also mention the fear that "good kids" are being "brainwashed" by new technology, referencing Ivory and Kalyanaraman's (2009) point that external cultural factors such as violent video games are called into play to explain why middle-class white kids such as the Columbine killers carry out mass shootings, but not to explain why less well-off young people from ethnic minorities perpetrate the same crimes. Up to that point their analysis thus shares many things in common with my own. However, even a cursory reader of the book reveals that the authors are very dismissive – often hyperbolically so – of any research that has purported to show links between game-playing and aggression, referring to all such work several times in terms such as "junk science" or "pseudoscientific muck", even when it has appeared in prestigious peer-reviewed journals. Detractors of a link between video games and violence have a tendency to see themselves as some kind of myth-busters bravely swimming against the tide of public opinion. In one revealingly purple passage of prose, the authors describe "younger pro-game researchers" (and, by implication, themselves) as engaged in "an epic struggle for truth as they attempt to challenge the much more powerful anti-video game empire" Markey & Ferguson (2017, p. 110). This is inevitably associated with a view of the older "anti-game" researchers as motivated by irrational fears, or a cynical desire for prestige and even funding, rather than accepting that they may have a rational basis for worrying about the risks posed by new technologies – or that the idea of "brainwashed" kids may tap into more emotional concerns about recent cultural changes. The closest that Markey and Ferguson come to accepting that moral panics can sometimes be at least partially rational is in their oldest historical example, when they mention 15th-century Catholics' fears that the new technology of the printing press could encourage misinterpretations of scripture, and point out that this fear was not unfounded, given that the printing of thousands of copies of the Bible in Europeans' everyday languages must have contributed to the Protestant Reformation less than a century late.

In the last few years, concerns raised about video game addiction, or internet or smartphone addiction more generally, have become another target for "pro-game" researchers who allege a moral panic. The most recent trigger for this reaction has been the inclusion of "gaming disorder" in the *International Classification of Diseases* (*ICD-11*) of the World Health Organization (WHO),[3] and the proposal to include it in the next version of the *Diagnostic and Statistical*

Manual of Mental Disorders (*DSM-5*) of the American Psychiatric Association (APA).[4] Among other comments, critics pointed to doubts over whether it's appropriate to use models from substance abuse to theorize behavioral disorders; to a lack of clarity over why video games (especially online ones) were being singled out over more traditional games as a target of this diagnosis; and to questions over the length of time that someone needed to show excessive interest in a game for them to be considered to have a disorder. Again, the notion of "moral panic" was explicitly invoked by some authors in questioning the motivations behind gaming disorder's inclusion. Bean et al. (2017), for instance, expressed cynicism about these motives, arguing that "Moral repugnance toward an issue, particularly by older adults, can incentivize scientific (or pseudoscientific) agendas, using the veneer of the scientific process as cover for moral or political causes" (p. 7). They cited personal communications with two WHO officials, who "reported receiving 'enormous pressure' to include video gaming as an addiction disorder particularly from Asian countries". Again, this assumption that moral panics are primarily motivated by "political pressure" and media storms contradicts the grassroots and interest group theories of moral panics, which see them more as grounded in everyday concerns about new technologies or cultural practices – particularly a loss of agency and productivity in young people who become "addicted" to games.

Influenced by accusations of moral panics over video game violence and addiction, researchers have recently begun alleging a moral panic over one of the newest technological bugbears: screen time. Over the last 20 years numerous studies purported to show links between total time spent online (especially by children and adolescents) and various mental health outcomes, notably depression and anxiety. However, later, larger-scale studies have often failed to find such effects, increasing the possibility that the original findings were false positives. Rather than accepting that the ideas guiding the earlier studies were theoretically plausible but mistaken – and acknowledging that the potential gravity of the situation made it worthwhile to test the hypothesis of a link between internet use and mental health – the skeptics have started to argue that perhaps this whole wave of research was driven by a moral panic that had gripped the wider society. Coyne et al. (authors of an excellent longitudinal study on adolescents' social media use and susceptibility to depression) put this question in their introduction: "are we engaged in a moral panic, perhaps not understanding the root of the problem [of the rise in young people's mental health issues]?" (2020, p. 1).

In the next chapter, I will return to the theme of how this and other studies have shown that total time spent in front of screens is too broad a target for a possible link with mental health. For now, what I want to emphasize is that this deployment of the term "moral panic" frames reaction to social change as an essentially irrational phenomenon that incentivizes researchers to go down empirical dead ends. What is missing is any recognition that the intuition many parents and educators have – that completely unregulated (whether by adult or child) screen time might be bad for children's cognitive development or teenagers' mental health – might still be valid, even if at present, the aggregate data available have not been shown to support it. Also missing, even assuming that this intuition is wrong, is any theoretical consideration of why it is so plausible to so many people, and why they are so worried about the younger generation losing their agency in being reduced to screen-goggling "zombies"; a consideration that is important if we want to replace this idea in lay minds with beliefs that (perhaps) have better empirical support.

* * *

To sum up the theoretical argument in this introductory chapter, I want to emphasize two things. First, reactions to the supposed threats posed by violent video games, internet gaming addiction, and screen time all fit the pattern of classic moral panics with one important caveat, which I will reiterate shortly. Second, the epithet "moral panic" has been attached by researchers to the reactions to these phenomena as a way of dismissing the possibility of any threat. This, I argue, is patronizing and counterproductive, in that it is unlikely to win over many people who feel intuitively that these phenomena are a threat. The point of this book is to try to find a middle way that will treat people's concerns as reasonable and emphasize that there is much that we still don't know, while also reassuring them that the threat may not be as great as they have thought, and opening up directions for future research that can help address their concerns more adequately in the future.

It is important to recognize that concerns about the three social phenomena described in this chapter do all fit the bill of moral panics. In addition to the properties highlighted by Littlewood (2003) – the presentation of the problem by the media in a highly stereotypical way, as a threat to social values, and the subsequent jumping by political and religious figures onto the bandwagon of concern – all three focus on something that would be of genuine social concern if it were a real danger, but about which worry seems to have been exaggerated well beyond what the evidence shows. One thing is different from the classic moral panic as described by Cohen, however, and that is the absence of "folk devils". However, if we accept the prototype-theory view of how concepts work, this need not affect our categorization of the reactions as moral panics. It is impossible to be sure why moral panics about new technology do not invoke folk devils, but one possibility is that new technology is sufficiently complex to be viewed intuitively as having a kind of agency (as seen, for example, when we swear at our computer if it takes too long to do a simple task) and thus itself plays the role of a folk devil. Importantly, the folk devil of new technology can be seen as implicitly taking away the agency of its young users, who are turned into hypo-aware "zombies" (in the screen time panic) or addicts (in the gaming addiction panic), at risk of mindlessly imitating the behavior that they see online (in the violent video game panic). This supposed loss of agency harks back to the cultural conservatism that lies behind many moral panics, and that may well be programmed into us by cultural group selection: children, adolescents, and young adults are not seen as having much choice in cleaving to new cultural forms, because if choice were accepted to be key it might become all too clear that their parents' culture is much less attractive than it was, and is being *voluntarily* rejected by young people wholesale; and, thus, might need to be radically changed in order to keep them adhering to it.

The focus of recent technology-related moral panics on the loss of agency by (mainly) young people helps explain, then, why the panics have occurred with these targets at this moment in time. As Jock Young (2011) has argued, explaining the fears that drive moral panics, and why they break out with specific targets in particular times and places, is critical if we are to avoid the "tendency in these neo-liberal times to view moral panics as simple mistakes in rationality generated perhaps by the mass media or rumour" (ibid., p. 245). Moral panics may not be rational, but nor is it realistic to assume that they are always (or even often) generated by media or political elites, in an attempt to dupe or distract an unsuspecting populace. As we have seen, the "interest group" and "grassroots" theories of moral panic do a better job of explaining why a particular panic takes hold in the population by appealing to real fears that people have: in the case of technological panics, their fear of rapid cultural change and loss of agency caused by new technological developments. Assuming that it is irrational to fear unrestricted internet use because there is no empirical evidence for harm also underestimates the important role that "discipline" – in this case, learning to restrict leisure time online in order to engage in more "productive" pursuits – has in marking middle-class distinction and privilege (ibid., p. 250). As Young puts it, "the targets of moral panics are not arbitrary and the passions they stir up understandable once seen in the wider context. There would be no panic if there wasn't something to panic about", which he locates in "the realm of excitement and spontaneity, of short-term hedonism and abandonment, of violent masculinity and daring" (ibid., p. 253). One of the three moral panics discussed in this chapter – the violent video games panic – clearly reflects fears about that realm, while the other two – centering on addiction and screen time – may be less graphic, but still allude to a fear of hedonistic unproductivity. This book is founded on the idea that the answer to such fears is not simply to dismiss them because of a lack of evidence for risks, but also to emphasize the opportunities that new technology carries for productivity and personal growth in young people.

1.4 Outline of the Argument

The three core chapters of this book are structured around three broad types of risk: those having to do with changes in young people's sense of identity; with their interest in new types of content; and with their formation of new social links and interactions. Each chapter will use the angle of identity, content, or interactions to consider the same three themes: changes (both developmental and historical) in adolescents' connections to people or content online; the new risks that these changes bring up; and examples of the opportunities that they also raise. Here I first explain these three themes before considering how they are tackled in the individual chapters.

1.4.1 Theme 1 – Connections

The changing nature of preadolescents' social networks is reflected in changing patterns of technology use, with a gradual shift away from solo game-playing and toward new interpersonal connections. Preadolescents (aged approximately 10–12 years) live in groups that are more gender-segregated than any other age, and this theme will therefore trace the differing paths that tend to be followed by girls and boys in their online activities as they pass into and through the teenage years, while acknowledging that many boys are also concerned with visual self-expression, and many girls also play video games. An important change in adolescence is that teenagers tend to show more interest in romantic partners as they get older, and, in the case of heterosexual people at least, to spend more time with the other sex. The way that new romantic relationships play out online will thus also be explored in this theme.

1.4.2 Theme 2 – Risks

In this theme, I will emphasize that young people do face real risks online, which increase as they go through adolescence, at the same time as their reporting of their own activities to adults decreases. I will outline the distribution of and cultural differences between three categories of risks (addiction, cyberbullying, and sexual material). I will also discuss my own work on age-related changes in the reporting of these risks by young people themselves, which is important because it helps us understand why adults can become so worried about their children's activities online.

1.4.3 Theme 3 – Opportunities

The final theme in each chapter will show how as well as creating risks, the internet also offers many opportunities for young people today, which augment the natural tendency of adolescents to form new social networks and develop their own sense of identity in the world. This is the case even in areas where people worry a lot about risks, such as depression and other mental health problems, academic achievement, and political discussions.

Chapter 2, New Identities: Visual Communication, Screen Time, and Adolescent Wellbeing, will focus on how the forging of a new personal identity during adolescence plays out online, and the difficulties that adults (especially parents) have in understanding changes in children's identities. It will start by looking at how teenagers express themselves visually using social media such as Instagram and Snapchat. Topics include changes in self-concept and self-esteem in adolescence, gender differences in online identity, the effects of Instagram use on body image, and the use of emoji and memes to form "private codes" for self-expression of identity within age-based peer groups, which adults can find hard to understand. Next, a major risk often cited by parents will be examined, namely the problem of "screen time": how much is too much? This is relevant to the topic of identity because parents often feel like the internet has taken their child away from them, as he/she may prefer to spend time there with friends rather than with families. I will show that panic about widespread smartphone addiction is overblown, since screen time is not related with adolescents' wellbeing across the general population. Nevertheless, I will also argue that in extreme cases internet addiction is a real thing and can cause people real problems. It is not the total time spent online that matters so much as the nature of the activities carried out online, and whether young people have opportunities for rewarding activities offline. In this context, social networking software and smartphones offer potential for clinicians to reach out to people at risk of mental health problems like depression and loneliness (both of which may be linked to changes in social identity during adolescence).

Chapter 3, New Content: Social Gaming, Explicit Material, and Knowledge Sharing, looks at risks associated with new types of content that young people become interested in during preadolescence and adolescence. Boys, in particular, begin to use online games as a kind of social networking software, often preferring them to venues like Facebook or Instagram. This initial part of the chapter draws on my own ethnographic and experimental studies of play in various games, especially *League of Legends*, as well as the gaming video-streaming platform Twitch. Topics include gender differences in gaming (and how these have diminished over time), reactions to antisocial behavior in games, identity as a "gamer" (and as an aficionado of particular games), and learning about cooperation through social gaming. One issue that has been extensively discussed with respect to gaming is whether violent video games can lead to real-world violence. I show that this is a classic example of a moral panic, though in isolated cases games may exacerbate the level of violence that someone engages in. A parallel worry is over widespread access to online pornography and whether this has negative effects on real-world sexual behavior. Risks to privacy from sharing sensitive sexual material are also reviewed. Finally, new technology brings new opportunities for acquiring knowledge and engaging with educational content online. The last part of the chapter will draw on my own research with high school pupils in Colombia. While many people worry that time spent on social networks can detract from academic achievement, we found instead that time spent online was balanced by a tendency for children with lower academic self-esteem to use WhatsApp and Facebook groups, and other resources, to gain relevant information from their more "academically able" peers.

Chapter 4, New Relationships: Online Dating, Cyberbullying, and Intergroup Contact, investigates the risks and opportunities associated with new types of personal connections online. In preadolescence, a natural tendency to form new social networks is reflected in changing patterns of technology use, with a gradual shift away from solo game-playing and toward new interpersonal connections. Then, as teenagers pass through adolescence they tend to show increased interest in the other sex (or an increasingly romantic interest in their own sex if they are homosexual), a development which of course can bring much anxiety for parents. These days such interest is reflected in changing patterns of use of social networks like Instagram and Snapchat, and eventually of online dating apps such as Tinder. This chapter will therefore draw from a study conducted with Tinder users in Colombia and the United States, and a review of research on Tinder use. Topics include the evolutionary origins of the differences between women's and men's self-expression in dating apps, changes in self-expression during adolescence as young people gain more experience of interactions with potential partners, and the effects of cultural and personality differences on the use of such apps. New social connections in adolescence also raise the possibility of unwelcome forms of interaction such as cyberbullying and cyberharrasment. Cyberbullying is associated with particular risks due to its inescapability, the tendency for certain individuals to become perpetrators who would be reluctant to perpetrate face-to-face bullying, and the possibility for online mob situations to develop where individuals take part in victimizing without even knowing the victim or necessarily realizing the gravity of what they are doing. Again, however, concerns about cyberbullying may represent something of a moral panic, since bullying is not a new phenomenon and cyberbullying simply represents its expression in a new environment. I conclude by discussing the establishment of new social connections in an increasingly globalized world. A large body of literature shows that children can naturally learn second languages and acquire useful information about other cultures through their interactions in online games. An online version of the "contact hypothesis" suggests that young people's online interactions, as they grow up in an increasingly globalized culture, can potentially help solve many of the problems of nationalism and cultural intolerance that we currently see in adult society.

Finally, in the concluding chapter of the book, I revisit the main ideas from this introductory chapter, reviewing the evidence explored in more detail in other chapters to argue that while the existence (and even growth) of online risks should not be denied, they are often exaggerated in popular and even academic discourse. The ability of adolescents to adapt the internet to their natural tendency to form new interpersonal connections creates a flip side of opportunities that receives less attention, but may outweigh the risks for the majority of young people (though the possibility of important differences for vulnerable individuals must be acknowledged). In order to calm public doubts about new media and recover a sense of optimism about the kind of future that they can help create, it is vital to emphasize opportunities as much as risks. To help parents, teachers, policymakers, and young people themselves make the most of such opportunities, I provide a set of concrete guidelines for communicating about online risks, identifying particularly at-risk individuals, and providing opportunities (online and offline) to enhance adolescents' wellbeing. I also consider how the COVID-19 pandemic has altered views on young people's internet use and conclude with some speculation about how internet use may change in the future.

Notes

1 See http://www.bbc.com/culture/story/20140515-when-two-tribes-went-to-war for an accessible account
2 http://www.modrockmusical.com/history-of-mods-rockers/
3 https://icd.who.int/browse11/l-m/en#/http%3a%2f%2fid.who.int%2ficd%2fentity%2f1448597234
4 https://www.psychiatry.org/patients-families/internet-gaming

References

Alexander, R. D. (1987). *The biology of moral systems*. Transaction.

Bean, A. M., Nielsen, R. K. L., van Rooij, A. J., & Ferguson, C. J. (2017). Video game addiction: The push to pathologize video games. *Professional Psychology: Research and Practice, 48*, 378–389. http://dx.doi.org/10.1037/pro0000150

Cohen, S. (1972). *Folk devils and moral panics*. Routledge.

Coyne, S. M., Rogers, A. A., Zurcher, J. D., Stockdale, L., & Booth, M. (2020). Does time spent using social media impact mental health? An eight year longitudinal study. *Computers in Human Behavior, 104*, 106160. https://doi.org/10.1016/j.chb.2019.106160

Critcher, C. (2008). Moral panic analysis: Past, present and future. *Sociology Compass, 2*, 1127–1144. https://doi.org/10.1111/j.1751-9020.2008.00122.x

Garland, D. (2008). On the concept of moral panic. *Crime, Media, Culture, 4*, 9–30. https://doi.org/10.1177/1741659007087270

Goode, E., & Ben-Yehuda, N. (2010). *Moral panics: The social construction of deviance*. Wiley (1st Ed., 1994).

Henrich, Joseph. (2015). *The secret of our success: How culture is driving human evolution, domesticating our species, and making us smarter*. Princeton University Press. https://doi.org/10.1515/9781400873296

Ivory, J. D., & Kalyanaraman, S. (2009). Video games make people violent—well, maybe not that game: Effects of content and person abstraction on perceptions of violent video games' effects and support of censorship. *Communication Reports, 22*, 1–12. https://doi.org/10.1080/08934210902798536

Littlewood, A. (2003). Cyberporn and moral panic: An evaluation of press reactions to pornography on the internet. *Library and Information Research*, *27*, 8–18. http://eprints.rclis.org/6070/

Markey, P. M., & Ferguson, C. J. (2017). *Moral combat: Why the war on violent video games is wrong*. BenBella.

Young, J. (2011). Moral panics and the transgressive other. *Crime Media Culture*, 7, 245–258. https://doi.org/10.1177/1741659011417604

2

NEW IDENTITIES

Visual Communication, Screen Time, and Young People's Wellbeing

2.1 Changes in Young People's Identities with Age

Adolescence has long been seen as a problematic stage of "storm and stress" (Arnett, 1999). This idea has been around since the time of Plato and Aristotle, if not earlier, and gained great cultural momentum with Romantic writers such as Rousseau and Goethe, who influenced one of the founding fathers of developmental psychology, G. Stanley Hall (1907). Teenagers are "liminal" beings, who do not fit easily into the categories of either children or adults, being more mature than children in many ways, but not yet ready for adult responsibilities – especially in contemporary developed societies that require a lot of training for people to achieve economic independence (Benjamin et al., 2014). Associated with their liminality is the idea that adolescents are naturally rebellious and prone to conflict with adults (especially parents and teachers). This idea has been heavily criticized in recent years, and indeed in popular consciousness it is often exaggerated. Pushing back against the stigmatization of adolescents in modern societies, many social scientists have gone so far as to argue that the very concept of adolescence is a "Western" cultural category that does not exist in other cultures (Baxter, 2011; Ben-Amos, 1995). However, the existence of protracted rites of passage between childhood and adulthood in many societies points to the cross-cultural construction of adolescence as a liminal category (Delaney, 1995). There are also notable biological features of adolescence, including the massive increase in levels of sex hormones at puberty (leading of course to secondary sexual differences between male and female bodies, which take several years to reach adult levels of difference), and the gradual maturation of the prefrontal cortex, thought to be responsible for self-control and fully mature forms of behavior (Caballero et al., 2016).

DOI: 10.4324/9781003019459-2

The biological nature of these differences reminds us that humans are not the only animals to show profound changes in behavior as they reach sexual maturity. Many animals, especially social mammals, go through a kind of stage transition in their juvenile period. From living with their natal group – often dependent on their mothers or other adult relatives for food – they may disperse to join other groups, live a partially solitary life, or even start their own group. This process of dispersal is theoretically important for understanding how communities of animals can colonize new areas (Wolff, 1994) and avoid inbreeding, and has been studied in species as diverse as feral horses (Marjamäki et al., 2013), lions (Funston et al., 2003), meerkats (Maag et al., 2019), and tamarins (Romano et al., 2019). Depending on the ecological conditions, dispersal can lead to advantages in obtaining access to mates or resources, or be a response to population pressure (often manifested in physical conflict with more mature individuals in the natal area).

Humans are no exception to this pattern of juvenile (or, in our case, adolescent and young adult) dispersal. However, from the viewpoint of cultural group selection – as we saw in the introductory chapter – human adaptations to the environment are universally mediated through culture and language. How does this relate to adolescent dispersal? We can analyze dispersal among humans in contemporary societies as not just involving geographical processes, in terms of migration into new physical territories (though historically this has been important, of course), but also social and cultural processes, in terms of creating new social identities. Focusing on the changes that individuals go through in adolescence, I have argued elsewhere (Ingram, 2014) that as their social network expands, a young person's reputation with cliques of peers becomes more important for evolutionary fitness than are relationships with parents. Evidence for this comes from studies of gossip and tattling, which shows that children are less likely to report the misbehavior (including online) of other children to adults as they get older (Ingram, 2019). This in turn can mean that parents find that they know less and less about the world that their adolescent child inhabits in their interactions with friends (including online) – and as we shall see in the next chapter, when parents do come into contact with that world it may be increasingly unfamiliar to them in terms of its cultural content.

In animals, dispersal is likely driven by hormonal changes. As mentioned above, the phenomenon of puberty shows that humans are no less prone to such changes. Indeed, hormonal changes during (and just before) puberty are known to have major effects on the brain. Blakemore and Mills (2014) reviewed evidence that many of these changes to areas of the "social brain" – such as the "mentalizing network" in the dorsomedial prefrontal cortex, involved in the representation of other people's states of mind – represent a new sensitivity to sociocultural processing. A key development is the ability to integrate other people's differing intentions and perspectives when making judgments about considerations of fairness in social transactions (Güroğlu et al., 2009). This could help enable adolescents to navigate the new world of social relations beyond the family group, ensuring that they can protect themselves against being unfairly exploited, and build their reputation by avoiding unjust treatment of others (and perhaps even by protecting others against exploitation). However, this new focus on peer reputation is a double-edged sword. A well-known topic of research with adolescents (dating all the way back to Hall, 1907) is their propensity for risk-taking, especially when subject to peer pressure. For example, in a famous study of behavior in a driving simulation, Gardner and Steinberg (2005) found that 13- to 16-year-olds, 18- to 22-year-olds, and adults over 24 years old took about as many risks when driving alone. Yet when driving with friends, adolescents took significantly more risks, an effect that was weaker in the group of young adults and absent in the group of older adults.

Nevertheless, as Blakemore and Mills (2014, p. 196) pointed out:

> Although risky decision making during adolescence is often framed as maladaptive and unavoidable, this perspective leaves out many key features of risky decision making, including the fact that the outcome can be positive and that some risky decision making is necessary in development and throughout life.

Blakemore and Mills proposed that risky behaviors can actually be a way of gaining social rewards, such as peer acceptance, and avoiding social punishments, such as ostracism. The propensity toward risky behavior may thus not be a deficiency (caused by an "immature" prefrontal cortex), so much as a by-product of adolescents' heightened desire for social acceptance – gaining a good reputation – at a pivotal point in their lives. In support of this, some studies (e.g., Fischhoff et al., 2010) have indicated that adolescents may perceive their risk of dying soon as higher than it actually is, suggesting that they are aware of the risks associated with their actions, but choose to ignore them. Part of the reason for that may be their desire to carve out a reputational space that is different from that of adults, leading them to engage disproportionately in activities that appear "deviant" to the dominant adult culture (Lonardo et al., 2009).

The desire to "disperse" away from adult culture and dependence on parents means that adolescents naturally attach more importance to peer relations. In a review of adolescent social relations, Giordano (2003, p. 261) argued that:

> In contrast to the hierarchical nature of the parent-child bond, friendships at their base are egalitarian—within friendships, reality is "cooperatively co-constructed". [...] Young people, through recurrent peer interactions, draw on elements within the existing adult/parent culture in a unique and selective manner.

An important element of these changing dynamics of peer and parental relations is that teenagers tend to feel more "accepted" by close friends than by their parents, who have a habit of focusing on the negative potential consequences of their child's behavior (Youniss & Smollar, 1985). Alongside this feeling of acceptance comes a sense of greater intimacy with friends, which tends to increase the social influence that the latter have. There are several additional reasons why friends can have greater social influence than parents in adolescence: (i) teenagers may interact and communicate with friends more frequently, compared with parents; (ii) they identify with friends more readily because they perceive them as more similar to themselves than their parents are; and (iii) friendships with peers are perceived by teens as both valuable and vulnerable, and thus they tend to accede readily to attempts by friendly peers to influence them, so as to preserve or enhance the friendship (Warr, 1993).

Besides close friendships, the wider peer network (and with it, "peer culture") is also very important for adolescents. According to Giordano (2003, p. 275):

> The latter types of relationships are more apt to encompass elements of distance and difference, in effect constituting a "tougher audience" for the developing adolescent. These social others frequently weigh in on the adolescent's apparent social worth/identity and engender feelings of awkwardness and insecurity.

That is, the adolescent has supplemented a "primary" affiliation to parents with a later-developing, "secondary" affiliation to a peer group. Peer relationships may feel more intimate and egalitarian, because individuals have more input to the peer culture that is co-constructed with friends; yet somewhat paradoxically, they can also be less forgiving and feel more fragile, because peers do not have the same vested interest in one's success that one's parents do. Simply put, at this age peer relationships tend to feel much more *intense* than family relationships: if they are going well, they can lead to wonderful highs; but equally if going badly, they can cause deeper lows – and of course they can flip between the two unpredictably and with alarming speed. This tension and chaotic potential, along with the inadequacy of the parental relationship to serve as a model for effective peer relationships (because of both cultural and psychological differences between the two), can contribute to something of a crisis of identity in the adolescent mind.

From an adolescent's point of view, they must actively resolve this crisis by constructing a personal identity that (unlike in early or middle childhood) incorporates a reflexive sense of how they are perceived and evaluated by peers (Siegel, 1982). This can include the selection of peer groups who are seen as enhancing their reputation by association and are thus desirable sources of influence (for an analysis of how this plays out with taking up smoking, see Snow & Bruce, 2003). Hence, "to some extent adolescents create the very environment that influences them ... The kinds of settings an adolescent chooses to enter also influence what models and reinforcements are experienced" (Miller, 1989, p. 27). In terms of the broader social context, Erikson (1980) suggested that the "identity crisis" of adolescence can intensify when society goes through difficult times, perhaps because peer sources of influence are rendered relatively unstable and chaotic. This lack of stability may interact with adolescents' own cognitive fluidity, their newfound capacity for perspective-taking and hypothetical thinking, and their tendency to experiment with different possible social roles (Inhelder & Piaget, 1958).

Moreover, adolescents' newfound understanding of how they are perceived and evaluated by other people may lead to problems of self-esteem, which peak around 13 years and are linked to the development of an "imaginary audience" (Elkind & Bowen, 1979):

> Because of their own preoccupation with their appearance and behavior, children entering adolescence often assume that others also are constantly observing them and evaluating them.... Teenagers constantly are on stage, playing to this audience and anticipating its reactions to their appearance and behavior. Thus, there is a cognitive basis to the self-consciousness of adolescence.
>
> *(Miller, 1989, pp. 34–35)*

An exaggerated self-consciousness can also lead to what Elkind (1967) called the "personal fable". This refers to an overestimation of exactly how unique the young person and their experiences are, sometimes in a positive sense (which can lead to risk-taking because of feelings of invincibility) and sometimes in a negative sense (which can lead to feelings of emotional isolation and fear of rejection if peers discover "what I'm really like"). While the imaginary audience and personal fable never entirely disappear, even during adulthood, they diminish in importance during the late teens as the young person becomes more intimate with peers and discovers that they share similar thoughts, feelings, and experiences. However, both phenomena can contribute to emotional distancing from parents earlier in adolescence, since the imaginary audience will tend to be dominated by peers rather than family members, and the personal fable means that adolescents may underestimate how much parents can relate to what they are going through, leading to a reluctance to talk through their problems with them.

From this brief theoretical review of some of the literature on adolescent development, the following points stand out. First, adolescents naturally move apart from their parents in many ways, in terms of both emotional dependence and frequency of communication. This can lead to an ignorance about their activities and emotional states on the part of their parents. Second, the shift in social dependence from parents to peers can cause problems of self-esteem that manifest themselves in various ways (both internalizing and externalizing problems). Third, adolescents have always created their own cultural worlds, which can be quite alien from the cultural worlds inhabited by older generations. And fourth, while most young people quickly become well adapted to those worlds, others can suffer from mental health problems, especially if they become associated with a "deviant" peer group or are rejected by all peer groups that they want to join.

The rest of this chapter examines how the forging of a new personal identity during adolescence plays out online, and the difficulties that adults (especially parents) have in understanding changes in children's identities. Just as scooters were a badge of identity for the Mods and motorbikes for the Rockers (see Chapter 1), so various uses of new technology can be badges of cultural identity today, in ways that are often opaque to older generations. I start by looking at how teenagers express themselves visually on social media. Themes include changes in self-concept and self-esteem in adolescence, gender differences in online identity, the effects of Instagram on body image, and the use of emoji and memes to form "private codes" for expressing identity within age-based peer groups. Next, a major risk often cited by parents is examined, namely, the problem of "screen time": how much is too much? This is relevant to the topic of identity because parents often feel like the internet has taken their child away from them, as due to identity changes they may prefer to spend time online with friends rather than offline with families. I show that panics about screen time and smartphone addiction are overblown, since screen time is not related with adolescents' wellbeing across the general population. Nevertheless, I also argue that in extreme cases internet addiction can be a real problem. It is not the total time spent online that matters so much as the nature of the activities carried out online, and whether young people also have opportunities for rewarding activities offline. In this context, social networking software and smartphones offer new opportunities for clinicians to reach out to people at risk of mental health problems like depression and loneliness (both of which may be linked to changes in social identity during adolescence).

2.2 Visual Communication Online: A Foreign Language for Parents

In this section I argue that one important aspect of the changes in identity that are taking place in today's teenagers is that they are building a new language for themselves online. This language is one that older generations find hard to understand because it is fundamentally multimodal, including not just text but many visual elements as well (Dancygier & Vandelanotte, 2017). The new multimodal language has many different idioms, which are of course used by distinct groups of young people to different degrees, and understood or appropriated by adults with varying levels of success. One highly current development is the increasing use of self-produced videos in adolescent communications, using tools such as Instagram Reels, Snapchat and TikTok (Mittmann et al., 2021). Since there is as yet little published research on these tools, I focus here on three visual elements that are simpler because they are more static: *emojis*, *memes*, and *selfies*.

Emojis are the oldest of these visual elements, especially if one takes their ancestors, *emoticons*, into account. Emoticons, or "emote icons" – simple patterns of punctuation that represent emotional reactions, such as *:-)* or *:)* to indicate a smiley face – were invented in 1982 by Scott Fahlman on the Carnegie-Mellon University electronic bulletin board, and quickly spread to Usenet and other text-based posting sites. Similar services in Japan a few years later saw the introduction of *kaomoji* emoticons based on katakana characters, which were able to depict faces more realistically. The exact origins of *emoji* proper – that is, a set of pictograms implemented as ASCII characters for use within text messages – are more obscure, but they are thought to have been developed independently by several Japanese cellphone providers in the late 1990s. Outside Japan, emojis were first used in mobile text messages and online messaging services such as AOL Messenger and MSN Messenger, but really took off with the popularity of social networking sites like Facebook and, especially, WhatsApp and other internet-based mobile messaging services. Both emoticons and emojis have several interesting "affordances", in the sense of allowing users to do things with technology-mediated communication that they otherwise would not easily be able to do. As Kaye et al. (2017) pointed out, both these forms can make the communicative intent of messages less ambiguous (see also Kaye et al., 2016), and thus serve important nonverbal functions in communication. In particular – as shown by the fact that the prototypical emoji is a smiley face – the most common function of an emoji is to convey a communicator's emotional state, serving as the symbolic equivalent of a facial expression or tone of voice:

> Users are highly aware of how emojis can reduce discourse ambiguity … [and] can aid expression through establishing an emotional tone that is often lost with the absence of face-to-face interaction, thus providing the user with a toolkit for clarifying emotional concepts.
>
> *(Kaye et al., 2017, pp. 66–67)*

In keeping with this idea, a neuroscientific study of people reading emojis by Yuasa et al. (2011) revealed activity in the inferior frontal gyrus (associated with inhibitory control) on both the left and the right sides of the brain, in contrast to the dominance of the left hemisphere that is typical of purely verbal tasks. The right hemisphere is heavily involved in emotion processing and in determining the context of linguistic expressions and social actions (Gur et al., 2002; Sabbagh, 1999; Van Overwalle, 2009). Thus, it is no surprise that emoji users are sensitive to the context of their use, using emojis more frequently with informal tools such as text messages to friends, and less often in formal platforms such as emails (Kaye et al., 2016). Indeed, even though they are often seen as a "youthful" means of expression, emojis have been enthusiastically adopted by many older adults in informal contexts (Gallud et al., 2018), while teenage users may prefer emoticons or memes (which often serve as "in-jokes", signaling up-to-date cultural knowledge; Rowett, 2018). Adolescents tend to be highly sensitive to behaviors that are seen as childlike, so their partial abandonment of emojis could be associated with a rejection of childhood forms of culture (perhaps because, being reminiscent of cartoons, emojis look visually attractive to young children and are so easy to use and experiment with; Davison, 2012). Ironically, since emojis tend to have quite a literal meaning and are easily understood by adults, this could contribute to a reduction in adolescents communicating their emotional state to parents and other formerly intimate adults.

Compared with emoji and related forms, a much richer medium of visual communication that is hugely popular with young people is the "selfie": an informal self-portrait with a cellphone that is quickly posted to a social network – these days, usually to Instagram or Snapchat. The popularity of selfies began with the first camera phones, around the year 2000, and really took off with the ability of smartphones to share photos rapidly on social media (especially after Apple's release of the first iPhone in 2007). As with combining emojis and text, selfies on Instagram tend to be multimodal communications. Yet unlike emojis, which play a secondary role in adding emotional expression to text, on Instagram images take precedence; nevertheless, they are usually accompanied by text in the form of a caption (and sometimes also comments), which is an important part of the total communication (Veum & Undrum, 2018). Captions often include hashtags, which can be a way for individuals to tap into a global discourse and feel part of something bigger than themselves, and to show that they are on top of the latest trends (Machin & Van Leeuwen, 2007).

In a discourse analysis of 100 randomly selected selfies from across Instagram (they simply searched for the hashtag *#selfie*), Veum and Undrum showed that selfies, in common with the stock images in corporate image banks, "typically depict people in a generalized, decontextualized and stylized way" (2018, p. 14). In their earlier study of image banks, Machin and Van Leeuwen had claimed that the easy manipulability of electronic media was "changing the world's visual language from one which emphasized the photograph as witness, as record of reality, to one which emphasized photography as a symbolic system" (2007, p. 151). Veum and Undrum (2018) argued that a similar process was currently taking place in personal social media displays such as selfies. They drew on Schwarz's (2010) analysis of decontextualized images on the Israeli social network Shox, in which he suggested that photos of the body, if sufficiently attractive, carry a form of social power that he called "corporeal capital":

> One conclusion of this study was that the user's capacity to make friends through the social network seems to depend on the extent to which users publish the 'right' photos. Thus, the teenagers seemed to exchange corporeal capital for social capital.
>
> *(Veum & Undrum, 2018, p. 4)*

The multimodality of the selfie is also seen in the way that "likes" are expected from viewers, as well as being offered back, at times, with the use of hashtags such as #likeforlike (whereby a poster promises to "like" the photos of whoever donates them "likes"). Selfie posters are therefore essentially constructing a language of exchange with their viewers, many (but not all) of whom are personally unknown to them.

Veum and Undrum (2018, p. 14) also pointed out that "On the one hand, this language appears internal and understandable only to a specific group of Instagram users. On the other, the language is used worldwide". Indeed, anthropological analysis has revealed a huge variety of different selfie genres, as well as cross-cultural variation between different countries (and subcultures) in terms of how these genres are deployed. Some of this variety was examined in the *Why We Post* project led by Daniel Miller, a large-scale digital ethnographic study by nine anthropologists of social media use in eight different countries. In England, for example, Miller and his fellow ethnographer Ciara Green found that as well as creating more aesthetically formalized selfies on Instagram to show off new outfits, etc., young women would play up the informal aspects of selfies with styles labeled as "groupies" (particularly common on Facebook, these showed a group of young people socializing) and "uglies" (a deliberate attempt to look unattractive for humorous effect, usually posted as a temporary story rather than being left online permanently). In contrast, in Latin American, Mediterranean, or Caribbean countries, such as Brazil, Italy, or Trinidad, it was common to take the selfie more seriously, for example by showing one's gym activities, going through many changes of makeup or outfit, or showing off the whole body (e.g., with a full-length "mirror selfie") rather than just the face. However, even in these cultures casual selfies were also possible, for example the "footie" in Chile which showed a horizontal view of the taker's lower legs and feet in front of a TV in the lounge or bedroom, indicating relaxation (a similar style of photo was often taken on the beach). In the two Chinese field sites, people often used innovative filters or hairstyles to augment their natural appearance, whereas in India and Turkey people often seemed reluctant to post selfies (at least to Facebook), apparently worrying that they were too informal or would not show them in a good light.

The two types of visual communication considered so far are quite formally constrained: particularly so in the case of emojis, which are limited to less than 4,000 different characters; a bit less so in the case of selfies, which allow almost limitless settings, stylings, makeup, filters, props, etc., but are still constrained by the focus on the selfie taker. In contrast, memes make up an increasingly important fusion of visual and textual media that can deal with an almost infinite variety of themes and visual content, and the sharing (and creative adaptation) of memes has rapidly become central to youth culture. The word "meme" was coined in 1976 by Richard Dawkins in his book *The Selfish Gene*, which showed how cooperative behavior in humans and other animals can be determined by self-replicating genes acting in their own interests. Dawkins speculated that since culture essentially replicates as it passes between minds, cultural patterns could be explained as favoring the replication of self-replicating units analogous to genes, which he called "memes". In a quirky instance of life imitating science, this term was eventually adopted by the internet community to refer to units of culture that spread rapidly online.

The origins of internet memes as a phenomenon are even harder to pin down than those of emojis or selfies. This is partly because the term is so general: even particular usages of emojis or styles of selfie can be considered memes. However, one of the first "pure" memes (meaning, it served no real function other than to be passed around) to become popular was the viral video *Dancing Baby* – an animated video of a baby dancing to the classic rock song "Hooked on a Feeling" – in 1996. In the era before social media, this was shared by email as an attached video file. In the words of its creator, Ron Lussier:

> I showed it to a few people and one of them asked me to forward it to them in e-mail. A week or so later I heard from fellow employees that the animation was traveling through the company via e-mail … then a bit later, I heard people say they had received it back again from people outside the company, across the country. From that it quickly traveled to the internet and became the strange phenomenon that it was.[1]

The *Dancing Baby* is a good example of one important quality of memes: they tend to be visually attention-grabbing and amusing. Davison (2012) referred to this as the *replicability* of memes: their ability to gain cultural influence by garnering views. Naturally, the replicability of memes increased massively with the invention of social networking sites (Shifman, 2014) and messaging apps.

Another key aspect of memes that perhaps helps with communicating emotional responses, and that certainly developed later than the aspect of replicability, is their *malleability*, which refers to how easy it is to transform and adapt them in a particular rhetorical context. Malleability is what distinguishes the most prototypical contemporary memes from "viral videos" such as the *Dancing Baby*. The classic example of a malleable meme is an *image macro* (Dancygier & Vandelanotte, 2017), which is usually a stock image with the ability to substitute text strings in standard placeholders. Originally the latter came in the form of "banner text" above and below the main image, but this has become much more flexible, with a more recent trope being to superimpose inventive textual "labels" on top of different visual elements of the image, as with the well-known (but controversial) *Distracted Boyfriend* meme.[2] Dancygier and Vandelanotte used construction grammar techniques from cognitive linguistics to analyze this type of meme as a *multimodal* construction: the standard image stays the same, hooking into a shared cultural understanding, while the text is varied in creative and sometimes surprising ways.

In keeping with the importance of malleability, recent work on memes has emphasized the flexibility and creativity involved in creating new cultural variants (Acerbi, 2019; Dancygier & Vandelanotte, 2017; Shifman, 2014; Wiggins & Bowers, 2015). In a sense, there are two kinds of memes. Viral videos on YouTube, to which users share links on social networks, and which routinely rack up hundreds of thousands of shares and millions of views, are memes in Dawkins's original sense of the world: culturally replicable content selected over other memes replicating in the same space. But these days, YouTube is also full of imitations: any viral video tends to inspire many others with a similar format (Shifman, 2014). These imitations are not all parodies: some are tributes, others "straight" copies (to learn techniques or to share in reflected glory), while still others are "riffs" that try to take the format of the meme in a new creative direction. All these different "stances" toward the original meme may be associated with different identity orientations. Shifman therefore recommended looking at memes not as single replicants like genes, but as groups of ideas that are historically related to each other and share certain characteristics in common. What is particularly interesting about how these groups of ideas evolve online is that metadata about the competition between variants is becoming increasingly visible, in terms of numbers of views, shares, etc. Indeed, when people put up new variants it is often expressly for the purpose of garnering such metrics. Memes, and visual self-expression on social networks in general, have thus become a means not only of expressing cultural identity but also of contesting and competing in it, in the way that adolescents always have done.

The three forms of visual communication discussed in this section express identity in different ways. Emoticons and emoji, the simplest form, offer an opportunity to add emotional tone and expression to text-based communication, allowing users to feel that they are expressing themselves more naturally. Young people have grown up with this form of communication but tend not to overuse it, perhaps because it can seem childish to them. Selfies offer a more sophisticated way for today's teens to express their identity visually, especially with the use of filters, which can add emotional tone and help to present an idealized version of the self (Bakhshi et al., 2015; Harris & Bardey, 2019; Olivera-La Rosa et al., 2019; Rousseau, 2021). As we saw, styles of selfie-taking and selfie-publishing can vary hugely between cultural groups, allowing them to be used to express group belonging as well as individual identity. And finally, with memes we see the expression of identity through humor (whether satirical or affiliative) and creativity, which can involve a form of competition – as can selfies. Current developments in these types of visual expression include Snapchat and Instagram "stories" (Li et al., 2021; McRoberts et al., 2017; Villaespesa & Wowkowych, 2020), which are more spontaneous and temporary forms of identity expression (important for adolescents because it means they don't have to be embarrassed by "immature" expressions lingering online after their authors have outgrown them). How adolescents choose which images to keep as part of their permanent record, and which to post only temporarily, is worth further academic investigation.

Social media "stories" are often videos, of course; and the latest, natively video form of self-expression to emerge is TikTok (Montag et al., 2021) – lately imitated by Instagram Reels and YouTube Shorts (Instagram, 2020; Khleif, 2021). This type of mobile video platform is interesting because it fuses the three forms of visual expression discussed so far. Many videos produced on TikTok are clearly memes (Zeng & Abidin, 2021), because they take a common soundtrack – and usually common visual and/or action elements as well – and result in the creation of multiple variants on the same theme. They are also selfies or selfie-like (Suárez-Álvarez & García-Jiménez, 2021), since they tend to be quite intimate portraits of one person or a small group of people – though of course since the subjects are moving, the camera tends to be either fixed or manipulated by another person. And finally, they often focus on emotional expressions (Montefalcon et al., 2021) – indeed, one popular form of TikTok is aimed at physically reproducing emojis (Zhang, 2021)! In a sense, then, the dynamic, video-based modality of TikTok represents a further evolution of the main themes of visual identity expression outlined in this section.

2.3 From "Screen Time" to Problematic Internet Use

As well as creating all these new forms of digital visual content – which is a relatively new development – children and young people of course are spending increasing amounts of time on the consumption of digital content via TVs, computers, games consoles, tablets, and, above all, their own smartphones. Worries about "screen time" date back to the invention of television, or at least to the first time that children's cartoons were broadcast through that medium; but the proliferation of devices that children can stare at, and types of content that they can watch (or play), have made it an even more pressing concern. In consequence, there are few parents these days – at least in high-income countries – who have no worries about the amount of time their children are spending in front of screens. The fact that adolescents are going through an age when they live increasingly separate lives from their parents (along with the historical and technological changes in content that mean adolescents speak a different, much more visual language from their parents) may help explain this worry – although the behavior of younger kids is also an increasing concern. Professional organizations have tried to formulate advice to help families with this issue. Many parents are aware of some version of the American Academy of Pediatrics' (AAP) 2×2 rule ("no child under 2 years old should be exposed to any screen media, and no child over 2 should watch more than two hours per day"; Blum-Ross & Livingstone, 2018, p. 180). But in practice this rule has become increasingly anachronistic and difficult to enforce with most children, let alone adolescents, meaning that parents end up using the rule more as a stick to beat themselves (and their child) with when it is almost inevitably violated – even though such restrictive time limits are surely out of date in an age of smartphones, video-calling the grandparents, and doing one's homework online (not to mention the virtual classes of the COVID-19 pandemic). The AAP did abandon these guidelines in October 2016, in favor of an online "Media Time Calculator"[3] that takes different forms of screen use into account. However, such changes can take time to filter through to public consciousness. And academically, as we shall see, the whole notion of limiting screen time is quite a controversial concept.

It must be acknowledged, first, that a lot of the moral panic around screen time comes from nostalgia because our children are not living the same kind of childhood that we had; particularly, in many cases, an "outdoors" kind of childhood (outdoors being where parents used to banish children to get them out from under their feet, whereas now they are plonked in front of a screen). It's important not to be too rose-tinted about our own childhoods here: much of the time that I spent knocking around outside alone or with friends as an early teenager, I felt quite bored and insecure, and this contributed to a real sense of ennui at times. Yet, there is a sense that we understand how we felt in our own childhood and adolescence, that we can see how it contributed to us being the sort of people that we are now, and that we don't understand so well how our children's childhood is going or what their novel, technologically mediated experiences will do to them.

Nevertheless, we must also accept that there are also real fears of children "missing out on something" behind this nostalgia. There are at least three types of things that people feel today's youth are missing out on by being so engrossed in their smartphones, but that they themselves had more of as children. First, people feel that their kids are missing a physical sense of connection with the outside world. Second, they may feat that they are missing social connections with their friends. And third, they may be missing out on learning practical skills, whether those involve reading books, tinkering with their dad's old car, or practicing music or sports. Whether or not these supposed differences in childhood are empirically supported is not always the point (I am only certain of the first one – it's indisputable that children these days play outside a lot less). The point is that representations of the differences reflect genuine (and not *prima facie* unreasonable) fears that many people have in connection with their kids' overuse of technology We can see in all three of them clear ways in which our children's adolescence might end up being somehow "deficient" compared with our own (even though they are also learning other, more technologically based skills and connections that we didn't have, of course). Moreover, the first two in particular – spending time outdoors and making face-to-face personal connections – seem like they could have real impacts on young people's wellbeing, not only in their later lives as adults but during adolescence.

What then is the evidence for a connection between "screen time" and children's and adolescents' wellbeing? Relatively early research on the subject (e.g., Page et al., 2010; Romer et al., 2013; Rosen et al., 2014; Yang et al., 2013) often suffered from small sample sizes, unvalidated measures, and ad hoc interpretations of the results, leading to accusations of publication bias obscuring a real null effect (Przybylski & Weinstein, 2017). This seemed plausible since although many of the studies cited in the previous sentence found an (often modest) effect of screen time on wellbeing, others found essentially null effects or even benefits of computer- or video game–based activities (reviewed by Granic et al., 2014; Valkenburg & Peter, 2009). With increasing skepticism over the existence of a real effect, Przybylski and Weinstein (2017) published a study based on a huge, nationally representative sample of over 120,000 English adolescents, showing that moderate screen use did not seem to affect wellbeing: what they termed the "Goldilocks effect" (a U-shaped curve, meaning that moderate use is not associated with negative outcomes, whereas extremely low or extremely high amounts of technology use could be linked to lower wellbeing). One of the leading proponents of the existence of negative effects of screen time, Jean Twenge, then published a large-scale study of about 40,000 US children and adolescents, acknowledging the existence of this type of non-monotonic effect, but showing that the "inflection point" for the curve was actually quite low: more than one hour of screen time per day already started to be damaging (Twenge & Campbell, 2018). And comparing those with very high amounts of screen time (seven hours plus per day) to those with relatively low amounts (one hour per day) revealed that the former group were more than twice as likely to have been diagnosed with mental health problems such as anxiety or depression, and to have taken medication for psychiatric issues.

However, the methodology behind these results, and behind many other studies which had found negative effects of screen time, was questioned by Orben & Przybylski (2019a; see also Orben & Przybylski, 2019b). They showed that the median effect size in the Twenge & Campbell study was relatively small, explaining less than 1% of the variance in wellbeing (comparable to the effect on wellbeing of wearing glasses, in the same dataset). Twenge et al. (2020) responded by pointing out some problems with Orben and Przybylski's reasoning (though see also Orben and Przybylski, 2020, for a reply to this reply), including the lack of consideration of non-monotonic effects; the lack of fine-grained distinctions in their analysis (e.g., between different types of screen use, or different genders); the focus on individual items, which weighted the median effect toward longer scales; the absence of analysis of an hours-per-week measure for screen time; the inclusion of "control variables" (e.g., time spent with parents) that might actually be mediator variables; and the use of R^2 values to indicate "proportion of variance explained". As Twenge et al. (2020) point out, such an approach is problematic because a factor can still be important even if it explains very little variance in a linear analysis: for example, in one study, being vaccinated against polio explained only 0.00001% of the variance in whether a child caught polio (because catching polio was such a rare event that the vast majority of both vaccinated and unvaccinated children did not catch it), and yet unvaccinated children were three times more likely to catch the disease than vaccinated children – an appreciably important difference.

A similar point is illustrated by a set of other factors provided by Orben and Przybylski (2019b) as comparators to show the supposed lack of importance of screen time. One already mentioned was whether someone wore glasses, which they used as an example as something that they wouldn't, *a priori*, expect to have much effect on wellbeing. Yet this may seem rather unimaginative to anyone who is mindful of adolescents' self-consciousness about their physical appearance; if wearing glasses had no impact on subjective wellbeing, would millions of adults wear uncomfortable contact lenses or shell out thousands of dollars for laser eye surgery? The same goes for some other comparison variables, such as asthma, that also don't have much more effect on wellbeing than screen time. Other variables have even less effect: as Twenge et al. (2020, p. 347) pointed out, "One could just as easily conclude that social media use is more important for well-being than hard drug use, exercise and obesity" (all of which also receive great attention from policymakers and the media).

How to adjudicate this debate? When results of individual studies conflict, as is the case for studies of screen time effects, one solution is to conduct a systematic review and meta-analysis of all the published studies on the topic under debate. But what happens when these reviews themselves have conflicting results? In a narrative "review of reviews", Orben (2020) shows that reviews of screen time studies have been weakened by the inclusion of many "low-quality" cross-sectional and correlational studies, possibly explaining why so many of them have inconsistent results. As well as reviews, Orben considers several influential single studies as well, and, based on their results, advocates including more focused research questions in studies of screen time, such as considering the differences between active and passive use of social networks, or between authentic and inauthentic self-presentation styles. She also advocates making methodological improvements such as carrying out more longitudinal studies, considering the practical importance of any effects that are found, analyzing for individual differences such as gender, age, and cultural background, and working with more strategic samples. These changes could help clarify any causal relationship between screen time and wellbeing; as she points out, "Across the board a small negative correlation between digital technology use and adolescent well-being can be located, but it is not clear whether this represents a clear causal relationship or an association driven by third factors" (p. 412).

Kaye et al. (2020) make similar points to Orben, and extend or introduce others. They also make a set of useful recommendations for studies of screen time, such as employing a wider range of research methodologies to inform a conceptualization of screen time that makes sense to users; differentiating between screen time as a numerical measurement and "screen use" as goal-directed behavior, to capture the different kinds of motivations behind using screens; making use of more direct measurements of time spent on screens, such as app usage logs; and carrying out more studies with control groups, for example made up of people who are restricted from carrying out certain activities online. Relatedly, they also advocate interdisciplinary work on the privacy and security challenges around getting objective access to online usage data; developing theoretical taxonomies for classifying different types of behavior online and how they relate to distinct psychological outcomes; and centering measurements on these theoretically driven behavior categories, rather than on the particular "features and functions" of an app that people are using – which have only a tangential relation to theory and can quickly become obsolete.

Despite the deficiencies in academic research on screen time, we should remember that the negative effects found, while small, do not disappear entirely when subjected to meta-analysis. Moreover, although grand effects of "screen time" may be small and elusive, it seems intuitive to many parents that individual children can become too obsessed with digital devices, and it seems unwise to ignore that intuition completely. Yet in the absence of basic research (informed by the principles set out by Kaye et al., 2020) that reveals what types and aspects of screen use are harmful, it seems premature to offer concrete advice to caregivers on the kinds of restrictions that they should put on the time that their kids are spending online (yet alone restrictions as simplistic as a "2+2 rule"). As well as examining the effects of restricting different kinds of screen usage on kids, applied research should analyze how to balance the large amounts of time that today's children inevitably spend online with access to beneficial offline activities as well. Only then can we come up with nuanced guidelines for caregivers that include positive recommendations for enhancing children's opportunities online, instead of focusing on the monolithic risk factor of spending time looking at screens.

It is therefore worth considering under which circumstances something as ubiquitous as screen use can turn problematic. Despite criticisms of studies of "screen time", many authors have in fact taken quite a nuanced view of internet use, focusing on the variables associated with risky ways of using the internet, and often noting explicitly that problematic use should not be conflated with overall amount of use. A good, relatively early example in the case of Facebook was a study by Lee-Won et al. (2015), which was premised on the idea of individual differences in problematic internet use (on items such as "I have difficulties in focusing on my academic work due to my Facebook use" and "My Facebook use interferes with doing social activities"). The authors started from the point of view that humans have a fundamental motivation for self-presentation – that is, to form and maintain positive impressions of themselves with other people. People differ, however, in their level of skill at self-presentation. Those individuals with relative deficits in social skills may find internet-based interaction safer and more comfortable than face-to-face interaction, leading them to prefer the former as a way of minimizing the social risks associated with self-presentation. They concluded that:

> it will be important to guide Facebook users to understand that their need for affiliation and companionship may be met in a more sustainable way if their social activities can achieve a healthy balance between the offline (face-to-face) and the online realms.
>
> *(Lee-Won et al., 2015, p. 572)*

In other words, the solution is not simply about reducing Facebook or other social network use, but instead making sure that these are not taking time away from healthy offline behaviors.

Several authors have tried to incorporate the idea of screen time taking time away from healthy offline behaviors into the development of scales of internet or gaming addiction. As mentioned in Chapter 1, the World Health Organization (2018) recently – and controversially – included "gaming disorder" (effectively, internet gaming addiction) in its ICD-11 manual of psychiatric disorders. According to the ICD-11, "the condition results in gamers having little control over gaming, gaming [taking] precedence over other life interests, and gaming being continued despite negative consequences" (Hawi et al., 2019). Related to this, academics including Hawi have developed addiction scales based on ICD-11 and *DSM-5* diagnostic criteria, and on Griffiths's (2005) model of the six core addiction criteria (preoccupation, tolerance, withdrawal, mood modification, conflict, and relapse; problems, deception, and displacement were added in the *DSM-5* criteria). The excellent internal consistency achieved by the scale developed by Hawi et al. suggests that these criteria form a meaningful cluster relating to the concept of addiction, though they did note that their study suffered from problems inherent to self-report measures, including short-term memory and social desirability biases.

As with screen time, controversy has beset the debate over addiction to the internet in general, and smartphones in particular. Whether or not the addiction model is the best way of conceptualizing the problems experienced by people who spend more time than is good for them online (a theme I will return to in the context of pornography addiction in the next chapter), it is clear that some individuals and/or their families do feel that they have problems in this area; and rather than quibbling over precise definitions of terms, it would be more productive to work out how best we can help them. The concept of addiction is tightly bound up with that of identity, since in a way the "addict" can suffer from a perceived division or conflict in their self, between what they most like spending time doing and the social expectations of those around them (as well as their own long-term goals and values). Programs of treatment for such individuals should therefore focus on finding a balance between their online behavior and other activities that help meet their needs, and from which they can derive lasting meaning.

2.4 The Dark Side of Visual Communication: Negative Social Comparison, Low Self-esteem, and Depression

The emphasis that social networks put on explicit comparison of how successful a post is at garnering attention (through metrics such as views, likes, shares, and replies) fits with the importance of social comparison in adolescents' offline social networks. Social comparisons take three forms, depending on the relative position of the target individual with whom one is comparing oneself: upward comparison, in which one perceives the target individual as better than oneself in the domain of interest; lateral comparison, in which the target individual is perceived as performing at a comparable level; and downward comparison, in which the target is perceived as doing worse than oneself (Couture Bue, 2020; Tiggemann & Polivy, 2010). Although the direction of social comparison is neutral in itself (upward comparisons may, for example, be an inspiration for change, while downward comparisons may involve feelings of guilt), upward comparisons tend to be seen as more problematic than downward comparisons. Upward social comparisons may be particularly associated with social media because of the tendency for people to follow "influencers" (who have many more followers than they follow themselves), and for all sorts of social media users (and perhaps especially influencers), to present an idealized version of themselves for public consumption. For example, Jain (2017) found that 64% of Americans who had shared a photo of themselves online had edited a photo before sharing it. Editing was reported to be even more frequent with selfie images, which, as we have seen above, are very commonly posted by young people on Instagram and other social networks.

An evolutionary theory of why upward social comparisons are particularly problematic, especially in online social networks, was proposed by Blease (2015), in an insightful discussion of why too much social network use might be conducive to depression. According to Blease, depression – while obviously distressing both for sufferers and for their close friends and family – should not always be seen as pathological: counterintuitively, evolutionary psychology proposes that the mental states it induces can sometimes be adaptive. This makes sense because depression has a high incidence in the population, especially among young people: roughly 8% of college students experience it in a given year, and as many as 30–50% of people do so at some point in their lifetime. And in certain traumatic life situations – especially a bereavement, the breakup of a long-term relationship, or a sudden job loss – a period of depression seems quite natural, or at least understandable. This forms one evolutionary theory of the adaptiveness of depression, known as the "analytical rumination hypothesis": depression is seen as a stress response to a disruptive (and potentially dangerous) change in social support, which might require a reconfiguration of social relations. This also explains why depression might be more common in adolescents. The other main theory discussed by Blease is the "social comparison hypothesis". According to this theory, depression signals submissiveness in the face of higher-status rivals when confronted with a loss of social status (such as might result from a loss of social support). The broad social comparison enabled by Facebook and other social networks may therefore increase the incidence of depression.

In terms of the evidence for a link between the two, however, what this mainly shows is not a simple increase, but a U-shaped curve, where the people most prone to depression are either using social networks the most or the least. One of the first articles to demonstrate this was by Moreno et al. (2012), using an experience-sampling method in which people were asked by text message at regular, randomized intervals – in this case, six times a day – whether they were currently using the internet or not. (This, of course, tends to be more reliable than asking people to estimate how many hours they have been online in the past week.) Meta-analyses have tended to bear out the relationship between depression and internet use, while not always explicitly analyzing for the presence of a U-shaped effect. But the presence of such an effect, combined with sampling differences (either side of the U being underrepresented in the participant sample, for whatever reasons), could partly explain the high heterogeneity in effects that is found between studies. The mechanism behind the effect remains unknown but could be due to people being addicted to internet use, at the right-hand side of the U, and suffering from a lack of meaningful interactions online, at the left-hand side.

As we have seen, young adolescents are still learning about how best to present themselves to others, a competence known as "impression management" (Goffman, 1959). This means that they tend to be worried about how others perceive them and sensitive to any critical appraisals. Young people who do better at self-presentation, and who have a more accurate picture of how they are seen by other people, are more likely to have positive outcomes such as high self-efficacy and a sense of wellbeing, as well as higher social status and more popularity (Lease et al., 2002). Of course, these days the process of learning about self-presentation increasingly takes place in online contexts (Valkenburg & Peter, 2011), where the absence of immediate visual feedback may encourage a more explicit, conscious form of self-representation, involving more self-reflection (Ellison & Boyd, 2013; Meeus et al., 2019). How might this more conscious form of self-representation impact self-esteem? Empirical results are mixed. Some studies have found that spending time on social networking sites or viewing one's own profile can raise self-esteem (Gentile et al., 2012; Gonzales & Hancock, 2011), while others have found less beneficial outcomes, including adverse effects on self-esteem or subjective wellbeing (Chen & Lee, 2013; Kross et al., 2013), or higher levels of depression and anxiety (Primack et al., 2017). In response to this ambiguous picture, various authors have attempted to carry out more fine-grained research on these relationships, since self-esteem is a complex, multiply determined construct that may be influenced in non-straightforward ways by several different factors (Pelham & Swann, 1989), and we would therefore not expect to see large, simple effects of media usage (Valkenburg & Peter, 2013).

Along these lines, many authors have postulated that social comparison may play an important mediating role (Chou & Edge, 2012; Hanna et al., 2017). The visibility of comments and reactions on social networking sites gives them a strongly normative component (Meeus et al., 2019), and indeed, positive reactions are much more frequent than negative ones (Koutamanis et al., 2015). However, this may make negative feedback all the more wounding, explaining why negative responses tend to be particularly linked to increases in depressive symptoms, stress, and other undesirable outcomes (Davila et al., 2012; Weinstein & Selman, 2016). As with the lack of instantaneous feedback, the result may be a disposition to consciously and continuously "perform" a public identity that is viewed favorably by other SNS users and will thus gain them more popularity (Manago, 2015; Trepte & Reinecke, 2013). Indeed, Meeus et al. (2019) found that when their preadolescent and young-adolescent participants posted content on SNS it generated a perception of positive appraisal by other users, which helped boost their self-esteem. They argued that this was consistent with previous findings of a link between self-esteem and receiving approval online (e.g., Burrow & Rainone, 2017). Interestingly, they also found a gender difference: boys reported more need for self-esteem and popularity, while girls were significantly more likely to engage in online browsing and self-presentational activities (Meeus et al., 2019).

Noting that studies of the relationship between social comparison and self-esteem have typically shown only weak and unreliable effects, Lim et al. (2021) recently proposed a novel, "evolutionary mismatch" hypothesis to account for this. According to this hypothesis, negative social comparison with the unrealistic, idealized depictions of other people's lives portrayed on social media only impacts self-esteem when an individual's social network is small enough to correspond to the sort of size it would have had in our evolutionary past. Indeed, these authors found a relationship between social media use and low self-esteem in people who had social networks of around 150 connections. Yet with many of their participants reporting networks numbering over 1,000 online "friends", it seems that in these individuals, social comparison was generally not perceived as taking place with real social connections, and thus social media use did not adversely affect self-esteem. As with other studies mentioned above, Lim et al.'s article demonstrates the complexity of the factors affecting negative outcomes such as depression. If effects of social media use on wellbeing depend on moderating variables like self-esteem and the type of social comparison being made – as well as on an individual's social network size and level of media use, with non-monotonic effects at lower and higher ends of the scale – then it is not surprising that overall effects of screen time tend to be "washed out" when looking at large samples, most of which will be somewhere in the middle with regard to network size, self-esteem, and media usage. We thus need more studies that focus on theoretically vulnerable populations and/or include interventions tested against randomized controls.

2.5 Body Image

Body image is another variable that may mediate negative outcomes of social network use, and that has interesting associations with the variables of gender and age – which of course may differ widely between study samples, further complicating efforts to build up a more general picture of media effects. The topic has recently been highlighted by the media furor (perhaps even moral panic) over the negative impact of social comparison via Instagram on teenage girls' levels of self-esteem in relation to their bodily appearance. As should not be surprising by now, there is much debate over the extent to which body image concern correlates with social network usage. The first studies on the issue focused on Facebook use. A meta-analysis by Frost and Rickwood (2017) of both observational (e.g., Stronge et al., 2015; Tiggemann & Slater, 2013) and experimental studies (e.g., Fardouly et al., 2015; Mabe et al., 2014) found associations between general Facebook use and body image dissatisfaction. A later meta-analysis by Saiphoo and Vahedi (2019) showed more heterogeneous effects, indicating that Facebook-based activities focused on appearance (e.g., browsing photos) perhaps have more of an effect on body image than Facebook use in general.

More recent research has focused on Instagram, as both the most visually oriented of the "big three" social networks (Facebook, Instagram, and Twitter) and the most popular of the three among adolescent girls. Indeed, it is possible that many Instagram users are *motivated* to use it by the potential for making upward social comparisons (e.g., with influencers). And in terms of body image, a recent study by Couture Bue (2020) showed that frequency of Instagram usage, but not frequency of Facebook usage, predicted increased attention to high-anxiety body regions. As the author argued:

> Following the argument that appearance-based activities on social media may be particularly problematic, the use of highly visual social media sites such as Instagram may be more likely to affect women's body satisfaction than low-visual social media, as they encourage more photo-related behaviors than text-based or text and photo platforms.
>
> *(Couture Bue, 2020)*

Along these lines, social media activities that focus on personal appearance tend to predict body image disturbances more than social media usage in general does (Fardouly & Vartanian, 2016; Saiphoo & Vahedi, 2019). For example, an experiment by Casale et al. (2019) asked people who did not already use Instagram to view either a series of Instagram profiles that focused on physical appearance, or no Instagram content, for one week. Women in the experimental group showed higher levels of body dissatisfaction and a greater emphasis on appearance when evaluating self-worth. The limitation of this finding to women is interesting, since females tend to spend more time looking at images of same-sex individuals (McAndrew & Jeong, 2012), and are more likely to engage in social comparison online than men are (Haferkamp et al., 2012; Saiphoo & Vahedi, 2019).

Young women may be particularly vulnerable: Hayes et al. (2015) found that younger users (between 18 and 29 years old) both used Facebook more often and reported greater body image disturbances than older users. Highlighting the importance of social comparison as a mediator of the negative effects of social media usage, some studies (Mackson et al., 2019; Yang, 2016) have linked Instagram use to psychological benefits, such as a reduction in loneliness or improvements in wellbeing, but only for those people who did not engage in frequent social comparison. In terms of offline behavior, frequent visual "body-checking" behaviors tend to correlate with negative feelings about the body (Kraus et al., 2015) and greater body dissatisfaction (Stefano et al., 2016). Translating this to a social media context, it could be that when women think of an online audience's reaction to a photo it prompts them to pay greater attention to areas of bodily insecurity that they fear might be critiqued. As a highly visual social media platform, then, Instagram may encourage its users (especially female ones) to focus on body regions that they have anxieties about, potentially leading to body dissatisfaction.

An important moderator for body image effects may be the extent to which people use Instagram either actively or passively. In theory, active use of Instagram, in which people regularly post updates to meet particular goals, and have meaningful conversations about their own and others' posts, should have more positive effects than passively "doom-scrolling" through image after image without interacting with them in meaningful ways – especially since the latter seems more typical of upward social comparison. Another moderator is whether people think of themselves as expressing their "authentic" selves on social networks such as Instagram, or more as putting on an act. Yet actual evidence of these kinds of moderating effects has been difficult to establish. With my student Steven Lara, I attempted to collect such evidence by comparing the results of surveys on active and passive uses of Instagram, along with authentic and inauthentic uses, with others on self-esteem and body image (Lara & Ingram, 2022). Although overall Instagram usage time had no impact on self-esteem or body image, active use was found to be positively related to self-esteem, but not body image. In terms of authenticity, we discovered a negative relationship between self-esteem and being more authentic online than in face-to-face interactions. Lastly, the data showed similar effects of Instagram use in men and women.

Loneliness is another important variable that has been connected to the use of Instagram and other social networks, and has become even more relevant with the COVID-19 pandemic. Even though we live in an era of increasing social connections, many researchers have suggested that people in general, and young people in particular, feel more alone than ever before (Turkle, 2011). With another student, Valentina Parada, I investigated how different uses of Instagram may be associated with either loneliness or feelings of social connection in young adults (Parada & Ingram, 2022). We used a mixed methodology involving a semi-structured interview alongside the Jong Gierveld loneliness questionnaire and the Active Facebook Use Measure (PAUM), adapted for Instagram use. Some 185 people aged 18–25 answered the questionnaires, with 16 of them also participating in the interview. Eight interview participants had high levels and eight had low levels of loneliness. The results showed that active and passive use did not correlate with levels of loneliness, but in the interviews some interesting differences emerged, which suggested that using social networks does not generate loneliness by itself, but that loneliness is more related to the quality of interactions that people have online.

As in other areas of media effects, the possible risks of using social networks such as Instagram in increasingly visual ways, and the social comparison processes that such usage triggers, appear to be influenced by many other variables from which they are difficult to disentangle. Although active use may be related to higher self-esteem, the direction of the causal arrow is unclear. Perhaps people with high self-esteem tend to use social networks to "show off" in more social ways, rather than the latter activity augmenting their self-esteem. Or it could be that users get stuck in vicious or virtuous circles, with more active usage patterns being both a cause and an effect of high self-esteem. Chasing small quantitative effects from ever-more detailed consideration of moderating variables seems like something of a losing game, since it will probably never be possible to disentangle the causal influences to everyone's satisfaction (given that realistic, ecologically valid experimental studies are very difficult when studying such complex social behavior, and longitudinal studies are also complicated hugely by rapid changes in the relevant technology during the study period). Furthermore, the sorts of social comparison processes that take place on social networks are not new: it is only the modality by which they play out that is new.

Yet it is also clear that some individuals can have psychological problems – whether with body image, self-esteem, depression, loneliness, or all of the above – that are exacerbated, at least subjectively, by their use of social networks. The way out of this impasse may be to find ways of identifying such individuals and work with them to clarify the ways in which they are using social networks pathologically, and (if necessary) to encourage them to find healthier, more productive ways of fitting these technologies into their lives. The lessons learned from such studies could then be incorporated into the design of the social networks themselves, and finally the use for quantitative studies could come in analyzing whether such changes have really made a difference. Such an approach would fit with the final topic to be covered in this chapter, which concerns the use of internet technology to deliver help with mental health problems in more scalable and cost-effective ways.

2.6 New Opportunities for Mental Health Interventions

Up to now in this chapter I have been focused on the potential risks to adolescents of using the internet. However, the internet also offers many new opportunities for improving health outcomes, via the provision of health services online, or cyberhealth. This is particularly true in the case of clinical psychology. Whereas most other areas of cyberhealth are essentially limited to referring people to health specialists and, at most, providing a diagnosis and medical advice, cyberhealth can provide full-fledged interventions and programs of treatment online. It thus offers a unique set of opportunities and challenges for psychologists and policymakers in the digital era. There are also particular advantages for adolescents in receiving treatment online, which relate to some of the features of adolescent identity explored at the start of this chapter.

Probably the most important advantage of online psychological treatment is its scalability: the low cost, compared to conventional face-to-face therapies or counseling, means that many more patients can be treated effectively. Not only that, but the reach of treatment can extend into less accessible geographical areas, far from a country's major cities, and to patients who have difficulties with leaving home (as adolescents may often do due to their school timetable and lack of independence from parents). A further advantage is that patients can be attended more rapidly and at any time of the day or night, due to the internet's "always-on" nature allowing access to an enormous pool of psychologists. And finally, the greater feeling of anonymity afforded by the internet is a great advantage for attracting patients to receive attention who might otherwise be too embarrassed by the "stigma" of their problems (a particular issue with mental health conditions, of course). This is a particular issue for adolescents because of issues like the personal fable and hypersensitivity to social comparison discussed earlier.

On the flip side, because of that very feeling of anonymity there can be a lack of emotional connection in online therapy or counseling sessions, which could lead to the therapist or counselor missing significant details in what a patient is telling them. Not only that, but the lack of personal connection can contribute to a lack of motivation in engaging with the sessions, contributing to high rates of patient attrition (Richards & Richardson, 2012) which is known to be a particular problem for adolescents, who, due to changing identities and motivations, may not always commit to a particular course of action (such as seeking treatment) with as much "staying power" as adults. It must also be admitted that the therapeutic environment may not be ideal: one or both participants may be in a public or semi-public place, such as a café, which is not ideal for psychological consultation (especially for adolescents who are sensitive to social comparison); and the session may also be interrupted, either by other people or by technical problems with the communication service. Finally, holding face-to-face sessions in a formal institutional setting such as a clinic provides a certain level of guarantee about the credentials of the psychologist administering the sessions.

It is much harder to regulate who is providing the service in newer, less formal, internet-based environments – which, as we shall see in Chapter 4 of this book, can be a risk for adolescents, who for developmental reasons may be particularly vulnerable to exploitation and abuse in online relationships.

We saw earlier in the chapter that due to the importance of social comparison and their relative lack of status, adolescents may be especially vulnerable to depression. Because of the advantages of online psychological treatment explored above and the particular difficulties that depressed people may have in seeking face-to-face treatment, efforts to develop virtual interventions for depression started early, with a 2012 systematic review and meta-analysis already finding that computer-based treatments were largely effective (Richards & Richardson, 2012), particularly in the case of supported interventions that included active virtual contact with a therapist (as opposed to self-paced online courses), which exhibited both larger effect sizes and more participant retention. A much more recent meta-analysis of randomized control trials by Moshe et al. (2021) echoed these findings, replicating the stronger effect size for therapist-supported studies and also showing that efficacy (the ability of an intervention to work in ideal conditions) was easier to demonstrate than effectiveness (the ability of an intervention to work in real-world conditions), with much higher effect sizes in efficacy trials. There thus remains a significant challenge for the future – familiar to educational researchers in many different domains – in terms of ensuring that programs of treatment developed by academics can be shown to function when removed from tightly controlled parameters and let loose on everyday people and situations.

2.7 Conclusion

I began this chapter by emphasizing that in common with most social mammals, human adolescents naturally tend to become somewhat more distant from their parents than they were in childhood. Some of the intimacy of the parental bond is replaced by new alliances with peers, and an important element in maintaining these new alliances is the construction of new forms of individual identity, which are linked to reputation and acceptance by peers. However, these new identities can be mysterious and sometimes worrying to parents, both because they conflict (implicitly or explicitly) with the previous image that they held of their child, and because they are often linked to new cultural worlds, mediated by novel forms of cultural content that contemporary adults find difficult to navigate (a theme I return to in more detail in the next chapter). Sometimes, moreover, parents are right to be worried, since the conflict between their earlier and current (never mind future) identities can cause problems of self-esteem and social adjustment in the adolescent mind, particularly if they are rejected or neglected by peers. In this sense, identity-related processes that are taking place today with digital culture are but the latest manifestation of a social and psychological phenomenon as old as the hills. Yet the advent of the internet, and particularly social networking software, has of course transformed these processes as well, not only because peer culture and individual identity now seem to be changing so rapidly, but also because they have become increasingly mediated by visual images rather than solely by language.

The ability to view and manipulate images of oneself and others in different contexts, constantly and at will, while one is growing up, is likely to have profound psychological consequences in terms of how individuals view their own identity. Indeed, it is possible that it will one day be seen as a transformational innovation to rival the internet itself, or even the invention of writing. What is clear is that this new ability is already being integrated with verbal language in interesting ways. The simplest example of this is the use of emoji to add nonverbal expressions to text-based language, which has undoubtedly helped make electronic communication feel more human and immediate for many millions of people over the years. However, in this chapter I argued that selfies and memes are two more important forms of visual "language" for young people. Both these communication forms are integrated with verbal language in far-reaching ways: selfies through captions, hashtags, and interactive comments and messages (Instagram's "Ask Me A Question" feature being a particularly powerful example of this); memes through the incorporation of editable text captions, and through posting, commenting on, and reposting them to social media. In the case of both memes and selfies, as we saw, the point is to master the visual language by posting them in a way that is at once "traditional" and creative, thus demonstrating one's identity and standing as a competent member of the community to which the language belongs. Ignorance of the rules of these languages can contribute to the exclusion of interested adults, including parents, from these communities of young people.

The fact that parents do not understand the kind of identity that their adolescent children are constructing online – and how this differs from their earlier, childhood identity – helps to explain some of the "moral panic" around screen time. We saw that the evidence for negative effects of screen time on wellbeing is weak and beset by methodological flaws; but also that there *is* a consistent effect found across many studies, and that the effects of such obviously wellbeing-decreasing things as bullying, asthma, or wearing glasses may not be all that much stronger. One reason for the negative effects of screen time may be that some (not all) children may be missing out on worthwhile offline activities that foster a sense of connection with other people, due to the amount of time that they are spending with screens. It is hard to come up with recommendations for parents without knowing more about the dynamics of such processes. In common with many other researchers in this area, I therefore advocate more controlled, longitudinal studies that systematically vary the kinds of activities that children are exposed to, both online and offline, and measure not only their quantitative effects on wellbeing but also the qualitative experiences of the children and families involved.

One factor that would be worth considering in such studies, because it may mediate the negative effects of screen time (and especially time spent on social networks), is the nature of the social comparison that young people engage in online. Too much "upward" social comparison can be problematic, and may even be associated with depression, because it can lead to negative assessment of an individual's own identity compared with the curated, unrealistically positive view that they have of influencers or popular peers when looking at their social media presence. Much work, both qualitative and quantitative, remains to be done in order to clarify how such social comparison is affected by contextual factors, such as the number of online friends that an individual has and how actively or passively they are using social networks. There remains much potential for investigating the different forms of social comparison that take place on social networks and how this has changed from pre-internet days. Important changes include the exposure to larger and more diverse audiences online, which would seem to require more complex forms of mentalizing to manage reputation effectively (Davis & Jurgenson, 2014; Hamilton & Lind, 2016), and the permanence of reputation-relevant information online, sometimes known as a "digital footprint" (Hinds & Joinson, 2019) which can lead people to self-censor their online reports of their activities (Davidson & Joinson, 2021), or even inhibit gossip-worthy aspects of their offline lives (Marder et al., 2016).

Young people's bodily self-image and self-esteem form another set of processes that fit in very well with the visual construction of identity discussed above. In theory, the incessant focus of "visual social networks" (particularly Instagram, Snapchat and TikTok) on images of the body, as exemplified by the proliferation of selfies found on these networks, combined with uncertainty and anxiety about bodily changes during adolescence, could contribute to psychological problems such as eating disorders associated with negative body image, especially among adolescent girls and young women. In fact, the evidence for such links is far from solid, and media preoccupation with the effect on girls may be problematic given that some recent studies have pointed to similar issues for young men. Again, systematic longitudinal and mixed-methods investigations of detailed factors that affect these relationships (in as controlled a way as possible) will be essential going forward.

On the other hand, it must also be considered that focused online activities can help adolescents come to terms with their identity. This is true of what might be called "youth-led" activities, such as multiplayer games and social network communities. Yet perhaps an even more striking demonstration is in the use of internet technology to provide mental health treatment and prevention programs to young people. These services have certain advantages, compared to offline services, which seem almost tailor-made for adolescents, such as the ability to connect from anywhere at any time of the day or night, and the relative anonymity of being able to talk to a mental health professional online instead of in person, helping to alleviate both the extreme self-consciousness that adolescents often feel and the stigma associated with mental illness. Online programs thus hold much promise for treating identity-related disorders that seem almost endemic to adolescence, such as depression, loneliness, social anxiety, addictive or compulsive behavior, and eating disorders.

In this chapter I have shown how adolescents naturally try to forge a separate identity from their parents, and how as a corollary of that they grow to identify more with peers. In the digital age, this means that they spend increasing amounts of time online, and that parents have less and less understanding of what they are engaged in and who they are interacting with online. In the next chapter, I show how this phenomenon can lead parents and other adults to worry about the effects of various kinds of online content on their children's attitudes and behavior. Some of these fears may be justified, but many may be exaggerated; and public discourse again has tended to ignore the opportunities that adolescents can enjoy from sharing certain kinds of content online.

Notes

1 https://knowyourmeme.com/memes/dancing-baby
2 https://knowyourmeme.com/memes/distracted-boyfriend
3 AAP Media Time Calculator: https://www.healthychildren.org/English/media/Pages/default.aspx

References

Acerbi, A. (2019). *Cultural evolution in the digital age*. Oxford University Press.

Arnett, J. J. (1999). Adolescent storm and stress, reconsidered. *American Psychologist, 54*(5), 317–326.

Bakhshi, S., Shamma, D. A., Kennedy, L., & Gilbert, E. (2015). Why we filter our photos and how it impacts engagement. *Proceedings of the Ninth International AAAI Conference on Web and Social Media*. Retrieved from https://ojs.aaai.org/index.php/ICWSM/article/view/14622

Baxter, K. (2011). *The modern age: Turn-of-the-century American culture and the invention of adolescence*. University of Alabama Press.

Ben-Amos, I. K. (1995). Adolescence as a cultural invention: Philippe Ariès and the sociology of youth. *History of the Human Sciences, 8*, 69–89. https://doi.org/10.1177/095269519500800204

Benjamin, A., Domene, J., & Landine, K. (2014). Constructing the future in the liminal spaces between adolescence and adulthood: Responsibilities, careers, and social contexts. *Canadian Journal of Career Development, 13*, 37–45. https://cjcd-rcdc.ceric.ca/index.php/cjcd/article/view/189

Blakemore, S. J., & Mills, K. L. (2014). Is adolescence a sensitive period for sociocultural processing? *Annual Review of Psychology, 65*, 187–207. https://doi.org/10.1146/annurev-psych-010213-115202

Blease, C. R. (2015). Too many 'friends,' too few 'likes'? Evolutionary psychology and 'Facebook depression'. *Review of General Psychology, 19*, 1–13. https://doi.org/10.1037/gpr0000030

Blum-Ross, A., & Livingstone, S. (2018). The trouble with "screen time" rules. In G. Mascheroni, C. Ponte, & A. Jorge (Eds.), *Digital parenting: The challenges for families in the digital age* (pp. 179–187). Nordicom.

Burrow, A. L., & Rainone, N. (2017). How many likes did I get? Purpose moderates links between positive social media feedback and self-esteem. *Journal of Experimental Social Psychology*, *69*, 232–236. https://doi.org/10.1016/j.jesp.2016.09.005

Caballero, A., Granberg, R., & Tseng, K. Y. (2016). Mechanisms contributing to pre-frontal cortex maturation during adolescence. *Neuroscience & Biobehavioral Reviews*, *70*, 4–12. https://doi.org/10.1016/j.neubiorev.2016.05.013

Casale, S., Gemelli, G., Calosi, C., Giangrasso, B., & Fioravanti, G. (2019). Multiple exposure to appearance-focused real accounts on Instagram: Effects on body image among both genders. *Current Psychology*, *40*, 2877–2886. https://doi.org/10.1007/s12144-019-00229-6

Chen, W., & Lee, K. H. (2013). Sharing, liking, commenting, and distressed? The pathway between Facebook interaction and psychological distress. *Cyberpsychology, Behavior, and Social Networking*, *16*, 728–734. https://doi.org/10.1089/cyber.2012.0272

Chou, H. T. G., & Edge, N. (2012). "They are happier and having better lives than I am": The impact of using Facebook on perceptions of others' lives. *Cyberpsychology, Behavior, and Social Networking*, *15*, 117–121. https://doi.org/10.1089/cyber.2011.0324

Couture Bue, A. C. (2020). The looking glass selfie: Instagram use frequency predicts visual attention to high-anxiety body regions in young women. *Computers in Human Behavior*, *108*, 106329. https://doi.org/10.1016/j.chb.2020.106329

Dancygier, B., & Vandelanotte, L. (2017). Internet memes as multimodal constructions. *Cognitive Linguistics*, *28*, 565–598. https://doi.org/10.1515/cog-2017-0074

Davila, J., Hershenberg, R., Feinstein, B. A., Gorman, K., Bhatia, V., & Starr, L. R. (2012). Frequency and quality of social networking among young adults: Associations with depressive symptoms, rumination, and corumination. *Psychology of Popular Media Culture*, *1*, 72–86. https://doi.org/10.1037/a0027512

Davidson, B. I., & Joinson, A. N. (2021). Shape shifting across social media. *Social Media and Society*, *7*, 1–11. https://doi.org/10.1177/2056305121990632

Davis, J. L., Jurgenson, N. (2014). Context collapse: Theorizing context collusions and collisions. *Information, Communication & Society*, *17*, 476–485. https://doi.org/10.1080/1369118X.2014.888458

Davison, P. (2012). The language of internet memes. In M. Mandiberg (Ed.), *The social media reader* (pp. 120–134). New York University Press.

Delaney, C. H. (1995). Rites of passage in adolescence. *Adolescence*, *30*, 891–898. http://link.gale.com/apps/doc/A17856544/AONE

Dickson, K., et al. (2018). *Screen-based activities and children and young people's mental health and psychosocial wellbeing: A systematic map of reviews*. EPPI-Centre, Social Science Research Unit, UCL Institute of Education. https://eppi.ioe.ac.uk/cms/Portals/0/PDF%20reviews%20and%20summaries/Systematic%20Map%20of%20Reviews%20on%20Screen-based%20activties_08.01.19.pdf?ver=2019-01-29-155200-517

Elkind, D. (1967). Egocentrism in adolescence. *Child Development*, *38*, 1025–1034. https://doi.org/10.2307/1127100

Elkind, D., & Bowen, R. (1979). Imaginary audience behavior in children and adolescents. *Developmental Psychology*, *15*, 38–44. https://doi.org/10.1037/0012-1649.15.1.38

Ellison, N. B., & Boyd, D. (2013). Sociality through social network sites. In W. H. Dutton (Ed.), *The Oxford handbook of internet studies* (pp. 151–172). Oxford University Press.

Erikson, E. H. (1980). *Identity and the life cycle*. W. W. Norton.

Fardouly, J., Diedrichs, P. C., Vartanian, L. R., & Halliwell, E. (2015). Social comparisons on social media: The impact of Facebook on young women's body image concerns and mood. *Body Image, 13*, 38–45. https://doi.org/10.1016/j.bodyim.2014.12.002

Fardouly, J., & Vartanian, L. R. (2016). Social media and body image concerns: Current research and future directions. *Current Opinion in Psychology, 9*, 1–5. https://doi.org/10.1016/j.copsyc.2015.09.005

Fischhoff, B., de Bruin, W. B., Parker, A. M., Millstein, S. G., & Halpern-Felsher, B. L. (2010). Adolescents' perceived risk of dying. *Journal of Adolescent Health, 46*, 265–269. https://doi.org/10.1016/j.jadohealth.2009.06.026

Frost, R. L., & Rickwood, D. J. (2017). A systematic review of the mental health outcomes associated with Facebook use. *Computers in Human Behavior, 76*, 576–600. https://doi.org/10.1016/j.chb.2017.08.001

Funston, P. J., Mills, M. G., Richardson, P. R., & van Jaarsveld, A. S. (2003). Reduced dispersal and opportunistic territory acquisition in male lions (*Panthera leo*). *Journal of Zoology, 259*(2), 131–142. https://doi.org/10.1017/S0952836902003126

Gallud, J. A., Fardoun, H. M., Andres, F., & Safa, N. (2018). A study on how older people use emojis. In *Proceedings of the XIX International Conference on Human Computer Interaction* (pp. 1–4). https://doi.org/10.1145/3233824.3233861

Gardner, M., & Steinberg, L. (2005). Peer influence on risk taking, risk preference, and risky decision making in adolescence and adulthood: An experimental study. *Developmental Psychology, 41*, 625–635. https://doi.org/10.1037/0012-1649.41.4.625

Gentile, B., Twenge, J. M., Freeman, E. C., & Campbell, W. K. (2012). The effect of social networking websites on positive self-views: An experimental investigation. *Computers in Human Behavior, 28*, 1929–1933. https://doi.org/10.1016/j.chb.2012.05.012

Giordano, P. C. (2003). Relationships in adolescence. *Annual Review of Sociology, 29*, 257–281. https://www.jstor.org/stable/30036968

Goffman, E. (1959). *The presentation of self in everyday life*. Anchor.

Gonzales, A. L., & Hancock, J. T. (2011). Mirror, mirror on my Facebook wall: Effects of exposure to Facebook on self-esteem. *Cyberpsychology, Behavior, and Social Networking, 14*, 79–83. https://doi.org/10.1089/cyber.2009.0411

Granic, I., Lobel, A., & Engels, R. C. (2014). The benefits of playing video games. *American Psychologist, 69*, 66–78. https://doi.org/10.1037/a0034857

Griffiths, M. (2005). A 'components' model of addiction within a biopsychosocial framework. *Journal of Substance Use, 10*, 191–197. https://doi.org/10.1080/14659890500114359

Gur, R. C., Schroeder, L., Turner, T., McGrath, C., Chan, R. M., Turetsky, B. I., … Gur, R. E. (2002). Brain activation during facial emotion processing. *Neuroimage, 16*(3), 651–662. https://doi.org/10.1006/nimg.2002.1097

Güroğlu, B., van den Bos, W., & Crone, E. A. (2009). Fairness considerations: Increasing understanding of intentionality during adolescence. *Journal of Experimental Child Psychology, 104*, 398–409. https://doi.org/10.1016/j.jecp.2009.07.002

Haferkamp, N., Eimler, S. C., Papadakis, A. M., & Kruck, J. V. (2012). Men are from Mars, women are from Venus? Examining gender differences in self-presentation on social networking sites. *Cyberpsychology, Behavior, and Social Networking, 15*, 91–98. https://doi.org/10.1089/cyber.2011.0151

Hall, G. S. (1907). *Adolescence: Its psychology and its relations to physiology, anthropology, sociology, sex, crime, religion and education*. Appleton.

Hamilton, A., & Lind, F. (2016). Audience effects: What can they tell us about social neuroscience, theory of mind and autism? *Culture and Brain, 4*, 159–177. https://doi.org/10.1007/s40167-016-0044-5

Hanna, E., Ward, L. M., Seabrook, R. C., Jerald, M., Reed, L., Giaccardi, S., & Lippman, J. R. (2017). Contributions of social comparison and self-objectification in mediating associations between Facebook use and emergent adults' psychological well-being. *Cyberpsychology, Behavior, and Social Networking*, *20*, 172–179. https://doi.org/10.1089/cyber.2016.0247

Harris, E., & Bardey, A. C. (2019). Do Instagram profiles accurately portray personality? An investigation into idealized online self-presentation. *Frontiers in Psychology*, *10*, 871. https://doi.org/10.3389/fpsyg.2019.00871

Hawi, N. S., Samaha, M., & Griffiths, M. D. (2019). The digital addiction scale for children: Development and validation. *Cyberpsychology, Behavior, and Social Networking*, *22*, 771–778. https://doi.org/10.1089/cyber.2019.0132

Hayes, M., van Stolk-Cooke, K., & Muench, F. (2015). Understanding Facebook use and the psychological affects of use across generations. *Computers in Human Behavior*, *49*, 507–511. https://doi.org/10.1016/j.chb.2015.03.040

Hinds, J., & Joinson, A. (2019). Human and computer personality prediction from digital footprints. *Current Directions in Psychological Science*, *28*, 204–211. https://doi.org/10.1177/0963721419827849

Ingram, G. P. D. (2014). From hitting to tattling to gossip: An evolutionary rationale for the development of indirect aggression. *Evolutionary Psychology*, *12*(2), 147470491401200205. https://doi.org/10.1177/147470491401200205

Ingram, G. P. D. (2019). Gossip and reputation in childhood. In F. Giardini & R. Wittek (Eds.), *The Oxford handbook of gossip and reputation* (pp. 132–151). Oxford University Press.

Inhelder, B., & Piaget, J. (1958). *The growth of logical thinking from childhood to adolescence*. Basic Books.

Instagram (2020). *Introducing Instagram Reels*. Retrieved from https://about.instagram.com/blog/announcements/introducing-instagram-reels-announcement

Jain, R. (2017, May 18). Photo editing makes people distrust social media, dating sites, report says. *International Business Times*. https://www.ibtimes.com/photo-editing-makes-people-distrust-social-media-dating-sites-report-says-2540439

Kaye, L. K., Malone, S. A., & Wall, H. J. (2017). Emojis: Insights, affordances, and possibilities for psychological science. *Trends in Cognitive Sciences*, *21*(2), 66–68. https://doi.org/10.1016/j.tics.2016.10.007

Kaye, L. K., Orben, A., Ellis, D. A., Hunter, S. C., & Houghton, S. (2020). The conceptual and methodological mayhem of "screen time". *International Journal of Environmental Research and Public Health*, *17*, 3661. https://doi.org/10.3390/ijerph17103661

Kaye, L. K., Wall, H. J., & Malone, S. A. (2016). "Turn that frown upside-down": A contextual account of emoticon usage on different virtual platforms. *Computers in Human Behavior*, *60*, 463–467. https://doi.org/10.1016/j.chb.2016.02.088

Khleif, N. (2021). *YouTube and its content production*. Unpublished thesis, Vaasan Ammattikorkeakoulu University of Applied Sciences. Retrieved from https://www.theseus.fi/bitstream/handle/10024/500527/Khleif_Nasser.pdf?sequence=2

Koutamanis, M., Vossen, H. G., & Valkenburg, P. M. (2015). Adolescents' comments in social media: Why do adolescents receive negative feedback and who is most at risk? *Computers in Human Behavior*, *53*, 486–494. https://doi.org/10.1016/j.chb.2015.07.016

Kraus, N., Lindenberg, J., Zeeck, A., Kosfelder, J., & Vocks, S. (2015). Immediate effects of body checking behaviour on negative and positive emotions in women with eating disorders: An ecological momentary assessment approach. *European Eating Disorders Review*, *23*, 399–407. https://doi.org/10.1002/erv.2380

Kross, E., Verduyn, P., Demiralp, E., Park, J., Lee, D. S., Lin, N., et al. (2013). Facebook use predicts declines in subjective well-being in young adults. *PloS One*, *8*, e69841. https://doi.org/10.1371/journal.pone.0069841

Lara, F. S., & Ingram, G. P. D. (2022). *Relationships between different types of Instagram use, self-esteem, and body image*. Manuscript Under Review.

Lease, A. M., Musgrove, K. T., & Axelrod, J. L. (2002). Dimensions of social status in preadolescent peer groups: Likability, perceived popularity, and social dominance. *Social Development*, *11*, 508–533. https://doi.org/10.1111/1467-9507.00213

Lee-Won, R. J., Herzog, L., & Park, S. G. (2015). Hooked on Facebook: The role of social anxiety and need for social assurance in problematic use of Facebook. *Cyberpsychology, Behavior, and Social Networking*, *18*, 567–574. https://doi.org/10.1089/cyber.2015.0002

Li, B., Scott, O. K., Naraine, M. L., & Ruihley, B. J. (2021). Tell me a story: Exploring elite female athletes' self-presentation via an analysis of Instagram Stories. *Journal of Interactive Advertising*, 1–19. https://doi.org/10.1080/15252019.2020.1837038

Lim, A. J., Lau, C., & Li, N. P. (2021). The moderating role of social network size on social media use and self-esteem: An evolutionary mismatch perspective. *Frontiers in Psychology*, 4286. https://doi.org/10.3389/fpsyg.2021.734206

Lonardo, R. A., Giordano, P. C., Longmore, M. A., & Manning, W. D. (2009). Parents, friends, and romantic partners: Enmeshment in deviant networks and adolescent delinquency involvement. *Journal of Youth and Adolescence*, *38*(3), 367–383. https://doi.org/10.1007/s10964-008-9333-4

Maag, N., Cozzi, G., Bateman, A., Heistermann, M., Ganswindt, A., Manser, M., … & Ozgul, A. (2019). Cost of dispersal in a social mammal: body mass loss and increased stress. *Proceedings of the Royal Society B*, *286*(1896), 20190033. https://doi.org/10.1098/rspb.2019.0033

Mabe, A. G., Forney, K. J., & Keel, P. K. (2014). Do you "like" my photo? Facebook use maintains eating disorder risk. *International Journal of Eating Disorders*, *47*, 516–523. https://doi.org/10.1002/eat.22254

Machin, D., & Van Leeuwen, T. (2007). *Global media discourse: A critical introduction*. Routledge.

Mackson, S. B., Brochu, P. M., & Schneider, B. A. (2019). Instagram: Friend or foe? The application's association with psychological well-being. *New Media & Society*, *21*, 2160–2182. https://doi.org/10.1177/1461444819840021

Manago, A. M. (2015). Identity development in the digital age: The case of social networking sites. In K. C. McLean & M. Syed (Eds.) *The Oxford handbook of identity development* (pp. 508–524). Oxford University Press.

Marder, B., Houghton, D., Joinson, A., Shankar, A., & Bull, E. (2016). Understanding the psychological process of avoidance-based self-regulation on Facebook. *Cyberpsychology, Behavior, and Social Networking*, *19*, 321–327. https://doi.org/10.1089/cyber.2015.0564

Marjamäki, P. H., Contasti, A. L., Coulson, T. N., & McLoughlin, P. D. (2013). Local density and group size interacts with age and sex to determine direction and rate of social dispersal in a polygynous mammal. *Ecology and Evolution*, *3*(9), 3073–3082. https://doi.org/10.1002/ece3.694

McAndrew, F. T., & Jeong, H. S. (2012). Who does what on Facebook? Age, sex, and relationship status as predictors of Facebook use. *Computers in Human Behavior*, *28*, 2359–2365. https://doi.org/10.1016/j.chb.2012.07.007

McRoberts, S., Ma, H., Hall, A., & Yarosh, S. (2017). Share first, save later: Performance of self through Snapchat stories. In *Proceedings of the 2017 CHI conference on human factors in computing systems* (pp. 6902–6911). https://doi.org/10.1145/3025453.3025771

Meeus, A., Beullens, K., & Eggermont, S. (2019). Like me (please?): Connecting online self-presentation to pre-and early adolescents' self-esteem. *New Media and Society, 21*, 2386–2403. https://doi.org/10.1177/1461444819847447
Miller, P. H. (1989). Theories of adolescent development. In J. Worrell & F. Danner (Eds.), *The adolescent as decision-maker* (pp. 13–46). Academic Press.
Mittmann, G., Woodcock, K., Dörfler, S., Krammer, I., Pollak, I., & Schrank, B. (2021). "TikTok is my life and Snapchat is my ventricle": A mixed-methods study on the role of online communication tools for friendships in early adolescents. *Journal of Early Adolescence*, 02724316211020368. https://doi.org/10.1177%2F02724316211020368
Montag, C., Yang, H., & Elhai, J. D. (2021). On the psychology of TikTok use: A first glimpse from empirical findings. *Frontiers in Public Health, 9*, 62. https://doi.org/10.3389/fpubh.2021.641673
Montefalcon, M. D., Padilla, J. R., Paulino, J., Go, J., Llabanes Rodriguez, R., & Imperial, J. M. (2021). Understanding facial expression expressing hate from online short-form videos. In *2021 5th International Conference on E-Society, E-Education and E-Technology* (pp. 201–207). https://doi.org/10.1145/3485768.3485785
Moreno, M. A., Jelenchick, L., Koff, R., Eikoff, J., Diermyer, C., & Christakis, D. A. (2012). Internet use and multitasking among older adolescents: An experience sampling approach. *Computers in Human Behavior, 28*, 1097–1102. https://doi.org/10.1016/j.chb.2012.01.016
Moshe, I., Terhorst, Y., Philippi, P., Domhardt, M., Cuijpers, P., Cristea, I., … & Sander, L. B. (2021). Digital interventions for the treatment of depression: A meta-analytic review. *Psychological Bulletin, 147*, 749–786. https://psycnet.apa.org/doi/10.1037/bul0000334
Olivera-La Rosa, A., Arango-Tobón, O. E., & Ingram, G. P. D. (2019). Swiping right: Face perception in the age of Tinder. *Heliyon, 5*(12), e02949. https://doi.org/10.1016/j.heliyon.2019.e02949
Orben, A. (2020). Teenagers, screens and social media: A narrative review of reviews and key studies. *Social Psychiatry and Psychiatric Epidemiology, 55*, 407–414. https://doi.org/10.1007/s00127-019-01825-4
Orben, A., & Przybylski, A. K. (2019a). Screens, teens, and psychological well-being: Evidence from three time-use-diary studies. *Psychological Science, 30*, 682–696. https://doi.org/10.1177%2F0956797619830329
Orben, A., & Przybylski, A. K. (2019b). The association between adolescent well-being and digital technology use. *Nature Human Behaviour, 3*, 173–182. https://doi.org/10.1038/s41562-018-0506-1
Orben, A., & Przybylski, A. K. (2020). Reply to: Underestimating digital media harm. *Nature Human Behaviour, 4*, 349–351. https://doi.org/10.1038/s41562-020-0840-y
Page, A. S., Cooper, A. R., Griew, P., & Jago, R. (2010). Children's screen viewing is related to psychological difficulties irrespective of physical activity. *Pediatrics, 126*, e1011–e1017. https://doi.org/10.1542/peds.2010-1154
Parada, V., & Ingram, G. P. D. (2022). *Instagram and loneliness: Young Colombian adults' uses and perception of Instagram during the COVID-19 pandemic*. Manuscript Under Review.
Pelham, B. W., & Swann, W. B. (1989). From self-conceptions to self-worth: On the sources and structure of global self-esteem. *Journal of Personality and Social Psychology, 57*, 672–680. https://doi.org/10.1037/0022-3514.57.4.672
Primack, B. A., Shensa, A., Escobar-Viera, C. G., Barrett, E. L., Sidani, J. E., Colditz, J. B., & James, A. E. (2017). Use of multiple social media platforms and

symptoms of depression and anxiety: A nationally-representative study among US young adults. *Computers in Human Behavior, 69*, 1–9. https://doi.org/10.1016/j.chb.2016.11.013

Przybylski, A. K., & Weinstein, N. (2017). A large-scale test of the Goldilocks hypothesis: Quantifying the relations between digital-screen use and the mental well-being of adolescents. *Psychological Science, 28*, 204–215. https://doi.org/10.1177/0956797616678438

Richards, D., & Richardson, T. (2012). Computer-based psychological treatments for depression: A systematic review and meta-analysis. *Clinical Psychology Review, 32*, 329–342. https://doi.org/10.1016/j.cpr.2012.02.004

Romano, V., Martins, A. F., & Ruiz-Miranda, C. R. (2019). Unraveling the dispersal patterns and the social drivers of natal emigration of a cooperative breeding mammal, the golden lion tamarin. *American Journal of Primatology, 81*(3), e22959. https://doi.org/10.1002/ajp.22959

Romer, D., Bagdasarov, Z., & More, E. (2013). Older versus newer media and the well-being of United States youth: Results from a national longitudinal panel. *Journal of Adolescent Health, 52*, 613–619. https://doi.org/10.1016/j.jadohealth.2012.11.012

Rosen, L. D., Lim, A. F., Felt, J., Carrier, L. M., Cheever, N. A., Lara-Ruiz, J. M., et al. (2014). Media and technology use predicts ill-being among children, preteens and teenagers independent of the negative health impacts of exercise and eating habits. *Computers in Human Behavior, 35*, 364–375. https://doi.org/10.1016/j.chb.2014.01.036

Rousseau, A. (2021). Adolescents' selfie-activities and idealized online self-presentation: An application of the sociocultural model. *Body Image, 36*, 16–26. https://doi.org/10.1016/j.bodyim.2020.10.005

Rowett, G. (2018). The strategic need to understand online memes and modern information warfare theory. In *2018 IEEE International Conference on Big Data (Big Data)* (pp. 4437–4442). IEEE. https://doi.org/10.1109/BigData.2018.8622051

Sabbagh, M. A. (1999). Communicative intentions and language: Evidence from right-hemisphere damage and autism. *Brain and Language, 70*(1), 29–69. https://doi.org/10.1006/brln.1999.2139

Saiphoo, A. N., & Vahedi, Z. (2019). A meta-analytic review of the relationship between social media use and body image disturbance. *Computers in Human Behavior, 101*, 259–275. https://doi.org/10.1016/j.chb.2019.07.028

Schwarz, O. (2010). On friendship, boobs and the logic of the catalogue: Online self-portraits as a means for the exchange of capital. *Convergence: The International Journal of Research into New Media Technologies, 16*, 163–183. https://doi.org/10.1177/1354856509357582

Shifman, L. (2014). *Memes in digital culture*. MIT Press.

Siegel, O. (1982). Personality development in adolescence. In B. B. Wolman (Ed.), *Handbook of developmental psychology* (pp. 537–548). Prentice-Hall.

Snow, P. C., & Bruce, D. D. (2003). Cigarette smoking in teenage girls: Exploring the role of peer reputations, self-concept and coping. *Health Education Research, 18*(4), 439–452. https://doi.org/10.1093/her/cyf029

Stefano, E. C., Hudson, D. L., Whisenhunt, B. L., Buchanan, E. M., & Latner, J. D. (2016). Examination of body checking, body image dissatisfaction, and negative affect using ecological momentary assessment. *Eating Behaviors, 22*, 51–54. https://doi.org/10.1016/j.eatbeh.2016.03.026

Stronge, S., Greaves, L. M., Milojev, P., West-Newman, T., Barlow, F. K., & Sibley, C. G. (2015). Facebook is linked to body dissatisfaction: Comparing users and non-users. *Sex Roles, 73*, 200–213. https://doi.org/10.1007/s11199-015-0517-6

Suárez-Álvarez, R., & García-Jiménez, A. (2021). Centennials on TikTok: Type of video. Analysis and comparative Spain-Great Britain by gender, age, and nationality. *Revista Latina de Comunicación Social, 79*, 1–21. https://doi.org/10.4185/RLCS-2021-1503

Tiggemann, M., & Polivy, J. (2010). Upward and downward: Social comparison processing of thin idealized media images. *Psychology of Women Quarterly, 34*,356–364. https://doi.org/10.1111/j.1471-6402.2010.01581.x

Tiggemann, M., & Slater, A. (2013). NetGirls: The internet, Facebook, and body image concern in adolescent girls. *International Journal of Eating Disorders, 46*. https://doi.org/10.1002/eat.22141

Trepte, S., & Reinecke, L. (2013). The reciprocal effects of social network site use and the disposition for self-disclosure: A longitudinal study. *Computers in Human Behavior, 29*, 1102–1112. https://doi.org/10.1016/j.chb.2012.10.002

Turkle, S. (2011). The tethered self: Technology reinvents intimacy and solitude. *Continuing Higher Education Review, 75*, 28–31. https://eric.ed.gov/?id=EJ967807

Twenge, J. M., & Campbell, W. K. (2018). Associations between screen time and lower psychological well-being among children and adolescents: Evidence from a population-based study. *Preventive Medicine Reports, 12*, 271–283. https://doi.org/10.1016/j.pmedr.2018.10.003

Twenge, J. M., Haidt, J., Joiner, T. E., & Campbell, W. K. (2020). *Underestimating digital media harm*. Universities Press. https://doi.org/10.1038/s41562-020-0839-4

Valkenburg, P. M., & Peter, J. (2009). Social consequences of the Internet for adolescents: A decade of research. *Current Directions in Psychological Science, 18*, 1 5. https://doi.org/10.1111/j.1467-8721.2009.01595.x

Valkenburg, P. M., & Peter, J. (2011). Online communication among adolescents: An integrated model of its attraction, opportunities, and risks. *Journal of Adolescent Health, 48*, 121–127. https://doi.org/10.1016/j.jadohealth.2010.08.020

Valkenburg, P. M., & Peter, J. (2013). Five challenges for the future of media-effects research. *International Journal of Communication*, 7, 197–215.

Van Overwalle, F. (2009). Social cognition and the brain: A meta-analysis. *Human Brain Mapping, 30*(3), 829–858. https://doi.org/10.1002/hbm.20547

Veum, A., & Undrum, L. V. M. (2018). The selfie as a global discourse. *Discourse and Society, 29*, 86–103. https://doi.org/10.1177/0957926517725979

Villaespesa, E., & Wowkowych, S. (2020). Ephemeral storytelling with social media: Snapchat and Instagram Stories at the Brooklyn Mfuseum *Social Media + Society, 6*(1), 2056305119898776. https://doi.org/10.1177%2F2056305119898776

Warr, M. (1993). Age, peers, and delinquency. *Criminology, 31*, 17–40. https://doi.org/10.1111/j.1745-9125.1993.tb01120.x

Weinstein, E. C., & Selman, R. L. (2016). Digital stress: Adolescents' personal accounts. *New Media and Society, 18*, 391–409. https://doi.org/10.1177/1461444814543989

Wiggins, B. E., & Bowers, G. B. (2015). Memes as genre: A structurational analysis of the memescape. *New Media & Society, 17*, 1886–1906. https://doi.org/10.1177/1461444814535194

Wolff, J. O. (1994). More on juvenile dispersal in mammals. *Oikos*, 349–352. https://doi.org/10.2307/3546284

World Health Organization. (2018). Gaming disorder. www.who.int/features/qa/gaming-disorder/en

Yang, C. C. (2016). Instagram use, loneliness, and social comparison orientation: Interact and browse on social media, but don't compare. *Cyberpsychology, Behavior, and Social Networking, 19*, 703–708. https://doi.org/10.1089/cyber.2016.0201

Yang, F., Helgason, A. R., Sigfusdottir, I. D., & Kristjansson, A. L. (2013). Electronic screen use and mental well-being of 10–12-year-old children. *European Journal of Public Health*, *23*, 492–498. https://doi.org/10.1093/eurpub/cks102

Youniss, J., & Smollar, J. (1985). *Adolescent relations with mothers, fathers, and friends*. University of Chicago Press.

Yuasa, M., Saito, K., & Mukawa, N. (2011). Brain activity when reading sentences and emoticons: An fMRI study of verbal and nonverbal communication. *Electronics and Communications in Japan*, *94*, 17–24. https://doi.org/10.1002/ecj.10311

Zeng, J., & Abidin, C. (2021). '# OkBoomer, time to meet the Zoomers': studying the memefication of intergenerational politics on TikTok. *Information, Communication & Society*, *24*(16), 2459–2481. https://doi.org/10.1080/1369118X.2021.1961007

Zhang, C. (2021). TikTok Face: Emoji once stood in for facial expressions; now we are moving in the other direction. *Real Life*, February 8, 2021. Retrieved from https://reallifemag.com/tiktok-face/

3

NEW CONTENT

Social Gaming, Online Pornography, and Knowledge Sharing

3.1 Why Is New Content So Threatening to Old Moral Values?

In this chapter, I examine some of the risks and opportunities presented by new forms of cultural content that have appeared online. Here, again, theories of cultural evolution can help us understand how these novel forms of content interact with our evolved cognitive architecture. As Acerbi (2019) has argued, cultural evolution can provide a "long view" to put in perspective the sudden cultural changes wrought by digital media:

> When put into perspective, the new phenomena that characterize our digital age appear to have their roots in deeper psychological and historical dynamics, and, to understand what is genuinely new and what is not, we may need to take seriously these dynamics.
>
> *(Acerbi, 2016)*

Two of the dynamics discussed by Acerbi are popularity bias and prestige bias. Popularity bias is the tendency to copy the predominant behavior seen in neighboring individuals, either in a directed way because it is the most common behavior and is therefore perceived as a social norm, or emergently because that behavior is more prevalent in the environment and thus more likely to be witnessed. Prestige bias is the tendency to imitate, or otherwise socially learn from, specific individuals who are "attractive" role models because they are seen to possess valued cultural knowledge and/or a positive reputation. This tendency is more likely to be consciously directed, although for various reasons, prestigious people might well be more noticeable in the environment (thinking for example of the reach of "influencers" on social networks; Hu et al., 2020).

DOI: 10.4324/9781003019459-3

It is easy to see how both biases might affect the content that is transmitted by digital media, especially considering potential differences in the local versus global nature of that content. In terms of popularity bias, the "neighboring" individuals are not only those who are physically close to an internet user, but also include people on the other side of the world linked by ties of age or such ephemeral preferences as taste in music, films, fashion, or even sexual inclinations. In terms of prestige bias, as Barkow et al. (2012) argued, traditional sources of prestige-based cultural authority and targets of aspirational imitations – such as village elders – are being replaced by social media influencers and YouTubers, pop and rap stars, and people who are "famous for being famous" such as the Kardashians. These different sources of influence are associated with obvious differences in the sort of content that is transmitted, and they may also create a (largely generational) divide between people who were brought up on a diet of more local, "traditional" cultural content, and those who were exposed to more distal content from online sources. As Mesoudi (2020) points out in a comment on Acerbi's (2019) book, cultural learning does not take place to equal degrees at different ages. Higher rates of copying in adolescence suggest that older people are often "wary [social] learners" who do not continue constantly updating their stores of cultural knowledge throughout their lifetimes: "Perhaps people show adaptive strategies of copying extensively when young, then focus on individual learning later in life once skills are acquired in order to refine those skills" (Mesoudi, 2020). The same phenomenon can even be seen in non-human social learning, as in the case of stone handling by Japanese macaques (Leca et al., 2007).

As argued in the introductory chapter on "moral panics", this generational disconnect in terms of online content can create fear and mistrust on the part of older generations toward younger ones. From a cultural evolutionary perspective, people who have spent a lifetime socially learning specialized skills when they are young, then refining them with minor individual innovations when they are older, are bound to be disappointed that their children and the latter's peers favor other types of cultural content from different sources. Yet not all types of content are treated equally. Older people may moan about new trends in music or clothing, but they reserve their strongest reactions for certain types of morally charged content. These include political and religious material, with worries about revolutionary tendencies or conversion to extremist faiths. In the current chapter, I want to focus on two other topics that are morally charged: violent and sexual content. The topic of violent digital material is particularly linked with the debate about whether video games cause young people to be more aggressive. Before summarizing that debate, I first examine the theme of video game content in general, the innovations that have taken place in that arena, and their relation to "gamer culture". I then consider the parallel issue of whether free availability of explicit sexual material online can be linked to sexual harassment, before considering issues of privacy in general and risks from the sharing of sexual material in particular. I also consider some opportunities that can arise from new forms of sharing content online, particularly regarding academic achievement. In the conclusion to the chapter, I reconsider the cultural evolutionary perspective, asking how biases in social learning can help us maximize opportunities and minimize risks for adolescents online.

3.2 The Rise of Gamer Culture

In his recent book, *Lost in a Good Game: Why We Play Video Games and What They Do to Us*, psychologist Pete Etchells (2019) tries to answer the question of what makes video games so attractive, as well as dispelling myths about their potentially harmful effects. His key argument is that games are popular because they contain an inherent element of *agency*: people forge their own path, create their own story, and choose their own adventure, creating a form of *interactive* content that is different from most other entertainment media (with the possible exception of social media). He quotes the novelist and game designer Naomi Alderman (2013):

> While all art forms can elicit powerful emotions, only games can make their audience feel the emotion of agency. A novel can make you feel sad, but only a game can make you feel guilty for your actions. A play can make you feel joyful, but only a game can make you feel proud of yourself. A movie can make you feel angry with a traitor, but only a game can make you feel personally betrayed.

For Etchells, this element of interactivity in games is what makes them uniquely attractive and, indeed, uniquely sophisticated as an art form: they allow players to explore different emotions, and even find their own moral compass. Yet this same connection with agency may be partly responsible for the negative attitudes that many people – particular in older generations – have toward video games. The problem is that if you are viewing someone who is immersed in a game, while not yourself immersed in it (and still more so if you have never had the experience of being immersed in a computer game at all), it can seem as if their agency is somehow taken over by the game, almost as if "the players are completely absorbed into the screen – zombies drooling at this thing that's playing out in front of them, their brains melting before your very eyes". As discussed at the end of the Introduction to my book, the idea of a loss of agency, or transfer of agency to the game, can help explain why the content of games is so often viewed as dangerous.

It can also explain some of the negative stereotypes associated with gamers, which are something that Etchells frequently rails against in his book, pointing out that games these days are no longer just the province of socially deficient nerds or armchair warriors, but can be played in beautifully creative ways, and often appeal to women and older people as much as men and youth. Nevertheless, something of the old subculture of the nerd does survive in what is known as "gamer culture", and this identity still self-consciously positions itself a little outside the mainstream in ways that may not be conducive to general acceptance of gaming as an activity. In many ways, "gamer culture" is where content and identity collide. The culture of gaming does not simply involve the activity of actually playing games: it also encompasses discussions via text, audio, or video during, before, and after the games, using services such as Discord; live-streaming, and recorded streams of games (often in a loose review or walkthrough format) which are commented on via services such as Twitch or YouTube; and more "reflective" discussions on fora like Reddit, 4chan, or Twitter; as well as in-person events at gaming conventions and e-sports tournaments, which regularly pull in tens or even hundreds of thousands of attendees. Apart from these interpersonal discussions, gamer culture is also associated with the creation of reams of more durable digital content, notably memes but also involving more traditional cartoon strips, animations, and video pastiches, the latter of which are often set to music, even sometimes original songs created for the purpose.

One complaint that has frequently been made about many of these forms of gamer culture is that they are deeply sexist (e.g., Consalvo, 2012). The sexism is alleged by Consalvo and other feminist scholars to be pervasive within gamer culture, although in the public consciousness it is also marked by furor over particular events, such as the infamous Gamergate controversy beginning in 2014 (see Elliot, 2018, for a review). The allegations of sexism are slightly paradoxical: if, as many feminist critics point out, 40% or more of people who play games are female, how can gaming culture still be hostile to their calls to make games more female-friendly? Paaßen et al. (2017) argued that the answer lies in the cultural stereotypes that people in general have about "gamers". Female gamers tend to have a different playing profile than male gamers, spending more time on puzzle games on cellphones such as the infamous *Candy Crush*, and less time on consoles playing big-budget "AAA" games such as *Call of Duty* (though this too may be changing; Lopez-Fernandez et al., 2019). And it is players of the AAA games who dominate gaming culture, personified in the form of online game reviewers and "Let's play..." streamers such as PewDiePie, many of whom number their followers or subscribers in the millions and receive hundreds of millions of views for each of their videos. Analyzing the gender balance of game reviewers, Paaßen et al. found that of a sample of 200 staff of the top 100 review sites as listed by Alexa (2016), only 14% were female. The imbalance in the amateur streamers (who, despite the "amateur" label, can often make substantial amounts of money and represent a major target of aspiration today's teenagers) was even more striking: out of the 100 most subscribed gaming channels on YouTube, only 2 featured female main hosts, while 84 had exclusively male hosts. They argued that the lack of female role models makes it difficult for girls to identify with the gamer stereotype:

> Men perceive a stronger overlap between their gendered identity and their gamer identity, facilitating social identification and self-stereotyping. For women, the opposite is likely to happen: because their gendered identity conflicts with the gamer identity they may be less likely to describe themselves in terms of the gamer-stereotype.
>
> *(Paaßen et al., 2017, p. 11)*

This lack of "fit" with the gamer stereotype filters down to everyday behavior, with only 28% of female adolescents (compared to 71% of males) using voice chat services such as Discord when playing online (Lenhart et al., 2015), and surveys showing that only 15–30% of e-sports viewers are female (Gera, 2014).

In addition to using more general video services such as YouTube, social media such as Twitter, and fora such as Reddit, video game streamers have made extensive use of the specialist streaming service Twitch, which serves as one as of the main centers for disseminating the visual content of gaming culture. As Hilvert-Bruce et al. (2018, p. 58) pointed out, "Unlike previous streaming services, such as television and YouTube, live-streaming offers real-time human interaction between the streamer and viewers, facilitating their ability to interact with each other". In a Uses and Gratifications study of the motivations behind watching streaming videos on Twitch, they found a clear difference between small channels and bigger ones, with audiences of smaller channels understandably showing more social motivations for watching them, reflecting more of a sense of community than in bigger venues. Streamers themselves report that with more than 100–150 participants (a number interestingly reminiscent of "Dunbar's number" for the maximum number of interpersonal connections an individual can maintain at any given time; Dunbar, 2010) this sense of community tends to break down. However, the stereotypical content used for communication on Twitch, including idiosyncratic, emoji-like "emotes", can be intimidating to new users (Fraser et al., 2019), while also reinforcing a sense of community through the "restricted code" (Bernstein, 1964) shared by established users.

Although they may exhibit more of a sense of community, smaller channels tend to be seen as less prestigious than larger channels, of course. In a piece of "netnographic" research with my student Joaquin Chaves, we examined the hierarchies of prestige that exist on Twitch, whereby some content creators are seen as more influential than others. In large part this prestige is decided by viewers themselves and measured with view counts and subscriber numbers: but in order for those figures to go up, word has to get out about a streamer or channel. This is done by viewers expressing their opinion on Reddit, game forums, and YouTube, highlighting the best new games, best playthroughs, or surprising or humorous situations that occur during the streams. In turn, a kind of prestige hierarchy can be established among viewers of a particular channel, since streamers establish different categories or "ranks" of subscribers, lists of top donors, and rankings by seniority of subscription time, and unique, personalized emotes that only certain followers can use there, as well as up to three status icons that appear before the username in the chat window. All of this establishes a reputation system that means more "voice" is given to the people whom the streamer sees as the channel's staunchest supporters. It is worth noting that all this prestige is not just notional: real benefits can potentially accrue (chiefly by carrying followers over to one's own channel) from being seen as a "top subscriber" of one of the top streamers, who can accrue extraordinary wealth from their online activities (several million dollars per year in some cases; Lawler, 2018).

Prestige was also a focus of research for another of my students, Kevin Zambrano, who carried out a series of semi-structured interviews with a club of undergraduates which met regularly in person to play MOBA (multiplayer online battle arena) games, principally *League of Legends*. He found that although participants obtained a lot of pleasure from playing games, they also reported many instances of "toxic" behavior, including prejudice and discrimination – in particular, negative comments about the physical and mental capacities of other players. These toxic comments detracted from positive feelings of immersion in the game, and impacted performance and enjoyment. Interestingly, such conflicts could also break out between friends in offline contexts surrounding game-playing, with similar use of aggressive comments when one was displeased with another's play; but participants said that they had gradually learned to manage these offline conflicts and had created a healthier, more lighthearted environment in which to play games on the university campus. Indeed, they had found it a good way to meet people from other courses within the university, due to their shared interest and passion for the game.

How do individuals manage such conflicts within a group? One important evolutionary perspective on this process is that in social animals, conflict is largely managed through social hierarchies. In another online ethnography, my student Daniel Castañeda focused on the operation of hierarchies of prestige in *League of Legends*. A social hierarchy is a set of social norms delimiting the behavior of individuals according to their rank or status (Cummins, 2006). Prestige is a conceptual factor for which people compete within social hierarchies, generating differences in hierarchy by granting rank and exclusive access to resources (Ingram, 2014). Individuals will fight to maintain and increase their prestige as if this itself were an important resource to protect, due to the benefits it provides. As well as proficiency in the game itself, social gamers have two sets of mechanisms to protect their prestige: one being prosocial behaviors, which are directed at maintaining systems of reciprocity with other players; and the other being "toxic" behaviors. This second set of behaviors consists partly of direct verbal aggression, and partly of indirect gossip and accusations of non-normative behavior to authorities (Ingram, 2014). There is also the possibility of using both mechanisms or strategies at the same time, meaning that some individuals are "bi-strategics", using both prosocial and coercive behaviors in order to acquire and maintain a strong position in the hierarchy (Hawley, 2007). The roles of both prestige hierarchies and aggressive interactions are illustrated in the following two quotations from participants:

"SANTIAGO":

> There is a deep prestige, it becomes a sports competition. A culture is formed around who plays more, they see a diamond [rank] and say 'Oof, he plays too much.' It becomes a culture of prestige. Bronze: 'Oh no, he plays very badly.' They generate that competition as if it were a sport. Prestige plays a fundamental role.

"MARTÍN":

> It is a very aggressive competition, there is malice to humiliate the other player. Put your finger on the sore, I'm better and that's it. This happens regardless of the team, everyone with everyone. The rival humiliates me, saying negative things to me, and a teammate from my same team says the same to me, nobody likes it.

Thus, one outstanding factor in this type of MOBA video game is the establishment of a prestige hierarchy associated with contextual factors, such as standing in the league and the collection of resources to help the team, among other things, which are encouraged by the never-ending struggle for prestige. Resources play a fundamental role in these types of games and are presented as something fundamental to the player's experience, efficient exploitation of resources being a factor that enhances prestige and gives a sense of validation to the player in the game.

How does this competition for prestige connect to the phenomenon of gamer culture discussed in the first section of this chapter? In a theoretical article published a few years ago, I argued that status competition plays out very differently in adolescents than in younger children (Ingram, 2014). In early and middle childhood children tend to form well-defined "dominance hierarchies" that structure their relations within the primary peer group that they belong to (these days, usually a school class). However, in the larger peer groups characteristic of adolescence, the structure of dominance relations becomes simultaneously more fragmented and more mediated by abstract conceptions of prestige in certain activities than by interpersonal dominance in an instrumental sense. Of course, since computer games occupy such a central place in the life of so many young adolescents, the ability to play them well naturally becomes a central arena for the formation of prestige hierarchies in their aficionados, and can lead to frequent players centering their identity on aspects of "gamer culture" as they end up spending so much time thinking about these prestige-based competitions and how to do better in them. However, the unfortunate flip side is that those who are seen as weaker in the competition, or have an identity that is perceived as more peripheral to gamer culture (such as girls), can be marginalized, ignored, or belittled. Indeed, such toxic behavior toward – and negative gossip about – marginal individuals may be part of how other gamers seek to enhance their own prestige.

3.3 Violent Video Games: A Classic Moral Panic?

In addition to toxic behavior within games, a parallel and probably even stronger concern, which has dominated headlines probably more than any other online "moral panic" in recent years, is the supposed link between playing violent video games and real-world aggression. This is especially true insofar as such a link relates to mass shootings (in particular, given the associations with young people, mass school shootings). This concern is now quite old: it has been around in one form or another since at least the 1980s (Markey & Ferguson, 2017) and gained a suddenly inflated currency in 1999 after the Columbine high school shooting in Colorado. The two senior students who shot dead twelve other students (as well as themselves) and one teacher in that massacre, Eric Harris and Dylan Klebold, were aficionados of the FPS (first-person shooter) game *Doom*. They were rumored (though this was subsequently debunked; Mikkelsen, 2008) to have adapted their own version of the game, complete with a map that resembled their school's floor plan, and customized enemies who couldn't fight back (Copenhaver, 2019; Markey & Ferguson, 2017).

A certain school of video game researchers was quick to respond. They built on an academic tradition that had long investigated links between violent TV content and real-world aggression, going back to the famous "Bobo doll" study of Albert Bandura (Bandura et al., 1961). This research had created a body of theory known as the "General Aggression Model" (Allen et al., 2018; Anderson & Bushman, 2002), which identified multiple pathways by which violent media could influence behavior: namely, by explicit teaching or modeling of aggressive strategies, "priming" aggressive behavioral scripts to make them feel more relevant and accessible, increasing physiological arousal, or increasing aggressive affect (emotions). A moment's thought makes it clear that all of these pathways could apply just as easily (if not more so) to games as to TV cartoons or dramas. Indeed, as early as 2001, Craig Anderson and Brad Bushman – two of the leading scholars in this tradition – were able to publish a meta-analytic study collating the findings of 35 research reports published up to and including the year 2000, on the relationship between video game use and aggression, arousal or (for comparison) prosocial behavior. Interestingly, already at that stage gaming industry figures were claiming that attacks on video games were something of a moral panic.

Anderson and Bushman (2001, p. 353) quoted a CNN interview given in 2000 by the then-president of the Interactive Digital Software Assocation, who said:

> I think the issue has been vastly overblown and overstated, often by politicians and others who don't fully understand, frankly, this industry. There is absolutely no evidence, none, that playing a violent video game leads to aggressive behavior.

However, this was not what their meta-analysis found. In the published literature up to that point, they instead discovered weak, but significant, correlations between playing video games and aggressive actions, thoughts and feelings, as well as a similarly positive correlation with arousal and a *negative* correlation with prosocial behavior (essentially, helpfulness).

Since meta-analytic studies, which in principle eliminate the chance findings and researcher bias of single studies by grouping them together in an overarching statistical analysis, are supposed to be the gold standard of academic research, this certainly looked like Round One to those who claimed a link between video games and aggression. But it was by no means the end of the fight. In 2007, concerns about a link between games and violence resurfaced with another tragic school shooting, this time at Virginia Tech University, where student Seung-Hui Cho shot dead 32 people (one of the deadliest mass shootings in history) before turning his gun on himself (Fallahi et al., 2009). There were initial suggestions that Cho might have been an avid player of FPS (first-person shooter) games, which turned out not to be substantiated. Moreover, video game researcher Chris Ferguson (2007, p. 310) was skeptical "that a behavior with such a high base rate (i.e. video game playing) is useful in explaining a behavior with a very low base rate (i.e. school shootings)". How could an everyday activity, which was already becoming near-universal in young men, explain such rare atrocities? He also pointed out that correlation does not imply causation: it might be the case that children in families that are predisposed to violence in other ways (e.g., by witnessing acts of aggression between their parents) are also more likely to play violent video games. Finally, school shooters as a population do not seem to be particularly disposed to play such games (Ferguson, 2008).

Ferguson (2007) therefore undertook his own meta-analysis of the literature up to that point, focusing on aggressive behavior rather than also including aggressive thoughts and feelings as Anderson and Bushman had. His analysis showed a similar effect size to the latter study for the relation between game-playing and aggression, though this virtually disappeared when controlling for publication bias. Thus, it seemed that studies were more likely to be published if they showed a link between video games and aggression, and that this factor was distorting the literature. Round Two to those who argued for video games' innocence! This was still far from the end of the bout, but Ferguson's study did have some impact on policy, with the *Brown v Entertainment Merchants*

Association (2011) US Supreme Court decision that prohibited the regulation of violent content in video games, declaring the research evidence linking games to aggression to be unconvincing (Ferguson, 2020). However, the fight continued, with a 2015 APA statement deploring the use of violent content in video games for young people, and arguing[1] that this could be linked to aggressive behavior (though a reanalysis of the data used for the meta-analysis that informed that statement revealed major mistakes; Ferguson et al., 2020).

Ferguson and other opponents of the idea that there is a link between video game and real-world violence have often criticized the lack of quality longitudinal (rather than cross-sectional, correlational) studies on the subject. Another target of their criticism has been studies that rely on the General Aggression Model (Anderson & Bushman, 2002), which implies a general effect on all young people, rather than looking at the impact of moderating variables that might explain why some young people are particularly vulnerable. It is true that up until recently such research was quite rare; but recently, proponents of a link between video games and aggression seem to have heeded the call and both types of studies have become much more common. For example, Coyne and Stockdale (2021) examined longitudinal changes in adolescents' usage of violent video games and their aggressive tendencies. Noting that there is much individual variation in the relationships between game-playing, aggressive cognition, arousal, and emotion, they took a person-centered rather than variable-centered approach, grouping individuals into different types of game-players to look at multiple typical trajectories of game-playing over time. They found three such trajectories: a "high initial violence" group that started off using violent games a lot during early adolescence, played them less in middle adolescence and then finally used them more again in early adulthood; a "moderate" group that followed a similar trajectory but started from a lower initial base; and a "low-increasing" group that always kept their usage of violent video games low, compared to the other two groups, but steadily increased the amount that they played them over time. Counterintuitively, the group that self-reported as highest in interpersonal aggression was the second group, which the authors suggest could be due to the "high initial violence" group showing the effects of some sort of intervention to reduce their usage of violent video games in middle adolescence (though this does seem like quite a post hoc argument).

Studies that analyze specific risk factors that might interact with violent video game usage to produce aggressive behavior are based on what has been called the Catalyst Model of negative media effects; the idea that violent video games do not function alone as a causal factor but interact with genetic predispositions, family environment, and pressure from delinquent peers to make a subset of young people vulnerable to turning violent (Verheijen et al., 2021). There is something of a consensus on the theoretical plausibility of this model (though the empirical evidence tends to be more debated): indeed, as far back as 15 years ago, Ferguson noted that

> Individuals already at risk for violent behavior may respond more negatively to violent games than the majority of individuals. Although violent games are not likely a cause of violent behavior in such individuals, it may be possible that violent games may moderate existing violence predilections.
>
> *(Ferguson, 2007, pp. 314–315)*

One recent study that included moderating variables argued for mediating effects of both anger and moral disengagement on proactive and reactive aggression, and a mediating effect of cognitive impulsivity on reactive aggression alone (Zhao et al., 2021). A problem with "slicing and dicing" types of aggression and the factors that influence them like this is that the effects discovered can be very small: in fact, the correlations between violent video game exposure (VVGE) and both types of aggression were insignificant in that study, while the correlations between VVGE and anger, on the one hand, and moral disengagement, on the other, were .08 and .12, respectively. Given such small main effects, it is questionable whether any mediating effects found were really that important.

Another type of moderating variable involves the relationship between the social network in which a young person is embedded, their exposure to violent video games, and their aggressive behavior. Individuals do not act in a vacuum but are influenced by how their friends and other social contacts behave. Could the attitudes that peers have toward both violent video games and aggression play a mediating role in any association between the two? After all, it is known that "falling in with the wrong crowd" can be a substantial risk factor for adolescents, since friends tend to have similar probabilities of suffering negative outcomes in diverse, interlinked areas of life (including violent behavior and academic achievement; Brendgen et al., 2002; Liem & Martin, 2011). One methodological problem that complicates study of risk factors is how to distinguish between *selection* – the tendency to develop and maintain friendships with peers who have similar habits and interests – and *socialization* – the tendency to imitate peers' behavior directly. If peer group similarity of outcomes is primarily caused by selection, that implies that an individual might have suffered similarly adverse outcomes even if they hadn't fallen in with a bad crowd; whereas if it is due to socialization, that means that the friends an adolescent chooses to hang with can have causal effects on their wellbeing. In a longitudinal social network study of video game play and aggression, Verheijen et al. (2021) attempted to separate how much both selection and socialization contributed to hypothesized connections between these two factors in friends. They found that both played a role in aggressive behavior, but that peer similarities in violent video game exposure were mainly driven by selection: "Adolescents who played violent games were more likely to choose friends who also played violent games, but adolescents did not adopt the violent game behavior of their friends" (p. 28).

This points to one slightly disappointing aspect of the debate on violent video games. Since Ferguson (2007), or even before, interested researchers have pointed out the need for high-quality, pre-registered longitudinal studies and for considering moderating factors. This is associated with the replacement of the General Aggression Model, in much theoretical work, by the Catalyst Model described above (Verheijen et al., 2021). However, the evidence used (on both sides) to test theories of a link between video game play and aggression has not really changed in line with this change in the theory. The debate still seems to turn more than anything on large-scale longitudinal and meta-analytic studies that analyze effects of time spent on violent video games in the general population of young people. This does not really make a lot of sense, because no one is seriously arguing that it is important whether playing video games for an extra half an hour per day, on average, influences one's everyday levels of non-extreme aggression toward other people. Yet this is basically what the large-scale studies of general samples are attempting to measure.

Perhaps what is needed are more qualitative and mixed-methods studies with vulnerable teenagers and those who seem to have an obsessive interest in video games, to understand what motivates them and what other areas of their lives may be suffering (or not) due to the time they put into gaming. Building from such an evidence base, interventions could be developed to improve the strategies that they use for dealing with personal problems, above and beyond burying themselves in violent games. These might help to reassure families who feel that they have "lost" a child who seems addicted to such games and are worried about what he or she might do, and who may have intuitions that the level of the child's interest is unhealthy, intuitions that are unlikely to be assuaged by showing them the conflicting results of various meta-analyses of the academic literature. On the other hand, it is worth remembering that ordinary young people's intense interest in such games is often driven by their instincts to engage in prestige-based competition (as described at the end of the previous section; see also Ingram, 2014), and, as such, can be a "natural" part of growing up. What may be more concerning is if such interest comes at the expense of other forms of interaction with peers, in teenagers who seem lonely, ostracized, or otherwise socially peripheral, since much research in adolescent developmental psychology has shown that such individuals are at high risk of both internalizing and externalizing problems (including violent behavior).

3.4 Problems with Pornography

Many of the same tropes found in the debate on video game violence also crop up in the debate over the negative effects of online pornography. As with extreme violence in games, here we have a very intense kind of content that activates strong emotions and may be seen as "corrupting" young minds in some sense. Of course, pornography has been with us for thousands of years. However, it cannot be denied that the internet has led to a massive increase in the accessibility of pornographic content. Instead of having to go to an adult bookstore to buy a "porno mag" off the top shelf, or to a video library to rent an X-rated VHS or DVD, anyone can access extremely graphic content from the privacy of their own home. As well as increasing the audience for porn by removing the element of shame involved in publicly purchasing it, this has also increased porn's availability to adolescents in particular, since online age checks have proven much less effective than those that existed in brick-and-mortar shops. Indeed, porn quickly became so ubiquitous that as early as 2001, 70% of one study's mid-adolescent sample said they had accidentally seen it online (Rideout, 2002; cited by Brown & L'Engle, 2009). A few years later, Sabina et al. (2008) suggested that viewing porn on the internet had already become a normative experience for US adolescent boys (93% having been exposed to it), though less so for girls (62%). The internet has also increased the intensity of pornographic content on offer: in the 1980s, while much more graphic videos were available, most "dirty magazines" simply featured nude shots of the female form (the most famous one, *Playboy*, did not usually even include detailed images of the vulva); whereas since the 2000s, it has been easy for anyone to access close-up videos of quite extreme sexual acts, with nothing more than a few clicks in a "porn portal" like Pornhub or Xvideos. Moreover, "the Internet provides space for discussion and depiction of unconventional and bizarre sexual interests (e.g., discussion groups on almost any sexual paraphilia)" (Brown & L'Engle, 2009, p. 131) – which is clearly a concern when the paraphilia is illegal, as with rape, pedophilia, or bestiality. Many academics and cultural commentators have put these two dramatic changes together and argued that the ready availability of extreme pornographic content could be having unprecedented effects on young people's sexual development.

In this section, I consider three of the main worries about online pornography, the first and third of which are similar to concerns about video games, while the second is perhaps unique to porn. The first worry is that pornographic content is so stimulating and readily available that adolescents can easily become addicted to it (mirroring worries about addiction to video games or smartphones). The second – less obviously paralleled in other areas of research on online risks, though it has an echo in the concerns about "gamer culture" mentioned in a previous section – is that pornography necessarily "degrades" women, thus having negative effects on the wider culture and both male and female psychology. And the final concern, closely mirroring worries about violent video games, is that viewing extreme forms of pornographic content could influence young men's sexual behavior, making them more likely to abuse or harass women. This will lead on to questions of privacy in the next section of this chapter, and on to questions of changes in relationship dynamics and "revenge porn" in the following chapter.

The question of whether internet porn is addictive, like that of whether video games make young people violent, has caused controversy ever since concerns began to be raised by the new, ready availability of images online. On the one side, some researchers and (even more so) clinical practitioners uncritically apply a model of the addiction process developed to understand and treat substance abuse (e.g., Love et al., 2015). On the other side, researchers who are critical of the "addiction" label may even reject the term "pornography", in favor of the wordier "visual sexual stimuli" (e.g., Ley et al., 2014). This exemplifies how the two sides can talk past one another to an unfortunate extent, with those on the anti-porn side failing to pay as much attention as they could to the differences between "behavioral addictions" and substance abuse; and those on the "pro-porn" (or perhaps anti-anti-porn) side sometimes seeming to deny that excessive pornography use could ever exacerbate an individual's psychological problems, rather than being merely a symptom of them. Some on the latter side have even claimed that visual sexual stimuli are "likely effective for emotion regulation" (Ley et al., 2014, p. 100) because they produce positive affect – apparently confusing the short-term "high" users can experience from such stimuli, when feeling down or stressed, with effective control and adaptive modulation of emotions. Fortunately, some recent systematic reviews (Duffy et al., 2016; Grubbs et al., 2020) have taken a more balanced approach in proposing routes in which researchers could avoid pathologizing pornography use, while also seeking ways to help people who believe that excessive use is causing them problems.

Regarding the concept of behavioral addiction, recall from our discussion of screen time in Chapter 2 that it is not the total time spent viewing pornography that is likely to cause people problems, so much as the compulsive nature of some people's viewing, especially if they feel it is taking away time from other, more valued activities. Duffy et al. (2016) quote the early recommendation of Cooper et al. (2000, p. 169) that "A distinction can thus be made between more common recreational users, where viewing has minimal costs and can even have positive effects, and the subsample of compulsive users, where viewing can be particularly harmful". In terms of sexual addiction more generally, Grubbs et al. (2020, p. 8) note that "substantial portions of the populace in a number of Western countries are expressing concerns about their ability to regulate their sexual behaviors", citing in particular the study of Dickenson et al. (2018), which found that 11% of US men felt distress about their own seemingly out-of-control sexual behaviors. Emphasizing the absence of broad effects across the general population, and making semantic arguments about the applicability of the concept of addiction, or quasi-political comments about the religious affiliations of some of the anti-pornography researchers, does not do much to help the lived experiences of those in the subpopulation that feels distressed.

The "culture war"–style attacks can go the other way as well, with Zitzman and Butler (2009; cited by Duffy et al., 2016) arguing that: "Resistance to using the term addiction is perhaps more a reflection of cultural sexual liberality and permissiveness than any lack of symptomatic and diagnostic correspondence with other forms of addiction" (p. 212). It would perhaps be preferable if researchers on both sides of the debate could stick to the science, instead of targeting the ideological motivations of their opponents. From a scientific point of view, indeed, it seems reasonable theoretically to analyze patterns of pornography use with a classical addiction model, split into distinct phases of bingeing, withdrawal, and preoccupation/anticipation (Love et al., 2015). Yet most critics of the addiction model do not target the theory behind it in a scientific way (e.g., by empirically rejecting hypotheses derived from the theory) but rather focus on the cross-sectional nature of most anti-porn studies and the lack of high-quality measures of pornography use. Proponents of the addiction model often inappropriately draw causal conclusions from a correlation between using porn and feeling negative affect, or suffering relationship problems or sexual dysfunction. Furthermore, they typically define an arbitrary amount of usage time (which varies widely between researchers) as "excessive", instead of incorporating perceived addiction or lack of control into their operationalization of problematic use. Another valid criticism is the lack of attention paid to moderator variables: Duffy et al. pointed out that "psychological distress might not occur from pornography use itself but might be due to the attitudes individuals hold about their pornography use" (2016, p. 772) – explaining, for example, why religious Americans might be more vulnerable than other groups to negative effects of pornography use.

Duffy et al. (2016) highlighted many gaps in the evidence base on pornography addiction, such as the lack of studies of women's use of pornography, which anecdotal evidence and theoretical considerations (based on the potential for more covert access to porn) suggest may have increased dramatically in the internet era: "Women are often excluded from samples, with researchers citing evidence to suggest they view pornography less frequently than men (Morgan, 2011); however, evidence for this is often based on methodologically poor research" (Duffy et al., 2016, p. 775). They suggest that the homogeneous samples and statistical analyses that tend to be used in studies of pornography addiction are inappropriate for what is a highly diverse population, with diverging styles of porn use. Another important limitation – especially for the purposes of this book – is that there are relatively few studies of pornography addiction with participants younger than 18 years of age (Brown & L'Engle, 2009), even though adolescence is often regarded as a sensitive period for the development of addictions (Crews et al., 2007) and clearly is a critical period for the development of sexual identity (Bonino et al., 2006; Tolman & McClelland, 2011). The latter authors (2011, p. 250) argued that this absence of data was partly due to "ideological and political squeamishness" about adolescent sexual behaviors (as well as the ethical difficulties of gaining institutional clearance; Peter & Valkenburg, 2016), meaning that reviewers may ask authors to confine their analysis to questions of sexual risks for minors, rather than their sexual preferences.

The absence of female participants in studies of pornography use is particularly problematic given the suggestions of many feminists that porn is inherently degrading to women. A key assumption behind this argument is that pornographic material tends to portray male and female sexual roles as unequal, with men playing a more active, dominant part in the sex act. However, this has more often been simply asserted than demonstrated empirically. In an analysis of 400 randomly selected videos from popular porn sites, Klaassen and Peter (2015) showed that in fact, the subjugation of women in the videos was less than might be expected, with depictions of violence and even physical aggression (other than spanking or gagging) rare, and some types of objectification (e.g., dehumanization by not showing the face) actually commoner for male than female characters. Nevertheless, it was more frequent for women to adopt a submissive role in the videos than it was for men, and all types of inequality were more often found in amateur than professional videos, raising concerns with regard to the increasing amateurization of porn (Paasonen, 2017).

Furthermore, a more recent analysis of a much larger sample of 4,000 videos from similar sites (Pornhub and Xvideos) found that around 40% of scenes contained physical aggression, which was almost always (97% of cases) directed toward women (Fritz et al., 2020). In general, we may conclude that depiction of women in pornography as unequal and as passive acceptors of aggression (the women who received it rarely responded negatively) is not inevitable but does occur frequently. Concerns about the cultural and psychological effects of demeaning treatment of women in porn may have some validity, since one study of female adolescents showed that those who more often viewed sexually objectified depictions of women on TV also reported feeling less "sexual agency" (control over sexual situations; Tolman et al., 2007); while in college students, several experimental studies from the 1980s – when ethical procedures were less stringent – showed that exposure to even nonviolent sexual content increased "sexual callousness" (associated with endorsement of the idea that women enjoy sexual violence and even rape; see Brown and L'Engle, 2009, for a review).

This matters because, in an echo of the debate on video games and violence, some researchers argue that consumption of pornography by men may promote sexual violence and harassment against women. Clearly, this seems more probable if the pornography itself contains images of sexual aggression, which according to the General Aggression Model (discussed in the previous section) could lead both to the arousal of users and to the normalization of their expression of aggressive impulses during sexual encounters (Malamuth et al., 2000). And as with the debate on violent video games, the arguments over whether this tends to happen have been long and intense. As Bonino et al. (2006) put it:

> The debate on this topic is still very animated in Western society and tends to polarize in two opposite positions: one claiming the cathartic role of pornography as a sign of freedom and a tolerant attitude toward sex (McNair, 1996); the other stressing the negative role of pornography, not in causing violence in itself, but rather in contributing to the trivialization and greater acceptance of sexually abusive attitudes.
>
> *(Dine et al., 1998, p. 266)*

These authors also highlighted the lack of research up to that point on the relationship between consumption of pornography and sexual violence in adolescents, despite around 15% of teenage girls and 10% of teenage boys in Europe and North America having suffered some form of sexual aggression or unwanted sexual attention, and 10–20% of teenage boys having admitted to inflicting such behaviors on girls (Hilton et al., 2003). The content of the pornography consumed may be an important means of sex education for many adolescents (Bonino et al., 2006; Brown & L'Engle, 2009; Zillmann, 2000), since school-based sex education tends to be minimally graphic and focused on biological facts. In this context, it is also noteworthy that pornography consumption tends to correlate with other risky behaviors such as drug-taking and delinquency (Bonino et al., 2006), meaning that it is reaching an audience who may already be less inhibited about carrying out risky and counter-normative acts such as sexual harassment.

Once again, as with studies of video games and violence, meta-analyses have been unable to assess the overall effects in this area. For example, Wright et al. (2016) found small effects of pornography use on sexual aggression in both correlational and longitudinal studies. However, in a more recent meta-analysis, Ferguson and Hartley (2020) argued that the preceding study was marred by use of an unusual "correction" for measurement error, as well as by a lack of control for the effects of covariates, and by not considering the quality of the study methods analyzed. In their own meta-analysis that did not suffer from these problems, they found no effect of nonviolent pornography, though there was a small correlation between watching violent pornography and sexual aggression, underlining the importance of distinguishing between different types of pornography that are used rather than treating amount of exposure as a monolithic variable.

Assuming that there is a correlation between pornography use and sexual aggression – which, as we have seen, is far from certain – the question remains of whether the former has a causal effect on the latter. As Tolman and McClelland (2011, p. 249) put it,

> Like all media impact research, studies evaluating the effects of seeing sexual media are plagued by a "chicken or egg" challenge – are adolescents who watch sexual media more "sexual" to begin with and thus drawn to it, or are they curious or unintentionally exposed and thus imposed upon by it?

This is a very difficult question to answer, because the usual method of testing for causality in science – the controlled experiment – is impossible to carry out adequately in this area. There are insurmountable ethical problems both with administering pornography to users (especially underage users) who would not normally access it, and with measuring sexual aggression in an ecologically valid way – not to mention the real risks associated with potentially increasing sexual aggression. The usual strategy is to fall back on longitudinal studies: while not as reliable indicators of causality as experiments, these can at least *suggest* causality if, over time, some individuals show increased levels of (self-reported) sexual aggression subsequent to increasing their consumption of pornography, while others show a decrease in the former behavior over the same time frame, after decreasing their porn use. A recent study by Kohut et al. (2021) found that this was not in fact the case: although sexual aggression increased longitudinally after a construct known as "hostile masculinity" (measured by agreement with statements such as "Women are responsible for most of my troubles") increased, it did not increase following higher levels of pornography use. However, it must be noted that this study, while commendable for its use of rigorous longitudinal analyses, did not include indicators of different pornographic preferences but only measured it through a single-item scale of frequency of use over the last six months. In order to test the hypothesis that using violent porn in particular can increase levels of sexual aggression in men, future studies will need to integrate measures of different types of porn use with longitudinal strategies of data collection.

This was one of the conclusions of an important integrative review by Peter and Valkenburg (2016). They showed that, as for other areas of research into adolescent technology use (such as the connection between video games and violence), there was a need for more longitudinal studies, as the field was dominated by cross-sectional, correlational studies that can say little about causality. There had also been little work driven by testable theories, explaining how exposure to pornographic media at different ages can affect developmental change. Moreover (again, similarly to the case of video games) researchers have treated pornography use as a monolithic variable, without paying attention to the differential effects of different pornographic content – even though there is some evidence, for example, that enjoying violent pornography might be particularly associated with sexual violence. Another omission is the absence of work on non-heteronormative porn (especially using quantitative methods) and on cultural differences in the effects of even heteronormative porn (with most studies before 2016 being carried out on participants from a handful of countries: the Netherlands, Sweden, the United States, and South Korea). Peter and Valkenburg also noted the need to investigate moderator variables that influence the resilience or susceptibility of different adolescents to pornography's damaging effects.

Despite all these criticisms, Peter and Valkenburg (2016) did draw some conclusions about the correlates of pornography use in adolescents (although the practice's actual *effects* are much murkier, given the lack of causal studies). The most frequent pornography users tended to be male and had passed puberty, age being a less significant predictor than pubertal stage. They often had problems with their family relations, and sometimes held permissive opinions about sexual behavior and (slightly contradictorily, perhaps) views about gender roles that conformed to traditional stereotypes. Both male and female porn users tended to have casual sex earlier and more frequently, though this could well be correlation rather than causation, since people who are more interested in sex are probably more likely to use pornography. Porn users were also more sexually aggressive (if male) or more often victims of sexual aggression (if female; Valkenburg & Peter suggest that the latter pattern could in part be driven by male sexual aggressors coercing their victims to watch porn before, or while, abusing them).

Concluding this section on pornography use, we can see that although there are already some interesting general results, a lot of finer-grained research remains to be done. Many studies have focused on the potential links between pornography use and sexual violence, which are intuitively clear to many people but run up against the problem that overall in the last few decades, porn has increased massively in volume and accessibility, while sexual aggression has actually decreased. As those societal trends would suggest, there seems to be little or no evidence of a general correlation between men who use porn frequently and those who engage in sexual abuse or violence against women, although a question mark remains over the use of violent porn in particular. As well as investigating this link further, an under-studied avenue of research concerns the development of pornography addiction in adolescents, since this is an age at which people are especially vulnerable to nascent addictions. In particular, there is a noticeable absence of high-quality, longitudinal research on how developing compulsive behaviors around porn use in the teenage years might impact on individuals' ability to have healthy sexual relationships with real human beings later in life.

3.5 Risks to Privacy from Sharing Content

So far in this chapter I have mainly been considering the risks of negative behavior change to young people who more or less deliberately seek out "risky" content, whether in the form of violent video games or extreme pornography. Yet as previously mentioned, many adolescents report having been accidentally exposed to pornography. Therefore we also need to ask what risk factors are associated with such exposure, as well as with exposure to other forms of sensitive content and malicious actors online. This was the subject of one of my own recent studies (Ingram, 2020) which was carried out with Colombian teenagers – Latin American adolescents being an understudied group in this area.

Exposure to all forms of online risks increases with age up to adulthood (Cabello-Hutt et al., 2018), partly because older adolescents just use the internet more, but also perhaps because they experiment more with their own preferences and are less subject to adult restrictions on their behavior online. Risky sexual behavior in response to sexual risks may also increase with age, again for the latter two reasons. Gender too has a part to play, with much evidence that girls are more exposed to sexual risks (in the form of unwelcome sexual advances) online than boys are, while possibly being less likely to act on them, at least if frequency of risk exposure is controlled for (Baumgartner et al., 2010). In addition to age and gender, personality has been examined as a possible source of variation in both exposure to risk and risky behavior. The trait most investigated has been sensation-seeking, which has been linked to sexting (Van Ouytsel et al., 2014), receiving sexual messages (Livingstone & Görzig, 2014), online gambling (White et al., 2018), online gaming addiction (Hu et al., 2017), online deception (Lu, 2008), risky self-presentation (Koutamanis et al., 2015), pornography use (Beyens et al., 2015), and meeting online contacts in offline contexts (Bayraktar et al., 2016).

However, it might seem almost tautologous to say that sensation-seeking is linked to exposure to risks online, since risky behavior tends to cause exciting sensations, and exposure often involves some form of active seeking. Perhaps for this reason, other authors have looked for relationships between more general personality traits (such as the "Big Five" traits of openness to experience, conscientiousness, extraversion, agreeableness, and neuroticism; Kayiş et al., 2016) and internet usage, with mixed results. For example, Öztürk et al. (2015) found higher rates of extraversion and openness to experience in those participants at risk of internet addiction, while in a meta-analytic review, Kayiş et al. (2016) found that only neuroticism was positively associated with internet addiction, with openness to experience, conscientiousness, extraversion, and agreeableness all showing negative links. On the other hand, sexting has been associated with high extraversion and low conscientiousness (Gámez-Guadix & De Santisteban, 2018). These results contrast with Kuss et al.'s (2013) findings that extraversion and conscientiousness were preventive factors against online gaming addiction, and the associations found by Van der Aa et al. (2009) between compulsive internet use, introversion, and low agreeability. Finally, the relative contributions of sensation-seeking and broader "Big Five" personality traits to online gambling among adolescents were directly compared by Reardon et al. (2019), who showed that low levels of conscientiousness and high levels of sensation-seeking formed separate routes to problematic gambling.

In addition to individual characteristics such as age, gender, and personality, a substantial literature has examined the effects of parental mediation on teenager's internet use, with a view to finding out what is the best strategy for parents to protect their children from online risks. In particular, researchers have debated whether it is better for parents to take a restrictive strategy to limit internet use by teenagers, or a more active, enabling strategy which co-constructs a form of safe internet usage with them (Ho et al., 2017). The large-scale EU Kids Online study found that restrictive strategies tend to be favored when parents' or children's digital skills are lower, and enabling strategies when they are higher, with enabling strategies increasing the risks but also the opportunities associated with internet use (Livingstone et al., 2017). A similar double-edged pattern of restrictive strategies lowering both risks and opportunities was reported recently from Brazil (Cabello-Hutt et al., 2018). In Singapore, Shin and Lwin (2017) found that active mediation by parents and teachers reduced the level of risk that participants encountered, whereas that by peers raised it. Mediation by parents also declined during adolescence, while peer mediation increased. Meanwhile, Ho et al. (2017) found that restrictive mediation worked better for primary school pupils than for secondary school pupils.

Nonetheless, almost all this literature has focused on mediation defined in terms of adults (or occasionally peers) talking to teenagers about how the latter should manage their internet use: very little research has examined how teenagers proactively report the risks that they encounter online or activities that they carry out there. An exception is Wisniewski et al.'s (2017) diary study of parent–adolescent pairs, which found that parents consistently underestimated not only their teenage children's exposure to risks online, but also their propensity to respond in risky ways, while overestimating their willingness to report the risks that they had encountered. Since understanding the level of risk that an adolescent is facing online requires communicating with them about the topic, it is critical to understand the functioning of these communication processes with parents and other adults.

Accordingly, in my study I focused on four key variables that have to do with the risks that Colombian adolescents face online. The first, *risk exposure*, was measured through asking participants how often they were exposed to people making requests that invaded privacy (such as for their real name or physical address) or sharing upsetting content. The second, *risk vulnerability*, was measured by asking participants if they typically acted on these risks, for example by giving out their personal details to a stranger, or clicking on a link that appeared to contain extreme content. For the third variable, *concern about risks*, I asked young people how worried they were about these kinds of phenomena online. Finally, to get at *communication about risks*, I asked how likely they would be to report such phenomena to three categories of people: adult family members, teachers and other school staff, and peers. A simplified model of the study variables, including only those that had significant correlations with other variables, is presented in Figure 3.1:

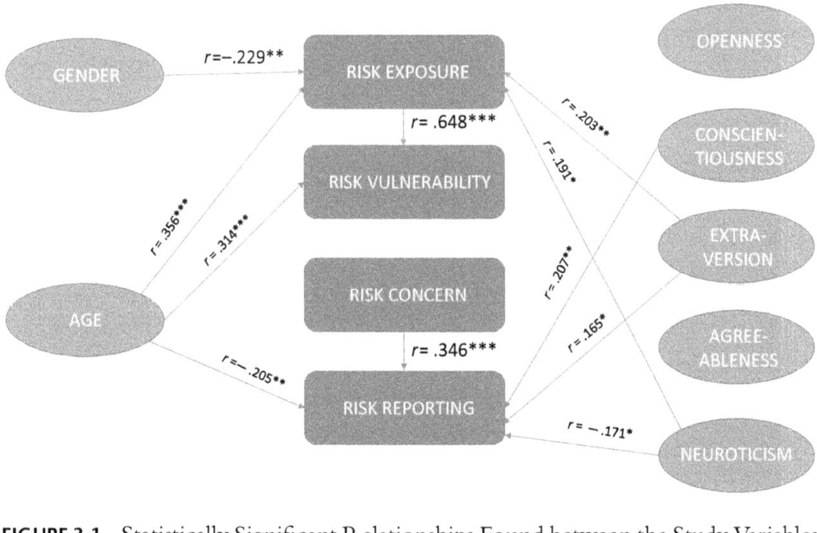

FIGURE 3.1 Statistically Significant Relationships Found between the Study Variables

Note: Reprinted with permission from Ingram (2020). * $p < .05$; ** $p < .01$; *** $p < .001$.

As shown in the diagram, there was a strong correlation between exposure and vulnerability to online risks. There are several possible explanations for this. It could be that with more exposure to risks, young people become "desensitized" to them, and are more likely to click on a link containing troublesome material, or provide their personal details to strangers. It could also be the case that people who are more vulnerable to risks actively seek out exposure to them (or to material associated with them). Finally, the link could be a methodological artifact, if those participants who were more likely to say that they were exposed to risks were also more likely to say that they were more likely to respond to them, interpreting the question as one of frequency (against this interpretation, note that risk exposure did not correlate with the similarly worded questions about risk concern and risk reporting). Another interesting finding was that age and (weakly) female gender, extraversion and neuroticism all correlated with risk exposure (in line with findings by Baumgartner et al., 2010; Cabello-Hutt et al., 2018; Gámez-Guadix & De Santisteban, 2018; and Kayiş et al., 2016), but that none of these correlated with risk vulnerability once risk exposure was controlled for. Thus, risk exposure appeared to mediate the relationship between age and risk vulnerability, suggesting tentatively that older adolescents' greater susceptibility to online risks may be less to do with developmental factors and more to do with desensitization.

Surprisingly, I found no link in this study between either exposure or vulnerability to online risks and concern about such risks. Risk reporting was the only study variable with which risk concern correlated significantly. Leaving out risk reporting (which a priori seems more likely to be causally predicted by risk concern than a predictor of it), all other variables in the study put together explained less than 3% of the variance in risk concern. The current study thus leaves a huge explanatory gap in accounting for what makes young adolescents more or less concerned about online risks. Since this does not seem to be linked to demographic or personality factors, nor exposure or vulnerability to risks, one candidate explanatory factor would be peer attitudes to these risks: whether the adolescent's friends see them as harmless fun or something to be avoided. Another would be the level and quality of education that adolescents have received about online risks: hypothetically, they might well be more worried about risks if they have unanswered questions about them. Future work could study the relationships between levels of concern and the communication that adolescents have received about risks, and integrate that with a study of adolescents' own reporting of risks. As well as being related to risk concern, the latter activity declined with age (in terms of reporting to parents and teachers, though not to peers) and was weakly correlated with conscientiousness, extraversion and (negatively) with neuroticism. These relationships should all be borne in mind when designing interventions to promote young people's communication about online risks.

A further limitation of this study was its reliance on self-report measures. This is a particular concern when working with young adolescents, who may be understandably hesitant to reveal much about their engagement in risky behavior online (or offline), particularly if it is sexual in nature. Further research should examine other possible methods for investigating this topic, including implicit methods, diary studies, or even access to smartphone logs (if complete anonymity is guaranteed). Nevertheless, this work was valuable in helping me to conceptualize risk-related activity as a process, or rather two processes, that vary in interesting ways through adolescence – with risk exposure strongly predicting risk vulnerability and risk concern strongly predicting risk reporting, and both exposure and reporting showing significant independent relationships with age. A focus on how young people communicate about online risks may help to uncover why some are more concerned than others, and possibly even help to develop interventions which alleviate their concerns and improve their overall wellbeing in online environments.

3.6 The Bright Side of Sharing Content: Informal Knowledge Networks

This chapter has focused on the risks to young people from the new and often extreme forms of content found online and in electronic media, such as video games, more generally. There is a positive side to the explosion of new content on the internet, however, namely that it has an enormous amount of educational potential. There are many ways that one could investigate how young people take advantage of these new educational opportunities. One which falls clearly within the scope of the current book is the way that young people use social media and other new technology to share educational content in informal peer networks. In the next chapter, I will examine how the internet helps young people to form new social relationships across national boundaries, educating them about life in different cultures and contributing to the globalization of human culture. In this chapter I focus instead on how social media are deployed in existing, local social networks – such as study groups within a university class – to disseminate formal and informal educational content.

As with the influence of internet use on adolescent wellbeing in general, on violence and on many other areas of behavior, studies of the relationship between internet use and academic achievement have found very mixed results (reviewed by Ainin et al., 2015; Liu et al., 2017). Also in line with the other areas, researchers have more often focused on negative effects of internet usage, with a meta-analysis by Kates et al. (2018) finding a small average effect. Amez and Baert (2020) point out four reasons why smartphones can take time away from study. First, visual and auditory notifications (e.g., of new social media messages) may be inherently distracting to students. Second, individuals could feel a constant social pressure to check these messages, due to "fear of missing out" (FOMO), leading to poor time management (Tsai & Liu, 2015). Students could also show a behavioral addiction to smartphone usage because of the sense of social validation that they provide, or use them to indulge in "cyberloafing" ("cyberslacking") if they find academic pursuits too boring (Gökçearslan et al., 2018; Saritepeci, 2019; Taneja et al., 2015). Additionally, smartphone use could have indirect negative effects by impacting students' health, through mediating variables, including sleep quality (Christensen et al., 2016), physical fitness (Jackson et al., 2011), or mental illness (Lepp et al., 2014), since all these health indicators have been linked to academic achievement.

Like Kates et al. (2018), Amez and Baert (2020) found an overall negative effect, in a systematic review of the educational effects of smartphone usage, that was robust to the geographical location of the study, the type of educational institution, and the presence of potentially confounding factors in the analysis, although they noted the lack of longitudinal compared to cross-sectional studies (a familiar complaint, as we have seen for studies of screen time, violent games and pornography use). Indeed, some studies have found that social media could have positive effects, due to the promotion of information sharing and collaborative working (Sharma et al., 2016). In parallel with other areas of technology use, these mixed findings could indicate that the practice has differential effects on different individuals and in differing social contexts.

In this area there have been some relevant and innovative studies in Colombia, including one by Peñuela Epalza et al. (2014), who studied the effect of smartphone usage on the social relations of university students in the city of Barranquilla. Although they found frequent conflicts relating to the overuse of smartphones, often relating to someone being distracted by their phone and ignoring an interlocutor, they also found that a majority of students said that smartphones were essential for keeping in touch with friends and family. It was very common for students to check their smartphones in class (in one in-depth Korean study, students did so every three to four minutes on average; Kim et al., 2019), and one in eight students said their smartphone was also essential for study-related purposes. This may be why Peñuela Epalza et al. found that people who checked their phones frequently were equally likely to do well academically in class. In a study with my student Luis Vallejo, we attempted to probe the relationship between academic achievement and internet usage more rigorously, focusing in particular on social media use. As stated above, studies in this area have found very mixed results, suggesting the involvement of as yet poorly understood mediating and/or moderating variables. Hence, Luis and I formed the idea of investigating two such variables: academic self-esteem as a mediator, and parenting style as a moderator.

A mediating variable is one that has an effect on a dependent variable if its values are raised or lowered by a third variable (which has no direct effect on the dependent variable). We hypothesized that academic self-esteem (essentially, how academically able a young person believes themselves to be) could function as such a mediator, and used an academic "self-concept" scale to measure it. This construct stems from the work of Covington (1984), who theorized that academic success is not due simply to IQ or the amount of work that students put in. The idea of academic self-concept or self-esteem points to the potential roles of home environment and interactions with parents and teachers in determining academic success (children from homes where academic learning seems more "natural" may feel more confident in their academic abilities and have easier interactions with teachers; Quintero & Vallejo, 2013). Thus, if academic self-esteem is a mediating variable, then interventions that raise it could potentially have effects on adolescents' academic achievement without needing to raise their IQ or asking them to study longer. Considering the importance of home environment, we also looked at parenting style (Baumrind, 1991) as a possible moderating variable: that is, a variable that determines whether an independent variable (such as use of social networks) has an effect on a dependent variable (such as academic success). This hypothesis was based on literature indicating that authoritative parents may have more success in encouraging their children's academic achievement than do authoritarian parents (Brown & Iyengar, 2008; Masud et al., 2015).

Some 176 students, aged between 15 and 18 years and attending 10th or 11th grade at a mixed, private high school in Bogota, took part in our study. To measure their social network use, following Vossen and Valkenburg (2016), we asked them the number of hours they typically spent using such software per day and the number of days per week, as well as having them complete the Internet Addiction Test (Widyanto & McMurran, 2004). Academic self-esteem was measured using the Academic Self-Concept subscale of the multidimensional Self-Concept scale AF5, developed in Spanish by Musitu and Navarro (2004), while parenting style was assessed with a Spanish translation of the PCRI-M questionnaire (Coffman et al., 2006). Finally, effects on academic performance were measured using a simple mean of students' end-of-year grades in mathematics and Spanish. We also conducted semi-structured interviews with 40 randomly selected participants, asking them questions including whether they had ever used social networks for academic purposes and how much their parents regulated their use of them.

As shown in Figure 3.2, there was a link between academic self-concept and social network use, with adolescents who thought of themselves as more academically able tending to use social networks less. There was also a solid link between academic self-concept and actual academic achievement. However, parenting style did not seem to have anything to do with either academic self-concept or academic achievement, and had only a weak link with social network usage, since children with either authoritarian or authoritative parents tended to use social networks less, presumably because of greater management of their time by parents. The most puzzling absence of a link, however, was between social network usage and academic achievement, given that both correlated positively with academic self-concept.

To explain this null result, we turn again to the idea that social network usage is multifaceted: adolescents can use it either as a distraction from academic work,

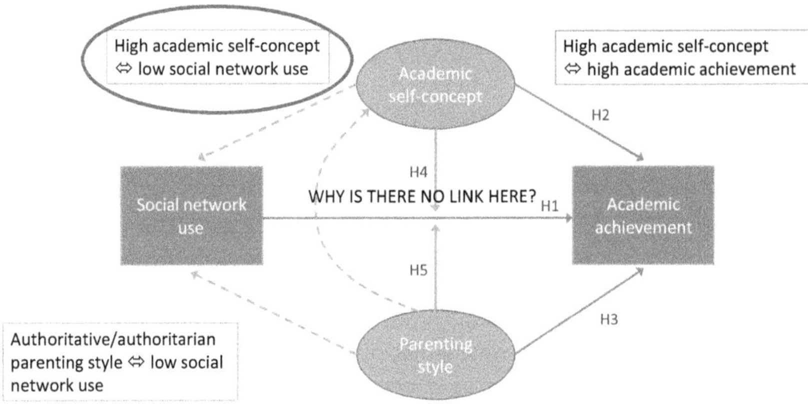

FIGURE 3.2 Hypothesized Links between Social Network Use, Parenting Style, Academic Self-Concept, and Academic Achievement

or as a support structure for knowledge sharing. This was supported by some of the students' statements in the qualitative interviews, which contained a mix of positive and negative opinions about social networks. For example, adolescents could see them as a distraction from work:

> Many times I do my work [at the same time as] social networks, so I take a lot of time doing a task; but then there comes a point where I take back control and say, no, wait a minute, I'm not doing anything; then I close my conversation and I put aside my cellphone and I concentrate on my work. But I often get distracted, I write a line and answer messages, write another line and answer messages.

But they could also point out how they could help them with their studies:

> For example, in my course we have a [group] chat, where we pass around homework, we ask each other questions about something that we haven't understood and if someone understands it they explain it. When a class ends we all meet, in the same conversation.

If social network use is not helping teenagers who have a high academic self-concept, but *is* helping those who have a lower self-esteem in the academic domain, this might explain why there is an overall null effect on academic achievement. This also raises the intriguing possibility that social networks could serve as an academic "leveler" in some sense, by promoting knowledge-sharing between young people with high academic self-esteem and their peers who feel less academically able.

3.7 Conclusion

This chapter started with the argument that many moral panics have their roots in the suspicions that older generations may feel about the production and consumption of new forms of cultural content by young people. Having learned about and adapted themselves to a given cultural milieu, older people can see cultural innovations as a replacement of their "traditional" knowledge that weakens the store of cultural capital they have built up for their families. I further argued that such anxieties tend to center on emotionally charged kinds of content, such as violent games and pornographic material (religious and political content are other possible targets for such anxieties, although perhaps given their roots in associations of people, concerns in these domains may center more on the social connections that young people are making than on the content per se that they are consuming). This argument was supported by my identification of "gamer culture" as a kind of adolescent counter-culture that explicitly goes against the norms of the dominant culture in important ways (for instance, in its alleged valorization of sexist tropes) and can therefore be seen as threatening to the dominant culture, contributing to the sense of moral panic that surrounds video gaming and other novel online activities.

However, while concerns over the psychological effects of exposure to extreme content via new technology might show many of the typical features of moral panics, it would be premature to exclude the possibility that violent video games do make young people more aggressive. Yet as we saw, the empirical evidence for this hypothesis is actually rather weak, and any effect must be small to tiny in size. Over and above these evidential problems, we also saw that violence overall has been decreasing in most developed countries even as rates of video game usage have been soaring. So, while it is technically possible that people who frequently play violent games do become slightly more aggressive, it would not seem to represent a huge potential crisis for these societies. Nevertheless, the Catalyst Model – which predicts that particular populations of disturbed individuals might be particularly vulnerable to the negative effects of violent games – does make some theoretical sense, even if it has as yet little empirical support behind it. Like many researchers in this field, I therefore advocate for more targeted qualitative and mixed-methods research with these sub-populations, as well as with individuals whose families, friends, or teachers suspect they might have an unhealthy interest in violent content. This could extend to testing interventions with such groups to see whether their interest in violent video games can be replaced with healthier pursuits, to positive effect. Pending the results of such academic studies, my main recommendation to parents is to try to involve themselves as much as possible in their children's lives, if they suspect they have issues with video game content, and to offer them possibilities for fulfilling activities in other domains – rather than trying to limit their use of video games in a confrontational way, which intuitively seems likely to have counterproductive effects.

It might seem that similar recommendations could be made for the consumption of pornography and other sexual content online, especially when the content is extreme. To an extent that is true, but it is complicated by the sensitivity of the material involved. Most teenagers – and many parents – would presumably rather not have a conversation about the detailed content of the porn that they consume, or even how often they are viewing it. For most adolescents, this may not be a serious problem: it seems that overall volume of pornography consumed does not have much negative impact on real-world sexual behavior. However, there are also suggestions from the research that an obsessive interest in extreme and (especially) violent porn may indicate a risk of engaging in offline abuse. This seems like one area in which government regulation might have a role to play. The old system of age ratings on videos and computer games, which relied on voluntary enforcement by parents and retailers, has been rendered obsolete by the ready availability of extreme material online, completely free of charge. Therefore it might make sense to introduce a new compulsory system of age verification, perhaps based on credit card checks or on data held by mobile internet providers about their clients, for popular sites such as Pornhub or Xvideos that host vast quantities of free hardcore porn. Whether such a move would do anything to limit offline sexual abuse is debatable and not something that academic research can answer definitively right now, if ever. It may also be difficult to implement given freedom-of-speech objections, especially in the United States (C. Ferguson, pers. comm.). But what exactly are the downsides? No one would seem to be harmed by such a measure, and it might at least give parents some reassurance over what their children are watching online, while sending a social signal that much of this content is deeply problematic and degrading to women, in particular.

As well as governments, technology companies also need to do more to protect young people from problematic content. In my study of online risk exposure (Ingram, 2020), I showed that many young people were concerned about material that they had been exposed to online, but that predictors of such concern were hard to account for, and might, in many cases, be determined by the nature of the content itself. Therefore – since my results also showed that young people are increasingly unwilling to talk with adults about their online viewing habits as they move through adolescence – the onus is on tech firms to include anonymized ways for users to flag disturbing content, and feed that into their algorithms to ensure that such content is de-emphasized or even completely hidden from young people. Since adolescents' willingness to talk with peers does not seem to be as affected as their willingness to talk with parents or teachers, interventions that use a "buddy" or peer community support system to deal with problems caused by risky content are another promising area of potential research.

A different sort of problem is posed by the tendency of young people to use social networks (along with messaging apps such as WhatsApp) to share academic content and strategies. What is most notable here is how this operates as a kind of "shadow" educational system, completely detached from official course requirements and didactic methods. Although numerous educational interventions (particularly in higher education) have tried to make use of social networks for pedagogical purposes, this tends to be done in a rather strained and top-down way (e.g., a course Facebook page where the students all have to leave comments). Researchers should attempt to investigate in more detail exactly how students are using technology to support their studies, and eventually test interventions that leverage the results of such research to provide more organically designed forms of teaching that integrate with students' actual practices (a medium like WhatsApp might be particularly suited to a peer-teaching exercise, for example). This kind of research also needs to be carried out much more frequently with high school as well as university students.

We know that adolescents like to choose their own path, form their own identity, and, in many cases, create whole new subcultures based on the practice of novel activities and the consumption of new kinds of content. Will we continue with the current system where they are left entirely free to find their own way in this? Or will we try to offer some guidance, tipping the needle of online content so that it is less easy to get hold of extreme material (particularly violent material, including that relating to sexual violence) and easier for young people to be genuinely educated, including about sensitive topics? This might seem too paternalistic, restricting young people's freedoms in unpalatable ways. Yet evolutionary science teaches us that adolescents have an instinct for freedom and that many of them will find ways to subvert such social control if they are really determined to do so. The promise of using both legislation and algorithms to tip the needle on content is that negative influences online can be reduced and positive influences augmented, on balance leading to better outcomes for young people in the aggregate, while also reassuring older generations that "something is being done" about the new dangers of the online world – and without depriving individuals of the possibility of viewing extreme content if they really, really want to. In the next chapter I consider how similar dynamics could apply not only to the content that young people consume online, but also to the new relationships that they form (and existing relationships that they consolidate) online.

Note

1 To many scholars' ire; see the open letter written by over 230 researchers in the field at https://www.scribd.com/doc/223284732/Scholar-s-Open-Letter-to-the-APA-Task-Force-On-Violent-Media-Opposing-APA-Policy-Statements-on-Violent-Media

References

Acerbi, A. (2016). A cultural evolution approach to digital media. *Frontiers in Human Neuroscience*, *10*, 636. https://doi.org/10.3389/fnhum.2016.00636

Acerbi, A. (2019). *Cultural evolution in the digital age*. Oxford University Press.

Ainin, S., Naqshbandi, M. M., Moghavvemi, S., & Jaafar, N. I. (2015). Facebook usage, socialization and academic performance. *Computers & Education*, *83*, 64–73. https://doi.org/10.1016/j.compedu.2014.12.018

Alderman, N. (2013). The existential me. BBC Radio Essay. Retrieved from https://www.bbc.co.uk/programmes/b03h3p4q

Alexa. (2016). *Top sites in video games*. Retrieved from http://www.alexa.com/topsites/category;0/Top/Games/Video_Games

Allen, J. J., Anderson, C. A., & Bushman, B. J. (2018). The general aggression model. *Current Opinion in Psychology*, *19*, 75–80. https://doi.org/10.1016/j.copsyc.2017.03.034

Amez, S., & Baert, S. (2020). Smartphone use and academic performance: A literature review. *International Journal of Educational Research*, *103*, 101618. https://doi.org/10.1016/j.ijer.2020.101618

Anderson, C. A., & Bushman, B. J. (2001). Effects of violent video games on aggressive behavior, aggressive cognition, aggressive affect, physiological arousal, and prosocial behavior: A meta-analytic review of the scientific literature. *Psychological Science*, *12*, 353–359. https://psycnet.apa.org/doi/10.1111/1467-9280.00366

Anderson, C. A., & Bushman, B. J. (2002). Human aggression. *Annual Review of Psychology*, *53*, 27–51. https://doi.org/10.1146/annurev.psych.53.100901.135231

Bandura, A., Ross, D., & Ross, S. A. (1961). Transmission of aggression through imitation of aggressive models. *Journal of Abnormal and Social Psychology*, *63*, 575–582. https://doi.org/10.1037/h0045925

Barkow, J. H., O'Gorman, R., & Rendell, L. (2012). Are the new mass media subverting cultural transmission? *Review of General Psychology*, *16*, 121–133. https://doi.org/10.1037/a0027907

Baumgartner, S. E., Valkenburg, P. M., & Peter, J. (2010). Unwanted online sexual solicitation and risky sexual online behavior across the lifespan. *Journal of Applied Developmental Psychology*, *31*, 439–447. https://doi.org/10.1016/j.appdev.2010.07.005

Baumrind, D. (1991). Effective parenting during the early adolescent transition. In P. A. Cowan & E. M. Hetherington (Eds.), *Family transitions* (pp. 111–143). Psychology Press.

Bayraktar, F., Barbovschi, M., & Kontrikova, V. (2016). Risky sociability and personal agency-offline meetings with online contacts among European children and adolescents. *Children and Youth Services Review*, *70*, 78–83. https://doi.org/10.1016/j.childyouth.2016.09.007

Bernstein, B. (1964). Elaborated and restricted codes: Their social origins and some consequences. *American Anthropologist*, *66*, 55–69. https://doi.org/10.1525/aa.1964.66.suppl_3.02a00030

Beyens, I., Vandenbosch, L., & Eggermont, S. (2015). Early adolescent boys' exposure to Internet pornography: Relationships to pubertal timing, sensation seeking, and academic performance. *Journal of Early Adolescence*, *35*, 1045–1068. https://doi.org/10.1177/0272431614548069

Bonino, S., Ciairano, S., Rabaglietti, E., & Cattelino, E. (2006). Use of pornography and self-reported engagement in sexual violence among adolescents. *European Journal of Developmental Psychology*, *3*(3), 265–288. https://doi.org/10.1080/17405620600562359

Brendgen, M., Vitaro, F., Tremblay, R. E., & Wanner, B. (2002). Parent and peer effects on delinquency-related violence and dating violence: A test of two mediational models. *Social Development*, *11*(2), 225–244. https://doi.org/10.1111/1467-9507.00196

Brown, L., & Iyengar, S. (2008). Parenting styles: The impact on student achievement. *Marriage & Family Review*, *43*(1–2), 14–38. https://doi.org/10.1080/01494920802010140

Brown, J. D., & L'Engle, K. L. (2009). X-rated: Sexual attitudes and behaviors associated with US early adolescents' exposure to sexually explicit media. *Communication Research*, *36*(1), 129–151. https://doi.org/10.1177/0093650208326465

Brown v. Entertainment Merchants Association, *131 S. Ct. 2729* (2011). http://www.supremecourt.gov/opinions/10pdf/08–1448.pdf

Cabello-Hutt, T., Cabello, P., & Claro, M. (2018). Online opportunities and risks for children and adolescents: The role of digital skills, age, gender and parental mediation in Brazil. *New Media and Society*, *20*, 2411–2431. https://doi.org/10.1177/1461444817724168

Christensen, M. A., Bettencourt, L., Kaye, L., Moturu, S. T., Nguyen, K. T., Olgin, J. E., Pletcher, M. J., & Marcus, G. M. (2016). Direct measurements of smartphone screen-time: Relationships with demographics and sleep. *PloS One*, *11*(11), e0165331. https://doi.org/10.1371/journal.pone.0165331

Coffman, J. K., Guerin, D. W., & Gottfried, A. W. (2006). Reliability and validity of the Parent-Child Relationship Inventory (PCRI): Evidence from a longitudinal cross-informant investigation. *Psychological Assessment*, *18*(2), 209–214. https://doi.org/10.1037/1040-3590.18.2.209

Consalvo, M. (2012). Confronting toxic gamer culture: A challenge for feminist game studies scholars. *Ada: A Journal of Gender, New Media & Technology*, *11*(1). https://adanewmedia.org/2012/11/issue1-consalvo/

Cooper, A., Delmonico, D. L., & Burg, R. (2000). Cybersex users, abusers, and compulsives: New findings and implications. *Sexual Addiction & Compulsivity*, 7(1–2), 5–29. https://doi.org/10.1080/10720160008400205

Copenhaver, A. (2019). Violent video games as scapegoat after school shootings in the United States. In G. A. Crews (Ed.), *Handbook of research on mass shootings and multiple victim violence* (pp. 243–266). IGI Global.

Covington, M. V. (1984). The self-worth theory of achievement motivation: Findings and implications. *The Elementary School Journal*, *85*(1), 5–20. https://doi.org/abs/10.1086/461388

Coyne, S. M., & Stockdale, L. (2021). Growing up with *Grand Theft Auto*: A 10-year study of longitudinal growth of violent video game play in adolescents. *Cyberpsychology, Behavior, and Social Networking*, *24*(1), 11–16. https://doi.org/10.1089/cyber.2020.0049

Crews, F., He, J., & Hodge, C. (2007). Adolescent cortical development: A critical period of vulnerability for addiction. *Pharmacology, Biochemistry and Behavior*, *86*(2), 189–199. https://doi.org/10.1016/j.pbb.2006.12.001

Cummins, D. (2006). Dominance, status, and social hierarchies. In D. M. Buss (Ed.), *The handbook of evolutionary psychology* (pp. 676–697). Wiley.

Dickenson, J. A., Gleason, N., Coleman, E., & Miner, M. H. (2018). Prevalence of distress associated with difficulty controlling sexual urges, feelings, and behaviors in the United States. *JAMA Network Open*, *1*(7), e184468. https://doi.org/10.1001/jamanetworkopen.2018.4468

Dine, G., Jensen, R., & Russo, A. (1998). *Pornography: The production and consumption of inequality*. Routledge.

Duffy, A., Dawson, D. L., & das Nair, R. (2016). Pornography addiction in adults: A systematic review of definitions and reported impact. *Journal of Sexual Medicine, 13*(5), 760–777. https://doi.org/10.1016/j.jsxm.2016.03.002

Dunbar, R. (2010). *How many friends does one person need? Dunbar's number and other evolutionary quirks*. Faber & Faber.

Elliot, A. (2018). Speaking to the other: Digital intimate publics and Gamergate. In A. S. Dobson, B. Robards, & N. Carah (Eds.), *Digital intimate publics and social media*. Palgrave Macmillan. https://doi.org/10.1007/978-3-319-97607-5_14

Etchells, P. (2019). *Lost in a good game: Why we play video games and what they can do for us*. Icon.

Fallahi, C. R., Austad, C. S., Fallon, M., & Leishman, L. (2009). A survey of perceptions of the Virginia Tech tragedy. *Journal of School Violence, 8*(2), 120–135. https://doi.org/10.1080/15388220802074017

Ferguson, C. J. (2007). The good, the bad and the ugly: A meta-analytic review of positive and negative effects of violent video games. *Psychiatric Quarterly, 78*(4), 309–316. https://doi.org/10.1007/s11126-007-9056-9

Ferguson, C. J. (2008). The school shooting/violent video game link: Causal relationship or moral panic? *Journal of Investigative Psychology and Offender Profiling, 5*(1–2), 25–37. https://doi.org/10.1002/jip.76

Ferguson, C. J. (2020). Aggressive video games research emerges from its replication crisis (sort of). *Current Opinion in Psychology, 36*, 1–6. https://doi.org/10.1016/j.copsyc.2020.01.002

Ferguson, C. J., Copenhaver, A., & Markey, P. (2020). Reexamining the findings of the American Psychological Association's 2015 task force on violent media: A meta-analysis. *Perspectives on Psychological Science, 15*, 1423–1443. https://doi.org/10.1177/1745691620927666

Ferguson, C. J., & Hartley, R. D. (2020). Pornography and sexual aggression: Can meta-analysis find a link? *Trauma, Violence, & Abuse*, 1524838020942754. https://doi.org/10.1177/1524838020942754

Fraser, C. A., Kim, J. O., Thornsberry, A., Klemmer, S., & Dontcheva, M. (2019). Sharing the studio: How creative livestreaming can inspire, educate, and engage. In *C&C '19: Proceedings of the 2019 Conference on Creativity and Cognition* (pp. 144–155). https://doi.org/10.1145/3325480.3325485

Fritz, N., Malic, V., Paul, B., & Zhou, Y. (2020). A descriptive analysis of the types, targets, and relative frequency of aggression in mainstream pornography. *Archives of Sexual Behavior, 49*(8), 3041–3053. https://doi.org/10.1007/s10508-020-01773-0

Gámez-Guadix, M., & de Santisteban, P. (2018). "Sex pics?": Longitudinal predictors of sexting among adolescents. *Journal of Adolescent Health, 63*, 608–614. https://doi.org/10.1016/j.jadohealth.2018.05.032

Gera, E. (2014). Where are the women in eSports? Retrieved from http://www.polygon.com/2014/5/27/5723446/women-inesports-professional-gaming-riot-games-blizzard-starcraft-lol

Gökçearslan, Ş., Uluyol, Ç., & Şahin, S. (2018). Smartphone addiction, cyberloafing, stress and social support among university students: A path analysis. *Children and Youth Services Review, 91*, 47–54. https://doi.org/10.1016/j.childyouth.2018.05.036

Grubbs, J. B., Grant, J. T., Lee, B. N., Hoagland, K. C., Davidson, P., Reid, R. C., & Kraus, S. W. (2020). Sexual addiction 25 years on: A systematic and methodological review of empirical literature and an agenda for future research. *Clinical Psychology Review*, 101925. https://doi.org/10.1016/j.cpr.2020.101925

Hawley, P. H. (2007). Social dominance in childhood and adolescence: Why social competence and aggression may go hand in hand. In T. D. Little, P. C. Rodkin, & P. H. Hawley (Eds.), *Aggression and adaptation: The bright side to bad behavior* (pp. 1–29). Routledge.

Hilton, N. Z., Harris, G. T., & Rice, M. E. (2003). Adolescents' perceptions of the seriousness of sexual aggression: Influence of gender, traditional attitudes, and self-reported experience. *Sexual Abuse: A Journal of Research and Treatment, 15*(3), 201–214. https://doi.org/10.1023/A:1023551417337

Hilvert-Bruce, Z., Neill, J. T., Sjöblom, M., & Hamari, J. (2018). Social motivations of live-streaming viewer engagement on Twitch. *Computers in Human Behavior, 84*, 58–67. https://doi.org/10.1016/j.chb.2018.02.013

Ho, S. S., Chen, L., & Ng, A. P. (2017). Comparing cyberbullying perpetration on social media between primary and secondary school students. *Computers and Education, 109*, 74–84. https://doi.org/10.1016/j.compedu.2017.02.004

Hu, J., Zhen, S., Yu, C., Zhang, Q., & Zhang, W. (2017). Sensation seeking and online gaming addiction in adolescents: A moderated mediation model of positive affective associations and impulsivity. *Frontiers in Psychology, 8*, 699. https://doi.org/10.3389/fpsyg.2017.00699

Hu, L., Min, Q., Han, S., & Liu, Z. (2020). Understanding followers' stickiness to digital influencers: The effect of psychological responses. *International Journal of Information Management, 54*, 102169. https://doi.org/10.1016/j.ijinfomgt.2020.102169

Ingram, G. P. D. (2014). From hitting to tattling to gossip: An evolutionary rationale for the development of indirect aggression. *Evolutionary Psychology, 12*(2), 147470491401200205. https://doi.org/10.1177%2F147470491401200205

Ingram, G. P. D. (2020). Influence of age, gender and personality on young adolescents' reporting of online risks to third parties. *Computers in Human Behavior Reports, 2*, 100040. https://doi.org/10.1016/j.chbr.2020.100040

Jackson, L. A., Von Eye, A., Fitzgerald, H. E., Witt, E. A., & Zhao, Y. (2011). Internet use, videogame playing and cell phone use as predictors of children's body mass index (BMI), body weight, academic performance, and social and overall self-esteem. *Computers in Human Behavior, 27*(1), 599–604. https://doi.org/10.1016/j.chb.2010.10.019

Kates, A. W., Wu, H., & Coryn, C. L. (2018). The effects of mobile phone use on academic performance: A meta-analysis. *Computers & Education, 127*, 107–112. https://doi.org/10.1016/j.compedu.2018.08.012

Kayiş, A. R., Satici, S. A., Yilmaz, M. F., Şimşek, D., Ceyhan, E., & Bakioğlu, F. (2016). Big five-personality trait and internet addiction: A meta-analytic review. *Computers in Human Behavior, 63*, 35–40. https://doi.org/10.1016/j.chb.2016.05.012

Kim, I., Kim, R., Kim, H., Kim, D., Han, K., Lee, P. H., Mark, G., & Lee, U. (2019). Understanding smartphone usage in college classrooms: A long-term measurement study. *Computers & Education, 141*, 103611. https://doi.org/10.1016/j.compedu.2019.103611

Klaassen, M. J., & Peter, J. (2015). Gender (in) equality in Internet pornography: A content analysis of popular pornographic Internet videos. *Journal of Sex Research, 52*(7), 721–735. https://doi.org/10.1080/00224499.2014.976781

Kohut, T., Landripet, I., & Štulhofer, A. (2021). Testing the confluence model of the association between pornography use and male sexual aggression: A longitudinal assessment in two independent adolescent samples from Croatia. *Archives of Sexual Behavior, 50*(2), 647–665. https://doi.org/10.1007/s10508-020-01824-6

Koutamanis, M., Vossen, H. G., & Valkenburg, P. M. (2015). Adolescents' comments in social media: Why do adolescents receive negative feedback and who is most at risk? *Computers in Human Behavior, 53*, 486–494. https://doi.org/10.1016/j.chb.2015.07.016

Kuss, D. J., Van Rooij, A. J., Shorter, G. W., Griffiths, M. D., & van de Mheen, D. (2013). Internet addiction in adolescents: Prevalence and risk factors. *Computers in Human Behavior, 29*, 1987–1996. https://doi.org/10.1016/j.chb.2013.04.002

Lawler, R. (2018). 'Fortnite' streamer breaks Twitch records with help from Drake. *Engadget*. https://www.engadget.com/2018-03-15-ninja-drake-twitch.html

Leca, J. B., Gunst, N., & Huffman, M. A. (2007). Age-related differences in the performance, diffusion, and maintenance of stone handling, a behavioral tradition in Japanese macaques. *Journal of Human Evolution, 53*, 691–708. https://doi.org/10.1016/j.jhevol.2007.05.009

Lenhart, A., Smith, A., Anderson, M., Duggan, M., & Perrin, A. (2015). *Teens, technology and friendships*. Pew Research Center. https://www.pewresearch.org/internet/2015/08/06/teens-technology-and-friendships/

Lepp, A., Barkley, J. E., & Karpinski, A. C. (2014). The relationship between cell phone use, academic performance, anxiety, and satisfaction with life in college students. *Computers in Human Behavior, 31*, 343–350. https://doi.org/10.1016/j.chb.2013.10.049

Ley, D., Prause, N., & Finn, P. (2014). The emperor has no clothes: A review of the 'pornography addiction' model. *Current Sexual Health Reports, 6*(2), 94–105. https://doi.org/10.1007/s11930-014-0016-8

Liem, G. A. D., & Martin, A. J. (2011). Peer relationships and adolescents' academic and non-academic outcomes: Same-sex and opposite-sex peer effects and the mediating role of school engagement. *British Journal of Educational Psychology, 81*(2), 183–206. https://doi.org/10.1111/j.2044-8279.2010.02013.x

Liu, D., Kirschner, P. A., & Karpinski, A. C. (2017). A meta-analysis of the relationship of academic performance and Social Network Site use among adolescents and young adults. *Computers in Human Behavior*, 77, 148–157. https://doi.org/10.1016/j.chb.2017.08.039

Livingstone, S., & Görzig, A. (2014). When adolescents receive sexual messages on the internet: Explaining experiences of risk and harm. *Computers in Human Behavior, 33*, 8–15. https://doi.org/10.1016/j.chb.2013.12.021

Livingstone, S., Ólafsson, K., Helsper, E. J., Lupiáñez-Villanueva, F., Veltri, G. A., & Folkvord, F. (2017). Maximizing opportunities and minimizing risks for children online: The role of digital skills in emerging strategies of parental mediation. *Journal of Communication, 67*, 82–105. https://doi.org/10.1111/jcom.12277

Lopez-Fernandez, O., Williams, A. J., & Kuss, D. J. (2019). Measuring female gaming: Gamer profile, predictors, prevalence, and characteristics from psychological and gender perspectives. *Frontiers in Psychology, 10*, 898. https://doi.org/10.3389/fpsyg.2019.00898

Love, T., Laier, C., Brand, M., Hatch, L., & Hajela, R. (2015). Neuroscience of Internet pornography addiction: A review and update. *Behavioral Sciences, 5*(3), 388–433. https://doi.org/10.3390/bs5030388

Lu, H. Y. (2008). Sensation-seeking, Internet dependency, and online interpersonal deception. *CyberPsychology and Behavior, 11*, 227–231. https://doi.org/10.1089/cpb.2007.0053

Malamuth, N. M., Addison, T., & Koss, M. (2000). Pornography and sexual aggression: Are there reliable effects and can we understand them? *Annual Review of Sex Research*, *11*(1), 26–91. https://doi.org/10.1080/10532528.2000.10559784

Markey, P. M., & Ferguson, C. J. (2017). *Moral combat: Why the war on violent video games is wrong*. BenBella.

Masud, H., Thurasamy, R., & Ahmad, M. S. (2015). Parenting styles and academic achievement of young adolescents: A systematic literature review. *Quality & Quantity*, *49*(6), 2411–2433. https://doi.org/10.1007/s11135-014-0120-x

McNair, B. (1996). *Mediated sex. Pornography and postmodern culture*. Arnold.

Mesoudi, A. (2020). *Are humans "wary learners"?* International Cognition and Culture Institute. Retrieved from http://cognitionandculture.net/webinars/cultural-evolution-in-the-digital-age/are-humans-wary-learners/

Mikkelsen, D. (2008). *Columbine Doom levels: Did one of the Columbine murderers prepare by designing new Doom levels that resembled his school?* Snopes. https://www.snopes.com/fact-check/the-harris-levels/

Morgan, E. M. (2011). Associations between young adults' use of sexually explicit materials and their sexual preferences, behaviors, and satisfaction. *Journal of Sex Research*, *48*(6), 520–530. https://doi.org/10.1080/00224499.2010.543960

Musitu, G., & Navarro, J. F. (2004). Consequences of the family socialization in the Spanish culture. *Psicotema*, *16*(2), 288–293. https://doi.org/10.1.1.538.6892

Öztürk, C., Bektas, M., Ayar, D., Öztornacı, B. Ö., & Yağcı, D. (2015). Association of personality traits and risk of internet addiction in adolescents. *Asian Nursing Research*, *9*, 120–124. https://doi.org/10.1016/j.anr.2015.01.001

Paaßen, B., Morgenroth, T., & Stratemeyer, M. (2017). What is a true gamer? The male gamer stereotype and the marginalization of women in video game culture. *Sex Roles*, *76*(7), 421–435. https://doi.org/10.1007/s11199-016-0678-y

Paasonen, S. (2017). User-generated pornography: Amateurs and the ambiguity of authenticity. In C. Smith, F. Attwood, & B. McNair (Eds.), *The Routledge companion to media, sex and sexuality* (pp. 174–182). Routledge.

Peñuela Epalza, M., Patemina Del Río, J., Moreno Santiago, D., Camacho Pérez, L., Acosta Barrios, L., & De León, L. (2014). El uso de los smartphones y las relaciones interpersonales de los jóvenes universitarios en la ciudad de Barranquilla (Colombia). *Salud Uninorte*, *30*(3), 335–346. Retrieved from http://www.redalyc.org/articulo.oa?id=81737153008

Peter, J., & Valkenburg, P. M. (2016). Adolescents and pornography: A review of 20 years of research. *Journal of Sex Research*, *53*(4–5), 509–531. https://doi.org/10.1080/00224499.2016.1143441

Quintero, M. T. Q., & Vallejo, G. M. O. (2013). El desempeño académico: Una opción para la cualificación de las instituciones educativas. *Plumilla Educativa*, *12*(2), 93–115. Retrieved from https://dialnet.unirioja.es/servlet/articulo?codigo=4756664

Reardon, K. W., Wang, M., Neighbors, C., & Tackett, J. L. (2019). The personality context of adolescent gambling: Better explained by the Big Five or sensation-seeking? *Journal of Psychopathology and Behavioral Assessment*, *41*, 69–80. https://doi.org/10.1007/s10862-018-9690-6

Rideout, V. (2002). Generation RX.com: What are young people really doing online? *Marketing Health Services*, *22*, 26–30.

Sabina, C., Wolak, J., & Finkelhor, D. (2008). The nature and dynamics of Internet pornography exposure for youth. *CyberPsychology & Behavior*, *11*(6), 691–693. https://doi.org/10.1089/cpb.2007.0179

Saritepeci, M. (2019). Predictors of cyberloafing among high school students: Unauthorized access to school network, metacognitive awareness and smartphone addiction. *Education and Information Technologies*, 1–19. https://doi.org/10.1007/s10639-019-10042-0

Sharma, S. K., Joshi, A., & Sharma, H. (2016). A multi-analytical approach to predict the Facebook usage in higher education. *Computers in Human Behavior*, *55*, 340–353. https://doi.org/10.1016/j.chb.2015.09.020

Shin, W., & Lwin, M. O. (2017). How does "talking about the Internet with others" affect teenagers' experience of online risks? The role of active mediation by parents, peers, and school teachers. *New Media and Society*, *19*, 1109–1126. https://doi.org/10.1177/1461444815626612

Taneja, A., Fiore, V., & Fischer, B. (2015). Cyber-slacking in the classroom: Potential for digital distraction in the new age. *Computers & Education*, *82*, 141–151. https://doi.org/10.1016/j.compedu.2014.11.009

Tolman, D. L., Kim, J. L., Schooler, D., & Sorsoli, C. L. (2007). Rethinking the associations between television viewing and adolescent sexuality development: Bringing gender into focus. *Journal of Adolescent Health*, *40*(1), 84.e9–e16. https://doi.org/10.1016/j.jadohealth.2006.08.002

Tolman, D. L., & McClelland, S. I. (2011). Normative sexuality development in adolescence: A decade in review, 2000–2009. *Journal of Research on Adolescence*, *21*(1), 242–255. https://doi.org/10.1111/j.1532-7795.2010.00726.x

Tsai, H. C., & Liu, S. H. (2015). Relationships between time-management skills, Facebook interpersonal skills and academic achievement among junior high school students. *Social Psychology of Education*, *18*(3), 503–516. https://doi.org/10.1007/s11218-015-9297-7

Van der Aa, N., Overbeek, G., Engels, R. C., Scholte, R. H., Meerkerk, G. J., & Van den Eijnden, R. J. (2009). Daily and compulsive internet use and well-being in adolescence: A diathesis-stress model based on big five personality traits. *Journal of Youth and Adolescence*, *38*, 765–776. https://doi.org/10.1007/s10964-008-9298-3

Van Ouytsel, J., Van Gool, E., Ponnet, K., & Walrave, M. (2014). The association between adolescents' characteristics and engagement in sexting. *Journal of Adolescence*, *37*, 1387–1391. https://doi.org/10.1016/j.adolescence.2014.10.004

Verheijen, G. P., Burk, W. J., Stoltz, S. E., van den Berg, Y. H., & Cillessen, A. H. (2021). A longitudinal social network perspective on adolescents' exposure to violent video games and aggression. *Cyberpsychology, Behavior, and Social Networking*, *24*(1), 24–31. https://doi.org/10.1089/cyber.2019.0776

Vossen, H. G., & Valkenburg, P. M. (2016). Do social media foster or curtail adolescents' empathy? A longitudinal study. *Computers in Human Behavior*, *63*, 118–124. https://doi.org/10.1016/j.chb.2016.05.040

White, C. M., Gummerum, M., & Hanoch, Y. (2018). Framing of online risk: Young adults' and adolescents' representations of risky gambles. *Decision*, *5*, 119–128. https://doi.org/10.1037/dec0000066

Widyanto, L., & McMurran, M. (2004). The psychometric properties of the Internet Addiction Test. *Cyberpsychology & Behavior*, 7(4), 443–450. http://doi.org/10.1089/cpb.2004.7.443

Wisniewski, P., Xu, H., Rosson, M. B., & Carroll, J. M. (2017). Parents just don't understand: Why teens don't talk to parents about their online risk experiences. In *CSCW '17: Proceedings of the 2017 ACM Conference on Computer Supported Cooperative Work and Social Computing* (pp. 523–540). https://doi.org/10.1145/2998181.2998236s

Wright, P. J., Tokunaga, R. S., & Kraus, A. (2016). A meta-analysis of pornography consumption and actual acts of sexual aggression in general population studies. *Journal of Communication*, *66*(1), 183–205. https://doi.org/10.1111/jcom.12201

Zhao, H., Zhou, J., Xu, X., Gong, X., Zheng, J., & Zhou, J. (2021). How to Be Aggressive from Virtual to Reality? Revisiting the Violent Video Games Exposure-Aggression Association and the Mediating Mechanisms. *Cyberpsychology, Behavior, and Social Networking*, *24*(1), 56–62. https://doi.org/10.1089/cyber.2019.0762

Zillmann, D. (2000). Influence of unrestrained access to erotica on adolescents' and young adults' dispositions toward sexuality. *Journal of Adolescent Health*, *27*(2), 41–44. https://doi.org/10.1016/S1054-139X(00)00137-3

Zitzman, S. T., & Butler, M. H. (2009). Wives' experience of husbands' pornography use and concomitant deception as an attachment threat in the adult pair-bond relationship. *Sexual Addiction and Compulsivity*, *16*(3), 210–240. https://doi.org/s10.1080/10720160903202679

4

NEW RELATIONSHIPS

Online Dating, Cyberbullying, and Intergroup Contact

4.1 Changes in Young People's Social Networks with Age

To understand how young people's social networks vary with age, it helps to revisit the model of adolescent development described at the start of Chapter 2. Recall that as young people move from childhood to adolescence, they become less focused on their parents to meet their social and other needs, and spend much more time with peers. Not only that, but the nature of their peer relationships also changes. The very youngest children, in preschool environments before five years of age, tend to be focused on one or two close playmates who typically share common interests and play preferences, and whom they call friends (Howes, 2009). The limited number of friendship relations at this early age reflects the social orientation of young children toward family: in more traditional societies, such relationships would mostly correspond to siblings, cousins, or neighboring families' children whose mothers essentially practice co-rearing with the child's own mother.

Between five and ten years, friendship circles normally expand, but are still limited by external categories such as those imposed by educational institutions, geography (e.g., a housing block), or the child's own age and gender (Hartup, 1992). For example, an eight-year-old boy might think of all the boys in his (age-limited) class as his "friends", even though within that group he might have one or two "best friends" with whom he spends more time than the rest. He might only vaguely know the names of kids in other classes at the same school, if it is a fairly big school, and might have more distant relations with most of the girls in his class, perhaps not even thinking of them as "friends". (In one study by Graham et al., 1998, about 60% of six-year-old children nominated a child of the same gender as their "best friend", and by age 12, 90% did so.)

DOI: 10.4324/9781003019459-4

Another big change comes in the stage of preadolescence (around 10–12 years) when children typically undergo a kind of reorganization of their friendship networks (Zimmer-Gembeck, 2002). This is a process that I studied during my time as a postdoctoral researcher about ten years ago. As part of a team working on designing a computer game to improve preadolescent children's conflict resolution skills, we interviewed British, Greek, and Portuguese children about situations when another child had made them angry, where they had made another child angry, and when they had observed a conflict between two or more other children (Ingram et al., 2012). We found that a common source of conflicts (especially in girls, but also among some boys) was when one child thought of another as her best friend, but the second child did something to make the first suspect that the second child was actually closer friends with a third child (e.g., breaking a promise, or betraying a secret that the first child had told her). It is often thought that this change in friendship networks is caused by the switch from primary to secondary school with the consequent breakup of peer groups (e.g., Felmlee et al., 2018); however, we found these conflicts already in children who were in their penultimate, not even final, year of primary school (Ingram et al., 2012); and anecdotally they are also present in countries like Colombia where children stay in the same schools and simply move between primary and secondary departments. Therefore, I have postulated elsewhere (Ingram, 2014; Ingram, 2019) that such conflicts are more likely caused by endogenous changes within children's minds, as they stop hanging out with a "default" friendship group based on early shared interests and common class membership, and begin the process of identity (re)construction that is one of the major tasks of adolescence (see discussion of relevant literature at the start of Chapter 2).

It is noteworthy that this newfound flexibility in friendship networks does not initially extend to cross-gender friendships. Indeed, children's tendency to associate with peers of the same gender actually peaks around 12 or 13 years (Pfaff, 2010). In preadolescence, boys more often play in large mixed-age groups, while girls prefer small same-age groups or pairs (Lever, 1978). Boys tend to like competitive team games, while girls focus on intimacy and exclusiveness (Maccoby, 2002). Exclusive same-sex cliques (numbering 3–9 people) are still common in early adolescence (Bukowski et al., 1993). In mid-adolescence these gradually merge into larger "gangs" (still usually with identifiable cliques within them), and finally into mixed-sex "crowds", made up of loose associations of male and female cliques, by late adolescence (Thornburg, 1971). During all this time, the importance of shared interests in bonding friends together never goes away, but the overall nature of these interests changes, increasingly becoming focused on activities that are more associated with adults (including, but not limited to, things that are illegal for children: sex, drugs, alcohol, tobacco, and gambling; Kandel & Davies, 1991). All of this means that adolescents are naturally open to experiencing novel activities and forming new social relationships. However, there is a dark side to this which I already alluded to, namely that such changes in activities and social relationships create a lot of potential for conflict. This reaches its peak in pre-adolescence or early adolescence (as does bullying; Pepler et al., 2006), before stabilizing in mid-adolescence and decreasing in later adolescence (Galambos & Almeida, 1992), as young people get better at perspective-taking and self-control, and also form well-defined social hierarchies mediated by the prestige they can win in different social activities (Ingram, 2014).

In the rest of this chapter I first examine how these relationships, interests, and sources of prestige have changed with the shift to online modes of social interactions. Apart from forging an identity, one of the main tasks of adolescence is, of course, developing a sexual identity and attracting a mate (Zimmer-Gembeck, 2002). This process is being transformed by hookup and dating apps such as Tinder, along with visually oriented social networks such as Instagram and Snapchat. These apps and networks may make it easier to find a partner, but they also have a dark side, in the troubling rise of cyberstalking, online harassment, and revenge porn. In one sense, such behaviors are a sexualized version of cyberbullying. I consider whether cyberbullying needs to be considered as a new and uniquely harmful form of bullying, or whether it more represents "natural", evolved patterns of behavior translated to a new, virtual modality. Finally, it would be a mistake to ignore the positive effects of the new relationships that young people are forming online. One very important aspect of this is the internationalization of the World Wide Web, especially in an era of increasing nationalism and closed borders: youth culture is increasingly globalized and transcends international frontiers, while, of course, still varying greatly between cultural regions. Could this contribute to a new, more peaceful era of global relations – what might be called a virtual contact effect?

4.2 New Kinds of Connections Online

We saw in the previous two chapters how video games have become hugely popular among adolescents and young adults, and even a central part of their identity, especially for males. There is a significant gender difference here, with about nine out of ten boys sometimes playing socially online but only just over 50% of girls doing the same (less than the number who played video games with friends offline; Lenhart, 2015a). Something that may not be obvious to readers without adolescent game-playing children is that online interactions around game-playing these days are not based solely on text chats but involve "real" audio conversations: almost 60% of teens who played online with others reported using a voice connection (such as Discord or Skype) while they played. Again, far more boys (c. 80%) than girls (c. 50%) reported the use of voice chat during gameplay. While video games are particularly important for boys' interactions with friends, social media networks are relatively more important for girls (Lenhart, 2015b; see also Goswami & Dutta, 2015; Krasnova et al., 2017; McAndrew & Jeong, 2012). By 2015, over three quarters of US teens had some sort of social media presence – a proportion that is only likely to have increased since then – with Facebook, Instagram, and Snapchat being the dominant platforms (more recent research indicates that Instagram has since overtaken Facebook among young people; e.g., Shane-Simpson et al., 2018).

Young people today very much blend online and face-to-face communication with their offline friends (even more so since the widespread lockdowns associated with the COVID-19 pandemic, of course; see Chapter 5). Since smartphones and other digital devices can be used to connect to peers "anywhere and at any time" (Thulin & Vilhelmson, 2009), encouraging users to be "always online" (Brkljačić et al., 2019), young people tend to use them to interact with offline friends, even sometimes while physically present with them (Granholm, 2016). Offline interactions are thus not completely replaced by online interactions, but rather tend to complement them. Nevertheless, some data, such as that from a longitudinal mixed-methods study in Luxembourg by Décieux et al. (2019), suggest that frequency of offline interactions may be declining as adolescents see less of a need for it and find it easier to connect online. Table 4.1 shows results, from the latter study, when young people (aged 15–25) were asked to rank leisure activities in order of importance to them.

From this table, it is clear that the importance of physically meeting up with friends had been to some extent supplanted (even before the pandemic) by surfing and chatting, playing games, visually creative activities (involving camera phones, presumably), and even just relaxing alone. Furthermore, about three quarters of participants said that they used the internet to interact with or stay in contact with others, representing the most common reason given for using the internet.

TABLE 4.1 Change in Luxembourgish Young People's Ranked Importance of Leisure Activities

Activity	*Rank in 2008*	*Rank in 2011*	*Rank in 2014*	*Rank in 2016*
Being together with friends	1	2	4	7
Listening to music	2	1	1	2
Surfing, chatting, mailing on the Internet	3	3	2	1
Reading newspapers or books	5	4	5	9
Relaxing alone	8	8	6	5
Playing a game on computer, cellphone or console	13	11	7	3
Painting, drawing, taking photos or videos	14	14	10	4

Note: Recompiled from Décieux et al. (2019).

As well as quantitative trends surveys, the study authors also conducted focus groups to try to understand what was driving the changes in these trends. Young people generally found it more convenient to be able to message people quickly and at any time (even while carrying out other activities) rather than having to organize themselves to leave the house and go somewhere to meet someone, perhaps after a tiring day at school or at a time when they had to do extracurricular activities.

> These activities are important opportunities to meet and to spend time with peers. Interviewees reported that the leisure activities are very time-consuming and sometimes stressful for them so that they need time to relax and to spend time alone.
>
> *(Décieux et al., 2019, p. 24)*

Another important dynamic was the lack of benefit from face-to-face interactions perceived by participants, given that they were constantly chatting and catching up with gossip online. Indeed, they tended to associate offline meetings more with particular activities, such as cinema, music, or sport, than with just hanging out, since they felt they could derive many of the informational and entertainment benefits that previously might have been obtained from hanging out, simply by chatting with friends on their phones while relaxing alone in their rooms. Nevertheless, the participants also described how they tended to have originally met most of their friends in offline contexts such as school or sports, and how getting to know people in person was still very important in becoming friends; thus, "the dissemination of social media and mobile devices has not led to a complete disappearance of offline interaction among peers" (Décieux et al., 2019, p. 26).

The blending of offline and online modalities in friendships can begin from the moment new friends meet: university undergraduates, for example, often carry out an extensive process of online "vetting" on someone they have just met at a party, in a lecture or through a mutual acquaintance, to find out if they (or, more particularly, their social and political views) are compatible. This process was described in detail by the participants in the online-ethnographic (via Facebook) and interview study of Standlee (2019), conducted at two US universities around the time of the 2016 presidential election. She explains how "Online expressions of social and political attitudes function as a filter to create networks of social and political homogeneity that are viewed as desirable and even essential among participants" (p. 771). This is an example of a wider phenomenon whereby people with "strong ties", implying similar social positions and social circles, tend to share homogenized opinions and attitudes online – the famous "echo chamber" effect (Wollebæk et al., 2019). These kinds of closed, strong ties function to the detriment of people's "weak ties" with casual acquaintances from different backgrounds, ensuring that they are only infrequently exposed to attitudes and perspectives that greatly differ from their own (Kim & Kim, 2017).

Regarding the vetting of potential friends, Standlee's (2019) participants fell into three main categories: those who "did their homework" on potential friends, without openly admitting to the latter that they were checking up on them online; those who "explicitly filtered" their circle of friends, seeing it as an imperative for their own personal safety; and the "creepers" who continued silently following people they had met for long periods of time, researching many areas of their lives in great detail. For all three groups, the importance attached to investigating potential new contacts' online profiles reflected the social desirability and emotional intensity attached to friendships at this time of life, and their importance for providing social support in an environment where students are suddenly cut off from immediate parental aid (Friedlander et al., 2007; Raacke & Bonds-Raacke, 2015). In this context, where people could easily meet new people one day but then lose contact with them the next, online social networks such as Facebook are vital because of their perceived permanence. Standlee (2019) suggested that this sense of permanence was partly why her participants believed that viewing people's online "footprint" on Facebook was useful for getting a sense of their true, permanent identity, with minimal social investment compared to spending time with them face to face. Interestingly, many participants (in the "do your homework" group) felt it was not socially acceptable to let someone know that they were not taking the friendship further based on the political valence of their posts. As one of her participants, "Oscar", put it: "you make the decision to avoid the person based on what they post, but you can't say that's why you are doing it, right?" (Standlee, 2019, p. 777). These participants did not seem to mention "unfriending" people online because of their political views, implying that in many (if not most) cases people with differing views were still part of their social networks in some way, even though things had not gone further offline, and presumably there was still a degree of exposure to their differing ideas on Facebook when continuing to view their posts. The micro-dynamics of decisions about when to unfriend someone, and when not, would seem to be a rewarding topic for future research (see Yang et al., 2017, for a study of how people can sometimes be unfriended for their political views).

Given the widespread nature of interaction with friends online, it is also reasonable to ask to what extent the behavior varies according to individual differences. One difference that is particularly relevant in this area is shyness: since the internet's infancy in the 1990s, researchers have asked whether shy people might find it easier to interact with other people in more "socially distanced" environments online, and have linked shyness (and associated behavioral traits) with frequency of video game playing or internet use in general (Chak & Leung, 2004; Roberts et al., 2000). A more recent line of research examined an important correlate of shyness, emotional sensitivity (Kowert et al., 2014), which involves a hypersensitivity to the emotional signals of others (for instance, thinking that they are bored or annoyed with you when in reality their discomfort has another source). Kowert et al. hypothesized that online video games could provide a relatively welcoming environment for emotionally sensitive individuals to engage with friends, since the shared activity focuses joint attention and guides the content of conversations; yet at the same time, "One's co-players can be more than just individuals who help achieve in-game instrumental goals; they can be close, trusted friends and valued sources of online advice" (p. 448).

Indeed, the authors found that although more emotionally sensitive people did not engage in any more social gaming than less emotionally sensitive people, they did have more online-only friends, more initially online friends whom they later met up with offline, and more offline friends whom they sometimes played with online. They conclude that:

> mediated social spaces, particularly online games, hold the potential to be socially advantageous for emotionally sensitive individuals by allowing them to overcome their traditional social difficulties, generate new friendships, and strengthen old ones.
>
> *(p. 451)*

Given this potential, more research – especially qualitative and mixed-methods research – is clearly needed into how and why people make online-only (or initially online) friends, and into what they get out of such relationships that they do not – or do not easily – find in their offline friendships or acquaintanceships. It also seems likely that "online-only friendships" are less common – or at least less intense – among social media users than among video gamers (but see Ellison & Vitak, 2015). The extent to which an online-only relationship on social media corresponds to a true friendship would seem to be an under-studied topic, and worthy of further investigation.

In conclusion, social media and online games are used by young people both to meet (and "do their homework on") new friends and to hang out with existing, "offline-first" friends. They do not necessarily draw much of a distinction between the two activities, although offline meet-ups are still clearly important as well. Online gaming may be particularly useful as a kind of "ice-breaker" for emotionally sensitive and shy people who have difficulty making (or interacting with) friends and acquaintances in everyday offline contexts (a phenomenon that could be deployed in interventions, e.g., that of Jarusriboonchai et al., 2016). More and richer research is needed into how and why people form online-only or online-first friendships, especially those that are formed in social media or discussion forums as opposed to video games. The open-ended and flexible nature of young people's online friendships is in keeping with their tendency to form new social networks as they establish a novel identity for themselves in adolescence. Although, in this context, it may seem worrying that they have a tendency to form "echo chambers" by checking out people they have met online and only taking the offline friendship further if they have similar political and other views, it is important to avoid exaggerating the extent of this polarization, since people may remain online "friends" even if they decide not to take things further offline.

4.3 Looking for the Right Swipe on Tinder

If adolescents are forming new social networks with friends, and taking advantage of internet technology to do so in an ever freer and more flexible way, then it is even more true that they are also using internet technology to make contacts for the purpose of romantic and/or sexual relationships, for the first time. As we saw in the first section of this chapter, from middle adolescence (15–16 years) same-sex "cliques" tend to club together into mixed-sex "gangs" (Thornburg, 1971), a development that coincides with the first serious boyfriend–girlfriend relationships and is also one of the most frequent ages at which people lose their virginity. Young people's use of the internet for romantic/sexual purposes encompasses spontaneous interactions with friends of friends on social networking sites such as Facebook, Snapchat, and (most of all) Instagram; researching potential offline partners' background and online presence on such sites (Frampton & Fox, 2021); and logging on to dating sites (some of which, such as MyLol, have been specifically aimed at teens; Pujazon-Zazik et al., 2012) that are explicitly designed to facilitate the search for romantic connections. However, as we saw in Chapter 3 with the topic of teenage use of online pornography, ethical issues mean that there is a noticeable lack of research on the use of any of these methods to initiate romantic relationships or sexual encounters in under-18s. In this section, I therefore focus on the use of dating and "hookup" apps by young people aged over 18 (though note that some under-18s lie about their age in order to use these apps, since there is little meaningful age verification; Stoicescu et al., 2019); and particularly the use of the most famous hookup app, Tinder.

With an estimated 50 million registered users in more than 190 countries, 10 million daily active users, and over 30 billion matches, Tinder has become one of the most popular mobile dating apps in the world. Although it is promoted as a social discovery platform that "empowers users around the world to create new connections that otherwise might never have been possible" (Tinder, 2019), the view that Tinder is primarily a hookup app which may also lead to romantic relationships remains prevalent among users (LeFebvre, 2018; Orosz et al., 2018; Sumter et al., 2017). Once the Tinder app has been downloaded to their cellphone, users have the possibility to link their account to other social networks (Facebook, Instagram, Spotify) or they can manually add some pictures and basic personal information (education, occupation, hobbies and interests) to their Tinder profile (Olivera-La Rosa et al., 2019). The Tinder app uses the location and the age of users as filters to offer them a particular dating "pool", displayed one at a time as a sequence of profile photos (or occasionally short videos) associated with first names. Hence:

> the user gets a photo and has to decide if he/she likes that person or not based on that photo. If he/she likes that person, he/she has to swipe the picture of this person right. If he/she does not like that individual, he/she has to swipe left. If both parties like each other and swipe right, they are 'matched' and conversations begin.
>
> *(Orosz et al., 2018, p. 302)*

Tinder's increasing popularity has attracted the attention of psychologists. For instance, casual sex, love, friendship, self-esteem enhancement, ease of communication, boredom, and trendiness have been identified as particular motivational factors behind the decision to use Tinder (Orosz et al., 2018; Sumter et al., 2017). Some results suggest that, compared to women, men are more likely to use the app for casual sex and relationships (Sumter et al., 2017), while women tend to use it for friendship and self-validation (Ranzini & Lutz, 2017). Women also appear to be more selective in their right-swiping decisions compared to men (Timmermans & Courtois, 2018). These results are in line with previous research showing that men are more likely than women to use social networks to form new relationships and find potential mates (Mazman & Usluel, 2011; McAndrew & Jeong, 2012; Muscanell & Guadagno, 2012). Insights from evolutionary theory can help to explain these sex differences in judgments of novel dating partners. According to parental investment theory (Trivers, 1972), females evolved to invest more time and effort in taking care of offspring than males. In this vein, the fact that women have much greater obligatory parental investment than men (due to pregnancy and breastfeeding), and, as a result, have potentially more to lose from a short-term, "casual" sexual encounter, ultimately, leads them to be more conservative and risk-averse in their mating choices. On the other hand, men tend to view short-term sexual relationships more favorably, prefer greater number of sexual partners over time, and require less time before consenting to sex (Buss & Schmitt, 1993; Piazza & Bering, 2009; Piazza & Ingram, 2015).

Indeed, gender differences in Tinder use are very apparent. Ranzini and Lutz (2017) found that men tended to use Tinder for sex, travel, and starting a relationship, whereas women used it more for friendship and self-validation. Similarly, Sumter et al. (2017) found that men were more likely than women to use Tinder for casual sex. Piazza & Ingram (2015) reviewed evidence suggesting that men were more likely than women to initiate "sexting" (exchanges of sexually explicit text messages). Such sex differences might be expected to extend to the presentation of the self in Tinder profiles. While separate from the question of who initiates sexual interactions, gender differences in self-presentation are also related to issues of parental investment and sexual strategies (Feingold, 1992). Gender dynamics in self-presentation and attraction may be complementary, in that women often try to attract men through visual means, emphasizing their value as short-term mating prospects, while men may try to convince women that they are reliable, low-risk, long-term mating prospects, a proposition that may involve a certain amount of verbal persuasion. Although Tinder is primarily a visual application, both visual and verbal means of self-presentation are available to users, and conversational exchanges on Tinder are an under-studied area (but see James, 2015; Markowitz & Hancock, 2018).

In a study with my students Nathalia Eraso, Maria José Garcia, and Isabela Enciso, inspired by parental investment theory, we hypothesized that women would try to attract men to right-swipe (i.e., potentially match) their profiles through largely visual means; while men would try to do so more by showing off their skills and interests in the textual information fields and by linking to Spotify accounts. In particular, showing pictures of the whole body should be more important for females who want to demonstrate their potential suitability as short-term mates, according to a large body of work on the importance of the waist/hip ratio in female attractiveness (Singh et al., 2010).

There were no significant differences either in the number of photos uploaded between sexes (in fact, this number was slightly higher for men!) or in the tendency to link to an Instagram account (greater for women, but not by much). However, whole-body selfies were more common among female users (see Table 4.2) and males more frequently linked to their Spotify account. Pictures of sporting activities and pets were found only for males – although proportions were low (6%) in both cases, so this difference may not be very reliable. Pictures taken while traveling (e.g., on vacation) were also significantly more common in men. Further, men were much more likely than women to include a verbal profile description, as well as information about their college major.

TABLE 4.2 Differing Proportions of Photos in Each Category (Not Exhaustive), Split by Gender

Photo Category	*Females (col %)*	*Males (col %)*
Selfies	34	30
Mirror selfies	11***	0
Travel	5	15**
With friends	5	5
Body	14***	0
Sports	0	6**
Pets	0	6**

Note: *** significant at the 0.001 level; ** significant at the 0.01 level.

The lack of differences in the numbers of photos uploaded by female and male users contrasts with other social media such as Facebook, where females have been found to upload many more photos than males (McAndrew & Jeong, 2012). This may be because Tinder initially asks users to upload a maximum of only six photos when they register with the app. While they can upload more, the user interface for this is not intuitive, and only 6% of our sample had done so. Future work could investigate whether the difference exists in dating apps/sites that make it easier for users to upload photos. In contrast, the lack of men uploading mirror selfies – or other photos that showed their whole body – suggested that rather than simple visual information such as photos in general marking a gender difference in sexual strategies, it may be certain types of visual information, such as waist–hip ratio (Buss & Schmitt, 1993), that are important. It should be investigated whether poses and clothing that heterosexual women use in photos on Tinder and other dating sites, compared with social networks where they are not specifically trying to attract men, serve to accentuate this ratio. It is also worth noting that correcting for the 55–45% male–female split in Spotify's user base would likely mean that the difference in Spotify linking is not significant either. With hindsight, we might expect much less of a gender difference in linking to other social network accounts than in text-based profile elements such as description of university major that allow males to demonstrate their earnings potential, or photographic elements that allow the same (such as travel pics) or demonstrate a more caring side (pictures with pets). However, these hypotheses occurred to us only after we carried out our exploratory analysis of Tinder profile elements. Since the results in these areas were not predicted, they would need careful replication before firm conclusions could be drawn from them.

Notwithstanding, our results in that study show the limitations of emphasizing the visual aspects of youth culture, as I have been doing at various points in this book (especially Chapter 2). Although Tinder is a highly visual app, users were not just deploying photos to project themselves to other users, but were also displaying various other kinds of information, including their educational background, career profile, musical preferences, and hobbies and interests. (This does also parallel the argument in Chapter 2 that selfies and memes represent the use of visual and textual modalities in integrated ways, rather than being purely visual media.) In Tinder, making a match is far from the be-all and end-all of the interaction, and it would also be worth examining how post-match conversations on Tinder tend to run their course – a hugely under-researched area (presumably due to the extremely private nature of this sort of conversational content), not just on Tinder but also with regard to flirtatious conversations in online social networks, messaging apps, and even multiplayer games. Another conclusion from our study is that even when looking at modern technology, some differences between sexes may have deep evolutionary roots in different sexual strategies of parental investment. Although the differences we found were relatively innocent, the sex differences caused by evolutionary drives can also have a dark side, as we shall see in the next two sections, on cyberharassment and cyberbullying.

4.4 Cyberharassment, Cyberstalking, and Revenge Porn

How common is sexual harassment, especially against young people? Several large-scale surveys in different countries have tried to put figures on the behavior. For example, Ståhl and Dennhag (2021) found that of about 600 Swedish adolescents drawn from the general population, almost 50% of girls and almost 30% of boys had experienced some form of sexual harassment. Perhaps surprisingly, despite data being collected as recently as 2018–2019, offline harassment (reported by 24% of individuals) was still much more common than online (8%; another 8% reported that their harasser used both modalities). They note that variation between studies on this topic may reflect cultural differences in definitions of sexual harassment. However, two common findings, reinforced by their own results, are that girls tend to be harassed more than boys and that offline victimization tends to predict online victimization. As they point out, there is a need for more studies on the differential effects of the two modalities of harassment – particularly given their finding that offline sexual harassment showed stronger correlations with mental health symptoms (anxiety and depression) than did online harassment, especially for boys.

Another recent study in the different cultural environment of Chile reported similar results, in some ways (Guerra et al., 2021): 16% of almost 19,000 Chilean adolescents (aged 12–17) said they had experienced online sexual harassment, with this again being a much more common experience for girls (25%) than for boys (9%). Conversely, perpetrators were more often male, although it should not be forgotten that both adolescent and adult females can also perpetrate such behavior (Douglass et al., 2020). Despite the stereotype of sexual "grooming" as conducted by adults, minors frequently experience online sexual harassment from peers (Lewis, 2018), with about 10% of young people admitting having sexually harassed someone online (Leemis et al., 2019). In particular, former sexual partners are a very common source of online harassment for adolescent girls (Reed et al., 2019). This can have serious effects: like Ståhl and Dennhag (2021), Guerra et al. (2021) found that adolescents who had suffered sexual harassment were more likely to show depressive symptoms than those who had not. An interesting finding was how victim gender related to the gender and age of the harasser: in general, girls were mostly harassed by male perpetrators, both adolescents and adults; whereas boys were mainly harassed by adolescent peers, of either sex. (Though note that over 20% of participants were not able to identify the age or gender of their harasser, underlining the problem of anonymity in internet-based harassment.) There were also effects of age and gender (both of harasser and victim) on depressive symptoms in the victim, with girl victims being more likely than boys to suffer from depression, especially if the perpetrator was unidentified or another adolescent girl. What is clear from both these studies is that there is a need for finer-grained studies that consider the particularities of experiences of sexual harassment depending on who the victim is, who the perpetrator is, and the behaviors that comprise the harassment.

When unwanted sexual attention is especially persistent and focused on one person in particular, it is known as stalking, and the corresponding behavior in online environments is *cyberstalking*. This pattern can cross over from unwanted sexual attention to attempts at sexual coercion, and even this extreme form may unfortunately be quite common. For example, Drouin et al. (2015) found that about 20% of their young adult sample had experienced some kind of attempted sexual coercion when they were recipients of sexting, ranging from the relatively subtle (such as repeated attempts at sexual persuasion even after previous attempts were rebuffed) to the more overt (such as threats of physical violence). It is surprisingly frequent for such behaviors to become so distressing to victims that legal action is taken: Department of Justice statistics showed that as early as 2009, 1.2 million adults in the United States (approximately 1 in every 200 adults at the time) had claimed to be victims of cyberstalking with legal services (Higgins & Wolfe, 2009). In contrast, perhaps, to popular stereotypes, most cyberstalkers are recent ex-partners who opposed or regretted the breakup (Dreßing et al., 2014), with a substantial proportion even being current partners who are experiencing jealousy or suspicion over their partner's behavior (Smoker & March, 2017). As Kwok and Wescott (2020, p. 663) recently pointed out, "young people are especially vulnerable to such cyber dating abuses given their heavy reliance on technology to facilitate relationships". There is also evidence that given the flexibility of young people's sex lives, cyberstalking left unchecked within a relationship can be associated with even more worrying forms of sexual behavior, such as online or offline dating abuse (Caridade et al., 2019; Stonard, 2019), psychological violence, or attempts at sexual coercion (Calvete et al., 2019; Rodríguez-Domínguez et al., 2020).

As well as being more common than stalking by strangers or acquaintances, "intimate partner stalking" (Smoker & March, 2017; Spitzberg & Cupach, 2007) by a current or former relationship partner can lead to more aggression and physical violence, as well as tending to be more persistent and involving a greater range of stalking behaviors (McEwan et al., 2009). It can involve sending repeated online messages to a victim, the creation of an anonymous profile to monitor the victim's online behavior, or even – in more severe cases – the deployment of technological aids such as spyware or hidden webcams to access their private data or offline activities. Compared to offline stalking, cyberstalking removes spatial and temporal barriers from the stalker's ability to harass someone (Tokunaga, 2016), potentially exacerbating the negative psychological effects on the victim (e.g., anxiety, depression, and stress) that can result from stalking (Kuehner et al., 2012).

Another aspect of cyberstalking that differs from the popular imagination is the gender of the perpetrators. The image of the stalker is typically of a male harassing a female, whereas in fact, this depends greatly on the nature of the stalking behavior: male offline stalkers are more likely to physically follow their victims, whereas females typically use more physically distanced forms of stalking, such as phone calls (Purcell et al., 2010). Men are also more likely to report being victims of cyberstalking (Fisher et al., 2014) while women in long-term relationships are more likely to read their partner's emails, check their web history, etc. (Helsper & Whitty, 2010), which can be regarded as forms of cyberstalking. Indeed, Smoker and March (2017) found that women reported engaging in slightly more intimate partner cyberstalking than men did. One problem with this study was that the authors did not use the word "stalk" with participants, thus leaving it open to question whether the sort of behaviors described really counted as cyberstalking at all. More aggressive, damaging types of cyberstalking – including toward strangers or acquaintances – may be more often perpetrated by men against women (but see March et al., 2022, who found that even "invasive" cyberstalking was more often conducted by women). More research is thus needed on gender differences in stalking. Regarding age differences, few studies have been carried out on cyberstalking (or even offline stalking) in adolescents. One exception was a longitudinal study by Wright (2018), which found that being a victim of cyberstalking at Time 1 – during fall semester of the 11th grade – predicted both depression (positively) and academic performance (negatively) at Time 2, around a year later.

Perhaps even more damaging to mental health than cyberstalking is the phenomenon of "revenge porn", which typically refers to the online posting of sexually explicit images of an ex-partner (in a majority of cases, according to Citron & Franks, 2014, including identifying information such as their real name or social media account) with the motive of extracting vengeance by damaging the victim's reputation. The term is now often used loosely to refer to any non-consensual posting of sexual images, including hacked material, with one legal article defining it simply as "sexually explicit images that are publicly shared online without the consent of the pictured individual" (Levendowski, 2013, p. 425). Yet the prototypical, vengeance-motivated form of the behavior is also unfortunately quite common, with a 2013 survey finding that about 10% of former partners in the United States threatened to post sexually explicit images of their exes online, and up to 60% of that group carried out their threats (Eichorn, 2013, cited by Levendowski, 2013).

The research of Bates (2017) is notable for being an in-depth, qualitative study that focused on the individual experiences of a group of women who had suffered from being exposed in revenge porn, before, during, and after the experience. Their stories are often harrowing, and illustrate the real psychological harms caused by non-consensual pornography. In many cases this harm was exacerbated by the difficulty of removing sexual images from the internet once they were distributed there – a fact that, combined with the frequent presence of identifying information, can lead some victims to delete their social media accounts altogether. Bates stressed that the mental health after-effects of revenge porn shown by the women in her study were very similar to those suffered by sexual abuse survivors – including trust issues, PTSD (post-traumatic stress disorder), anxiety, and depression, as a well as loss of confidence, self-esteem, and sense of control. She pointed out that these problems help justify treating the distribution of such material as a sexual offense – an approach that lawmakers are now taking in many states (Cole et al., 2020).

Even though it probably does represent a sexual offense, an uncomfortable fact about revenge porn – as with cyberstalking and many other forms of online sexual harassment – is that it is not primarily generated by adult strangers "grooming" youngsters on the internet, but tends to be embedded in real or potential sexual relationships that then turn sour. Particularly relevant to this aspect of revenge porn is the phenomenon of sexting (the sending of sexual content by electronic means – usually visual images or videos – to a particular individual with whom one is in a sexual or quasi-sexual relationship; Gordon-Messer et al., 2013; Madigan et al., 2018). An important link between sexting and revenge porn was examined by Englander & McCoy (2017) in the phenomenon of "pressured sexting". In this form of sexting, one adolescent (usually female) feels pressured to send sexual or nude images to another (usually male) *before* they have started a serious relationship (qualitative evidence from their study suggested that some popular male teens might use these images almost like a kind of "audition reel", to decide whether to start a relationship with the sender). If the receiver then decided not to start a relationship with the sender, or the relationship ended in a non-amicable way, the receiver might then end up publishing or disseminating the images more widely.

One startling finding from this longitudinal study of 18- to 20-year-old undergraduates in Massachusetts was that sexting always or sometimes "under pressure" was actually more common than sexting purely voluntarily and "for fun" (Englander & McCoy, 2017). Less surprisingly, there was a marked gender difference in these motivations, with no males saying that they always felt pressured to sext, and more than twice as many males as females saying that they always did so voluntarily. There was also a difference between voluntary and pressured sexters in terms of whom they were sending the images to, with voluntary sexters considerably more likely to send them to an actual boyfriend, and pressured sexters much more likely to send them to a potential boyfriend. More relevantly to revenge porn, Englander & McCoy also analyzed possible risk factors for unwanted distribution of the resulting images, finding that this was three times as common among pressured sexters than among voluntary sexters, and was much more likely among participants who had sent images to more than one person and those who began sexting before turning 18.

A related, but distinct, phenomenon to revenge porn is known as "sextortion", which has been defined as "the threatened dissemination of explicit, intimate, or embarrassing images of a sexual nature without consent, usually for the purpose of procuring additional images, sexual acts, money, or something else" (Patchin & Hinduja, 2020, p. 31). The two phenomena differ in that revenge porn involves the public release of such images, while sextortion tends to be a private, covert behavior. The overlap between sextortion and revenge porn occurs when threats are carried out if the victim refuses to pay up, in which case the former can essentially evolve into the latter. One surprising finding of Patchin and Hinduja (2020) was that in contrast to the gender difference in revenge porn distribution, male adolescents were slightly more likely to be victims of sextortion than females (5.8% of males and 4.1% of females in the sample). A possible explanation is that some girls may have been using sextortion to gain revenge against boys who had sent them intimate, but sexually harassing, material (such as "dick pics"; Ringrose et al., 2021). This highlights the importance of examining cyber abusive behaviors in the full context of adolescent romantic, sexual, and social relationships, which can be very different from the sorts of relationships most of us are used to as adults. Patchin and Hinduja (2020) point to the importance of emphasizing to young people that sextortion is neither very rare nor very widespread, thus both empowering victims to communicate problems they are experiencing to peers or adults, and deterring potential aggressors by showing that it is an atypical, counter-normative behavior.

One thing that is clear from this section is that there many distinct behaviors in the area of problematic or abusive sexual behavior online – an area sometimes referred to broadly as *cyberdating violence*, and which can include things like online sexual harassment, cyberstalking, revenge porn, and sextortion (as well as other behaviors such as online grooming by strangers, which I have not had space to discuss in detail here). These behaviors interrelate in interesting ways and have different demographic characteristics. In a recent systematic review, Rodríguez-deArriba et al. (2021) try to disentangle some of these behavior patterns (see also Rocha-Silva et al., 2021, who carried out a similar exercise). As the former authors point out (p. 1):

> The terms aggression/violence and abuse are used interchangeably, but they are not the same. Thus, as noted by Geffner (2016), the term abuse implies not an isolated behavior, but the context, motivation, and consequences for victims. However, these characteristics are not addressed in the available measures, which are more focused on the analysis of specific behaviors.

This matters because abuse by definition involves a major imbalance of power between abuser and victim (Buchhandler-Raphael, 2010), and probably also a repeated pattern of behavior (Brassard et al., 2000). There is a world of difference between a middle-aged adult repeatedly coercing a minor into sexual displays online and a teenage boy texting an explicit picture to a female of about the same age whom he also knows offline, in the mistaken hope that she will reciprocate. The first case is clearly a serious form of sexual abuse; while the second, although clearly wrong, seems more likely motivated by naivety. Yet current questionnaires tend to ignore this sort of context and focus on the behavior itself, meaning that perpetrators in both cases could answer "yes" to the question, "Have you ever asked someone to send you a sexual image of themselves online". Measures of such phenomena need to become more sophisticated, defining, and operationalizing terms in theory-driven ways, rather than using the current ad hoc approach.

Likewise, studies in this area need to focus more on victims' own experiences of problematic online sexual behavior: what makes them disturbing to the recipients, and how can we more effectively detect and discourage perpetrators, and help potential victims avoid or recover from such unpleasant experiences. As in other areas of risks and opportunities for adolescents online, there is a lack of mixed-methods studies that try to integrate this kind of qualitative analysis with quantitative measures. One area that should be investigated more are the particular characteristics of online as opposed to offline abuse. Rodríguez-deArriba et al. (2021) point out that both tend to involve similar kinds of psychological aggression (emotional manipulation, insults, threats, and the like), but that cyberabuse is often exacerbated by factors including more opportunities to monitor a victim's behavior; potentially having access to the victim at any time and place; less exposure to a victim's negative emotional reactions, discouraging empathy with their plight; intensified shame and humiliation of the victim if they are broadcast to a wider audience (as with revenge porn); and even possibly impersonating the victim to harm their relationships with third parties, which, of course, is near-impossible offline. On the other hand, because of the element of physical violation and fear involved, offline abuse can be intensely damaging in different ways. Parallel differences between online and offline patterns of aggression have been explored more extensively, among adolescents, in the case of non-sexual cyberbullying.

4.5 Cyberbullying: New Problems or Old Patterns?

Several parallel features to those that mark the relationship between "cyberdating violence" and offline intimate partner abuse – the correlations between offending in the two environments, the similar mental health effects, and the exacerbating features of the "always-on" virtual modality – are found in the relationship between "traditional", offline bullying, and cyberbullying. The latter would be a daunting topic to tackle in a whole chapter of this book, let alone one section of a chapter. This is not only because research on cyberbullying has exploded in the last decade, with annual Google Scholar entries rising more than tenfold in ten years (from 727 articles mentioning "cyberbullying" published in the year 2010 to almost 8000 in the year 2020 alone); and the number of systematic reviews of cyberbullying studies becoming so large that researchers now need to publish "maps" of the reviews (Kwan et al., 2020). It is also because so much of this research is of dubious (or blatantly low) quality, making it a real challenge to sift through it all and separate the wheat from the chaff, in order to work out which factors are important for explaining and tackling the phenomenon. In contrast to other areas of online behavior – notably those that have to do with sex, such as cyber-dating violence and pornography use – there is also a wealth of evidence (of varying quality, as already mentioned) on cyberbullying among children and young people: of the 19 systematic reviews mapped by Kwan et al. (2020), 18 focused on this age group, while just one article reviewed bullying at all ages.

What is clear is that cyberbullying is associated with several damaging mental health problems, with a majority of the articles reviewed by Kwan et al. (2020) showing links between online victimization and outcomes including depression, suicidal ideation, anxiety, and peer relationship problems. Unfortunately, it is hard to disentangle whether cyberbullying was actually causing these negative outcomes in victims, since none of the reviews focused on longitudinal or experimental studies (the latter being ethically very difficult to carry out, of course), and most of them lacked adequate critical consideration of possible sources of bias in the studies reviewed and how such bias might affect the overall pattern of results found in the review. Furthermore, so far there seems to be no systematic review of qualitative studies of cyberbullying, which are very important for understanding the lived experiences of people who become victims of the behavior, and the ways in which they feel it can harm them. As the authors point out,

> Perceptions and experiences of cyberbullying are crucial to the understanding of the impact of cyberbullying as these data can inform clinicians working with CYP [children and young people] to identify and assess their mental health needs, a first step toward planning effective intervention.
>
> *(Kwan et al., 2020, p. 77)*

A related problem is that of finding a generally accepted definition of cyberbullying that can be operationalized in similar ways between studies. A relatively early attempt to solve this problem was made by Tokunaga (2010), who conducted a qualitative, but systematic, "meta-synthesis" of the comparatively few studies (only about 75 met his criteria of being peer-reviewed studies that contained some original quantitative analysis) published on the subject in the preceding decade. One important aspect highlighted in his research was the diversity of definitions of cyberbullying – he quoted nine, from nine different articles – that already existed in the literature. As he pointed out, divergences between these conceptual definitions might be at least partly responsible for divergence in the rates of cyberbullying incidence that had been found by various studies, and which already occupied a very wide range (between 6% and 75% of participants claiming to have experienced it, depending on the study). After reviewing these definitions, Tokunaga came up with his own definition of cyberbullying as "any behavior performed through electronic or digital media by individuals or groups that repeatedly communicates hostile or aggressive messages intended to inflict harm or discomfort on others" (p. 278). As he pointed out, this definition included the theoretically important elements of *repeated offending* and *intention to harm* (the former speaking to the painful ways that many victims can feel trapped by the behavior; the latter connecting with the problematic intentions of the perpetrators). Several previous definitions had left out one or even both of these elements; however, Tokunaga's definition in turn omitted another important element, namely the *power imbalance* that exists between bully and victim (Aalsma & Brown, 2008; Cuadrado-Gordillo, 2012). A bully is not just any person who intentionally, repeatedly aggresses against another person, since the latter could be giving as good as they get, and this definition would therefore encompass conflicts between enemies or rivals of equal status. A bully is someone whom the victim actively fears, because of the latter's inability (or unwillingness) to retaliate effectively.

It is clear that inconsistencies in definitions of cyberbullying can contribute to the already-mentioned divergence in rates of online victimization that different studies have found. Yet the problem is more fundamental than that. Definitions of cyberbullying are inconsistent not only between studies but even within studies, in the sense that the theoretical definitions supposedly employed by researchers are not always reflected in the specific items deployed in questionnaires. For instance, one relatively early, highly cited article on cyberbullying (Calvete et al., 2010) included items such as "writing embarrassing jokes, rumors, gossip, or comments about a classmate on the Internet" and "Deliberately excluding someone from an online group". Not only does the phrasing of these items not necessarily imply repeated offences or power differences, but it is not even clear that such behaviors always involve an intention to harm a victim. Yet in measuring the prevalence of cyberbullying, Calvete et al. counted someone as having engaged in the behavior if they answered "Yes" to just one of the items on their questionnaire. This has been a widespread practice in such studies, and unfortunately – per the wide range of prevalence values found by Kwan et al. (2020) in their reviews – it does not seem to have been eradicated over time. Researchers need to move to an approach of examining normative values on such questionnaires, instead of counting the occasional spreading of gossip for entertainment purposes, without real intent to harm, as a pathological behavior.

Bullying is, of course, as old as humanity itself – if not older – and thus the moral panic (or justified worries, depending on one's point of view) over cyberbullying is not so much about the intent to harm people via gossip and related behaviors in their own right, as about the potential for bullying that takes place through virtual modalities to be more harmful than "traditional" offline bullying (see Dooley et al., 2009). There are a variety of reasons why cyberbullying might be particularly harmful that make a lot of sense in theoretical terms. First, the perceived anonymity of online interactions might turn some less socially dominant individuals, who might otherwise be too afraid of the negative consequences, into bullies (Barlett et al., 2016) – especially when combined with the freedom from adult supervision that children and adolescents often enjoy online. Second, the reduced cues of distress that are transmitted online might increase the severity of bullying incidents, as bullies do not hold back because they don't witness how much their words are hurting their victims (Nesi et al., in press). Third, the "always-on" nature of online life means that victims have no "safe haven" where they can retreat from their harassers (Adams, 2007; Nesi et al., in press), unlike in the past when they could escape from offline peer bullies in the home. And, finally, but perhaps most significantly, the huge audiences online can increase victims' sense of humiliation, amplifying their distress (Festl, 2016).

On the other hand, it has perhaps not been acknowledged frequently enough that face-to-face bullying also has its downsides when compared with the online variety (Mishna et al., 2021). As the old schoolyard rhyme goes, "Sticks and stones may break my bones, but names will never hurt me" – and achieving real physical harm against someone is quite difficult online. Moreover, although it may seem that cyberbullying can invade a victim's personal space more than physical bullying, since modern online privacy tools are now so ubiquitous and easy to use in social networks, it may actually be easier for someone to block a serial harasser online than to stop someone from physically intercepting them on the way home from school, say (Byrne, 2021; Khairy et al., 2021). In general, despite the existence of literally thousands of academic investigations of cyberbullying, there is still a lack of qualitative or mixed-methods studies that truly examine which type of bullying is perceived as worse by young people (though one recent study did examine which kinds of bullying are perceived as most serious by adults, which has clear implications for the latter group's likelihood of intervening; Popovac et al., 2021). And when researchers have asked whether the perpetrators of online bullying are the same as those of offline bullying, they often find a significant overlap (up to 85% in some studies; Menesini et al., 2012; Waasdorp & Bradshaw, 2015; Wang et al., 2019), which goes against the argument that cyber-interactions have spawned a new army of bullies.

In fact, cyberbullying activities pertain to a category of aggression that is probably as old as humanity, and has been shown to increase steadily during middle childhood and adolescence (Ingram, 2014). This has been referred to by various terms including indirect, relational, or social aggression (Archer & Coyne, 2005), and entails the carrying out of intentional harm against a victim in such a way that the identity of the perpetrator is to some extent concealed, and the nature of the harm is more social and/or psychological than physical. The switch to indirect aggression led to the prediction that less dominant individuals would engage in cyberbullying when compared to those responsible for face-to-face bullying (Piazza & Ingram, 2015). Research evidence for that is mixed: in particular, the finding that there is considerable overlap between face-to-face bullies and cyberbullies is an important one to bear in mind here. A related prediction is that a relatively higher proportion of cyberbullies will be female, since meta-analyses have found the proportions of female and male adolescents engaging in indirect aggression to be more or less equal (Björkqvist, 2018; Card et al., 2008). This hypothesis has enjoyed more support (e.g., Connell et al., 2014), though the gender difference seems clearer for victims than perpetrators, with a recent analysis of several cross-cultural surveys finding that girls were comparatively more likely than boys to be victims of online relative to offline bullying (Smith et al., 2019).

Although some degree of bullying, and indeed cyberbullying, may be unavoidable in society, springing as these phenomena do from natural aggressive impulses, norm enforcement, and competition within dominance hierarchies (Ingram, 2014), that does not mean that we need to accept it. Added to the multitude of interventions against bullying in youth (some of the most promising of which were reviewed by Menesini & Salmivalli, 2017), there are already many interventions specifically against cyberbullying (reviewed by Espelage & Hong, 2017). However, there has been limited success with targeting either perpetrators or victims in these interventions, since to do so would require changing quite established patterns of behavior. A promising recent approach instead targets bystanders and aims to influence the peer culture to make bullying less acceptable. An example of this type of intervention which has had considerable success in Colombia is the *Ciberhéroes* program (adapted from the German *Medienhelden* program whose name means essentially the same thing: *Media Heroes*). The intervention is mainly aimed at sixth-grade children (aged 11–13 years). Its goals are that young adolescents expand their knowledge about the risks of cyberbullying, and about technological strategies to prevent and report it; develop their empathy toward possible victims of cyberaggression; develop their ability to assertively defend others against possible cyberattacks; and identify and criticize possible moral misunderstandings (rationalizations) that perpetrators could use to justify cyberbullying. Interestingly, as well as decreasing rates of cyberbullying, this approach was also found to have spillover effects in terms of also decreasing face-to-face bullying (Chaux et al., 2016).

Of course, the effectiveness of cyberbullying prevention and mitigation programs is hampered by our lack of secure knowledge of the mental health effects of cyberbullying: as Kwan et al. (2020) point out, there is not an absence of basic research on cyberbullying, but rather a lack of an effective research synthesis that can lead to a useful knowledge base on the subject. As well as the paucity of longitudinal and qualitative studies appearing in systematic reviews, they also note that we need more information on the long-term effects of cyberbullying on mental health; whether the effects get worse with a bigger "dose" of cyberbullying; and the influence of possible moderating factors (including cultural differences and the effects on minority groups such as LGBT youth). All this evidence would be needed to inform the design of a truly comprehensive program aimed at reducing the frequency and severity of cyberbullying and mitigating its adverse effects, in place of the current, rather ad hoc, approaches.

4.6 International Networking: An Online Contact Hypothesis

As with the two other main chapters in this book, I have spent most of this chapter describing the risks to young people that can result from new types of interactions online. Again, as in the other chapters, this is understandable because most of the public discourse and academic debate around online interactions has centered on risky interactions such as cyberbullying and sexual harassment. Nevertheless, I believe that while the risks are real, there are also many potential opportunities to reap new kinds of benefits from online interactions in the digital age. One important and (in my opinion) understudied aspect of such opportunities is the potential for online modalities to support interactions between people from very different cultural backgrounds and geographical locations in a newly globalized world. This is something that was at the forefront of people's minds when the internet first exploded in popularity in the early-to-mid-1990s, but lately seems to have been largely taken for granted, as research attention has instead tended to focus on the potential for online fora to exacerbate political differences and polarize opinions.

Increased contact between people from different cultural backgrounds online as a way of reducing intergroup conflict makes sense as an extension of the famous "contact hypothesis" in social psychology (Amir, 1969). The key idea of the contact hypothesis, originally elaborated by Allport (1954), is that abstract knowledge about another group is not sufficient to reduce prejudice against them, but direct contact with members of another group can override preexisting stereotypes and lead to the generation of new, more positive schemas about their behavior. This applies (in theory) as long as the contact involves cooperation rather than competition, common goals, equal status, and support from authorities (White et al., 2020). Even before the era of ubiquitous online interactions, there was evidence that "parasocial contact" with individuals from other groups – for example, viewing homosexual people in *Will and Grace* and *Queer Eye for the Straight Guy* – could reduce prejudice (Schiappa et al., 2005). In theory, then, bidirectional contact with online groups in properly organized online interactions should be even more effective, as was argued by Amichai-Hamburger and McKenna (2006). They pointed out that as well as being cheaper, more practical and easier to organize on repeated occasions, online contact meetings could fulfill many of the criteria originally put forward by Allport (1954) for successful contact interactions. In particular, since contact with members of other groups can often generate anxiety, this could be ameliorated by inviting participants to connect from a safe, comfortable environment (typically their own homes). The online environment also gives participants plenty of control over the extent to which they self-disclose in these interactions, helping to eliminate obvious signs of status differences (one of the preconditions set by Allport for successful interactions was that participants should be seen to have an equal a status as possible). And since there may be fewer personal details disclosed, this should aid with the generalization of the interaction to create more positive perceptions about other group members as a collective.

In a later study, Amichai-Hamburger et al. (2015) reviewed some of the evidence for what worked in terms of online contact-based interventions, particularly with regard to the differences between structured interventions (managed by experienced workers in conflict resolution and related fields) and unstructured interventions (which rely on naturalistic interactions between individuals from different groups on social networks such as Facebook, and which had become much more common with the massive growth in online social networks between 2006 and 2015). They identified seven characteristics of online modalities that can create a more protective environment for intergroup contact than with offline modalities, and can thus help to achieve more positive interactions and more effective prejudice reduction. These factors include anonymity, control over physical (e.g., visual) exposure, control over the interaction process, ease of finding similar individuals, widespread and constant accessibility, equality, and fun. Interestingly, some of these properties (such as anonymity, control over exposure, control over the interaction, and equality) seem to work better with structured activities, while the others (finding similar others, accessibility, and fun) are often easier to achieve with unstructured activities, underlining the importance of a sort of "horses for courses" approach whereby organizers decide in advance which aspects of the contact interactions are more important to them. Amichai-Hamburger et al. also provide good examples of both types of contact interventions, ranging from *Dissolving Boundaries*, a purpose-built online educational platform aimed at involving school pupils from across Northern Ireland and the Republic of Ireland in collaborative projects, to *Games for Peace*, which relies more on promoting naturalistic interactions between young people playing well-known online games.

In terms of structured contact activities, one approach that seems to have worked very well is to carry out these activities purely by text. White et al. (2020) showed in a meta-analysis that such interventions had a strong effect on cognitive measures of prejudice, on average, and a medium-sized effect on affective and behavioral measures of prejudice. The text-based medium especially helps to promote some of the factors identified by Amichai-Hamburger et al. (2015) as contributing to the success of structured contact interventions, notably anonymity, control over physical/visual exposure, and perceived equality. In contrast, unstructured forms of contact have not been nearly as well studied (Dajer &

Reilly, 2021). However, in public discussions on social media by opposing sides in post-conflict societies like Colombia and Northern Ireland – as also pointed out by Dajer and Reilly – one tends to see not an agonistic coming together in respectful rivalry, but rather an antagonistic deployment of insults, bad-faith arguments, and outright intentional falsehoods ("fake news") about the other side. Going all the way back to Allport's (1954) original identification of the factors that might help with a successful contact intervention, we can see how this problem might be linked to the lack of common goals and a cooperative environment online: instead of coming together to cooperate, people from rival groups are coming together on Facebook and (perhaps especially) Twitter mainly in order to *compete* with each other. The question then is how to harness the potential for finding similar others, accessibility, and fun inherent to social networks (see Amichai-Hamburger et al., 2015, as discussed above) while avoiding the pitfalls of the antagonistic interactions that all too often take place between different groups in such environments. To answer this question, I will briefly look at research into informal language learning online, especially through the medium of games.

As with online contact interactions, the concept of anonymity is central to why people might naturally pick up a second language (L2) in online contexts. According to Joseph Walther's (2014) social information processing theory, people adapt easily to new communications media because they have a strong intrinsic drive to develop new social relationships. This leads them to compensate for their perceived anonymity online by actually disclosing more about themselves and generally being more explicit in their conversational style – what he calls "hyperpersonal" communication. (For instance, two people who meet on an online dating site will tend to be much more open and loquacious with each other, initially, than if they meet face-to-face on a speed date.) Applied to online language learning, this means that L2 learners should find it natural to have internet-based conversations in their new language, opening up more about personal details and opinions and attempting more complex linguistic structures to compensate for their feelings of anonymity and lack of nonverbal cues. Not surprisingly, then, impromptu language learning by young people was shown to occur in the early days of both Facebook (Kabilan et al., 2010) and Twitter (Ruipérez et al., 2011). Even YouTube can be considered a social network for these purposes, since in the comments sections beneath its videos extensive discussions often take place between named, recognizable users, and these discussions often involve "translanguaging" (communication across linguistic barriers) which can result in language learning (Benson, 2015). Adding to the complexity of the analysis, different social networks can potentially be of benefit for language education in a wide variety of ways, ranging from mere exposure to posts or tweets in a foreign language by contacts in another country, to the setting up of a private Facebook group by a teacher where a class can informally practice their language skills.

However, one of the most powerful ways to learn a language online is undoubtedly through the medium of an online game. Computer games have a long tradition of being used in language education and have often been mass-produced specifically for that purpose (see Godwin-Jones, 2014, for a review). Furthermore, principles of game interaction were explicitly applied to popular language-learning apps such as Duolingo (von Ahn, 2013). Such apps reflect a shift in emphasis from the use of the clunky "edutainment" type of games to support the formal learning of static educational content, to the informal learning of dynamic concepts through "serious games", which aim to provide a commercial-quality gaming experience (Egenfeldt-Nielsen, 2011). A systematic review by Connolly et al. (2012) and a meta-analysis by Wouters et al. (2013) showed that serious games can be remarkably successful in imparting a wide variety of educational concepts (including foreign languages; e.g., Butler et al., 2014; Johnson, 2010). Possible reasons for this include enhanced motivation to learn due to the fun experience of playing the game (Garris et al., 2002) and a sensation of "flow" resulting in a heightened sensitivity to the ambient content of the game (Kiili et al., 2012). If these factors work for serious games, they might conceivably also hold for games that have not been designed with any educational connection in mind, but which offer opportunities for ambient learning in the form of exposure to the languages spoken by other players.

Indeed, this is what many studies have tried to show, using MMORPGs (massively multiplayer online role playing games) such as *Second Life* (Liou, 2012; Wehner et al., 2011), *World of Warcraft* (Rama et al., 2012; Thorne & Fischer, 2012), and *EverQuest* (Rankin et al., 2009). While many of these authors worked with quite small samples, and there is a need for larger-scale, systematically controlled studies, they do show the potential for young people to learn about other languages (and indeed cultures) online in ambient, unstructured ways. This being the case, it seems reasonable to suppose that over the long term, online game-playing (particularly by male adolescents and young men, perhaps) could be important for reducing hostility between nations in a massively multiplayer version of the online contact hypothesis. In terms of providing a positive space for online contact, MMORPGs would seem to fit with the properties identified by Amichai-Hamburger et al. (2015) of finding similar individuals, ease of access, and fun; as well as tying in with the properties originally identified by Allport (1954) of cooperation, common goals, and equality within the contact environment.

4.7 Conclusion

This chapter has focused on the expansion in social relations that naturally takes place during adolescence, and that these days is increasingly facilitated by online connections, particularly through social media. As children get older, and particularly as they enter adolescence, their friendship circles expand, from being limited to family friends and school classmates to being based more on deliberate selection due to shared interests and identity, leading to the formation of ever-larger cliques, gangs, and bands. Clearly the use of social networks and online games expands the potential for encountering other individuals who share interests and attitudes and thus can make good friendship partners. It also facilitates a biologically driven shift to showing more romantic and/or sexual interest in peers, in many cases those of the other sex, who were relatively ignored in middle childhood and (especially) pre-adolescence.

Looking at friendship-related activities online, we saw that the line between online and offline friendships is becoming increasingly blurred. It is not the case that online friendships are completely replacing offline ones, but it does seem to be true that unstructured forms of "hanging out" offline are being partially replaced by chatting to friends through social media, online messaging services, and video calls. Nevertheless, shared activities such as sports, cinema, musical performances, or (in later adolescence) going out drinking are still important for bonding with friends, and especially in the initial "getting-to-know-each-other" phase of a relationship. This relates to the identity exploration aspect of adolescence described in Chapter 2: shared activities remain very important to adolescents for defining their membership in particular cliques. Conversely, the same sort of dynamics can also play out online, with people using social media information to "research" potential friends and see whether their identity fits with their own, before deciding whether to spend more time with them offline. An important topic for future research, which does not seem to have investigated much so far, is when, why, and how online friendships turn into offline friendships, and what types of friendships remain as "online-only". In particular, it will be important to look at individual differences in these processes and the potential for online interactions to help shy or socially impaired adolescents form new friendships, whether these stay online or move offline as well.

An important gender difference in online friendships during earlier adolescence is that many boys' friendships center around the playing of video games, an activity in which they often make new friends; whereas girls are more likely than boys to have a social media presence, particularly on Instagram. In later adolescence, both sexes make increasing use of social media to find potential romantic partners and check out aspects of their interests and identity, just as they do when initiating new platonic friendships. Again, however, individuals' use of social media and online dating apps for romantic purposes is marked by gender differences that likely have an evolutionary basis in parental investment theory, with women often focusing on displaying their visual attractiveness while men typically try to attract a partner with textual information and links to other social media profiles. The integration of visual and textual information in an app like Tinder highlights the complexity of the new visual languages that young people are speaking online; and the transitions from visual and kinesthetic-based "swiping" and "matching" to real online conversations with potential partners, whether on dating apps like Tinder, on social media such as Instagram, or on online messaging services like WhatsApp, would make a valuable topic for future research. In general, age differences between adolescent minors and young adults over 18 with regard to romantic and sexual behavior online are also very poorly understood, largely due to ethical issues with this research. There is thus a need to elaborate ethically sound methodologies to study the development of this vital behavioral domain in today's adolescents.

Ethical problems also limit the conclusions of the broad area of research known as "cyberdating violence", which centers on the study of what happens when sexual interactions take a dark turn into abusive behavior online, and encompasses online sexual harassment, sextortion, revenge porn, cyberstalking, and grooming. We saw that all these phenomena are interrelated and to some extent overlapping. As in other areas of cyberpsychology, there is a need for more application of theory in defining exactly how they differ from each other and how they can be operationalized in research instruments – for example, including the criteria of imbalance of power and repeated offending in the operationalization of abusive behavior. Alongside this more systematic, theory-driven application of definitions in empirical studies, we also need more qualitative and mixed-methods studies that report on the lived experiences of victims of cyberdating violence, including what makes their experiences both different from and similar to those of offline victims, how we can help people avoid and/or recover from cyberabuse, and how we can help potential and actual perpetrators avoid committing such behavior.

It also seems clear from the research reviewed in this chapter that there is a need to distinguish truly predatory behavior in the area of online dating violence – such as the "grooming" of underage victims by much older adults – from the kind of missteps (albeit very serious ones) that adolescents can make as they learn about romantic relationships. Again, a good way to do this would be to listen to victims' (and perpetrators') stories in an attempt to understand the different ways in which such behaviors can come to pass. Perhaps such stories could then be used to elaborate educational materials for adolescents that could help prevent potential perpetrators and victims from becoming enmeshed in these kinds of behaviors. Rather than assuming that perpetrators are always male and victims always female, such educational work should also take into account the varying gender dynamics of different forms of online dating violence, with victims of revenge porn or pressured sexting being much more likely to be female, while victims of sextortion or intimate partner stalking may be at least as likely to be male as female. In terms of the more serious forms of online dating violence, the evidence on victims' experiences would justify treating them as crimes on the same order as offline sexual abuse, while providing specialist psychological help to support victims through the depression, anxiety, and even PTSD that often result – especially if identifying images relating to the violence are widely disseminated, amplifying feelings of humiliation and shame.

In contrast to research on cyberdating violence, where there has been relatively little work with young people under the age of 18, studies of cyberbullying have largely focused on this age group. Hence, the situation with cyberbullying is almost a mirror image of the situation with online sexual abuse and related behaviors, where there is a lack of knowledge on how they relate to missteps in learning about romantic and sexual relationships. In the case of non-sexual online aggression, a parallel problem results from not knowing how cyberbullying and related behaviors continue to develop in adulthood, and thus how most individuals come to restrain their own impulses to victimize peers online. More long-term longitudinal studies of cyberbullying, continuing after participants leave school, would help with this, as would more qualitative and mixed-methods studies to understand the difficulties suffered by victims and the motivations of aggressors. In all studies of cyberbullying, more attention needs to be paid to definitions which are widely agreed in theory but not always operationalized in practice, such as the tendency for bullying to involve repeated, intentionally harmful aggression from a position of differential power. Again, however, qualitative methods should be used to check whether these aspects matter the most to victims and how online bullying compares to more "traditional" offline forms.

In this context, a particularly important area of study might be the effect of audience amplification that is found in cyberbullying, which can both intensify the harmful effects for victims and change the power dynamics for aggressors (e.g., in the recruitment of "Twitter mobs" to attack more prestigious figures on Twitter). Despite the thousands of studies on cyberbullying, perhaps because of the fast-changing nature of the subject matter there is still a lack of an effective research synthesis that could help inform truly effective interventions, and would include such factors as the involvement of third-party bystanders (or online audiences), the moderating effects of demographic and other variables, and the long-term effects of cyberbullying on mental health. In this chapter, as elsewhere in this book, I have suggested that such interventions should be based on a deeper understanding of young people's normal psychological changes during adolescence – as reflected, for example, in the shift from more direct to more indirect forms of aggression.

In the final section of this chapter, I looked at some of the more positive aspects of interpersonal relationships online, especially in terms of the (still under-studied) potential for learning about people from different cultural and national backgrounds. A precedent for this lies in the evidence for the potential of online games (particularly MMORPGs) for encouraging informal language-learning, when players from different linguistic backgrounds play together. I showed how online games could help promote many of the properties identified in the social psychological literature as necessary for successful intergroup contact, including a common goal, cooperation, and perceived equality (facilitated by the relative anonymity of online interactions). One way in which technology companies could facilitate these kinds of more productive interactions, when people of different cultural (and perhaps even political) backgrounds meet, is by learning some lessons from online games. From a developmental point of view, gender would be an important aspect to consider here, since we know that young male adolescents often prefer to interact online via games, while girls of the same age tend to prefer visually oriented social networks such as Instagram and TikTok. Perhaps the next wave of social networking software will try to attract more boys by integrating visual communication with online gaming. In the process, software architects could try to take advantage of the features of games that can facilitate intergroup contact, rather than leaving this to chance.

As with the areas of the reformulation of identity and the proliferation of new forms of content consumption, there have always been major shifts in social relationships as children pass into and through adolescence. Young people's friendship networks tend to change, grow, and diversify, while they may also show a newfound interest in finding romantic partners, including of the (previously rather ignored) opposite gender if they are heterosexual. We saw that in the former case, competition for prestige through indirect aggression may be associated with cyberbullying and online victimization; while in the latter case, difficulties in managing newfound impulses and a lack of experience with partners' expectations may contribute to online sexual harassment and cyberdating violence. In both cases, there is clearly a role for educational interventions in fostering a culture in which such behaviors are not tolerated among or by adolescents. There is also a role for structured interventions in promoting positive forms of contact online between young people of different groups and cultural backgrounds. In the concluding chapter to the book, I focus on making a few recommendations that caregivers, educators, policymakers, and technology providers could follow to help bring about positive changes in young people's online lives.

References

Aalsma, M. C., & Brown, J. R. (2008). What is bullying? *Journal of Adolescent Health, 43*(2), 101–102. https://doi.org/10.1016/j.jadohealth.2008.06.001

Adams, S. (2007). Cyberbullying: An emerging form of student aggression for the "always-on" generation. *Australian Educational Leader, 29*(2).

Allport, G. W. (1954). *The nature of prejudice*. Addison-Wesley.

Amichai-Hamburger, Y., & McKenna, K. Y. A. (2006). The contact hypothesis reconsidered: Interacting via the Internet. *Journal of Computer-Mediated Communication, 11*, 825–843. https://doi.org/10.1111/j.1083-6101.2006.00037.x

Amichai-Hamburger, Y., Hasler, B. S., & Shani-Sherman, T. (2015). Structured and unstructured intergroup contact in the digital age. *Computers in Human Behavior, 52*, 515–522. https://doi.org/10.1016/j.chb.2015.02.022

Amir, Y. (1969). Contact hypothesis in ethnic relations. *Psychological Bulletin, 71*, 319–342. https://doi.org/10.1037/h0027352

Archer, J., & Coyne, S. M. (2005). An integrated review of indirect, relational, and social aggression. *Personality and Social Psychology Review, 9*, 212–230. https://doi.org/10.1207/s15327957pspr0903_2

Barlett, C. P., Gentile, D. A., & Chew, C. (2016). Predicting cyberbullying from anonymity. *Psychology of Popular Media Culture, 5*(2), 171. https://doi.org/10.1037/ppm0000055

Bates, S. (2017). Revenge porn and mental health: A qualitative analysis of the mental health effects of revenge porn on female survivors. *Feminist Criminology, 12*(1), 22–42. https://doi.org/10.1177/1557085116654565

Benson, P. (2015). Commenting to learn: Evidence of language and intercultural learning in comments on YouTube videos. *Language Learning and Technology, 19*, 88–105. Retrieved from https://scholarspace.manoa.hawaii.edu/bitstream/10125/44435/19_03_benson.pdf

Björkqvist, K. (2018). Gender differences in aggression. *Current Opinion in Psychology, 19*, 39–42. https://doi.org/10.1016/j.copsyc.2017.03.030

Brassard, M. R., Hart, S. N., & Hardy, D. B. (2000). Psychological and emotional abuse of children. In R. T. Ammerman & M. Hersen (Eds.), *Case studies in family violence* (pp. 293–319). Springer.

Brkljačić, T., Majetić, F., & Wertag, A. (2019). I'm always online: Well-being and main sources of life dis/satisfaction of heavy Internet users. In M. Khosrow-Pour (Ed.), *Internet and technology addiction: Breakthroughs in research and practice* (pp. 455–472). IGI Global.

Buchhandler-Raphael, M. (2010). Sexual abuse of power. *U. Florida Journal of Law & Public Policy, 21*, 77. Retrieved from https://heinonline.org/HOL/LandingPage?handle=hein.journals/ufpp21&div=5

Bukowski, W. M., Gauze, C., Hoza, B., & Newcomb, A. F. (1993). Differences and consistency between same-sex and other-sex peer relationships during early adolescence. *Developmental Psychology, 29*(2), 255. https://doi.org/10.1037/0012-1649.29.2.255

Buss, D. M., & Schmitt, D. P. (1993). Sexual strategies theory: An evolutionary perspective on human mating. *Psychological Review, 100*(2), 204. https://doi.org/10.1037/0033-295X.100.2.204

Butler, Y. G., Someya, Y., & Fukuhara, E. (2014). Online games for young learners' foreign language learning. *ELT Journal, 68*, 265–275. https://doi.org/10.1093/elt/ccu008

Byrne, V. L. (2021). Blocking and self-silencing: Undergraduate students' cyberbullying victimization and coping strategies. *TechTrends, 65*(2), 164–173. https://doi.org/10.1007/s11528-020-00560-x

Calvete, E., Orue, I., Estévez, A., Villardón, L., & Padilla, P. (2010). Cyberbullying in adolescents: Modalities and aggressors' profile. *Computers in Human Behavior, 26*(5), 1128–1135. https://doi.org/10.1016/j.chb.2010.03.017

Calvete, E., Gámez-Guadix, M., & Borrajo, E. (2019). Cyberbullying in romantic relationships. In G. W. Giumetti & R. M. Kowalski (Eds.), *Cyberbullying in schools, workplaces, and romantic relationships: The many lenses and perspectives of electronic mistreatment*. Routledge.

Card, N. A., Stucky, B. D., Sawalani, G. M., & Little, T. D. (2008). Direct and indirect aggression during childhood and adolescence: A meta-analytic review of gender differences, intercorrelations, and relations to maladjustment. *Child Development, 79*, 1185–1229. https://doi.org/10.1111/j.1467-8624.2008.01184.x

Caridade, S., Braga, T., & Borrajo, E. (2019). Cyber dating abuse (CDA): Evidence from a systematic review. *Aggression and Violent Behavior, 48*, 152–168. https://doi.org/10.1016/j.avb.2019.08.018

Chak, K., & Leung, L. (2004). Shyness and locus of control as predictors of internet addiction and internet use. *CyberPsychology & Behavior, 7*(5), 559–570. https://doi.org/10.1089/cpb.2004.7.559

Chaux, E., Velásquez, A. M., Schultze-Krumbholz, A., & Scheithauer, H. (2016). Effects of the cyberbullying prevention program *Media Heroes* (*Medienhelden*) on traditional bullying. *Aggressive Behavior, 42*(2), 157–165. https://doi.org/10.1002/ab.21637

Citron, D. K., & Franks, M. A. (2014). Criminalizing revenge porn. *Wake Forest Law Review, 49*, 345. Retrieved from https://heinonline.org/HOL/LandingPage?handle=hein.journals/wflr49&div=15

Cole, T., Policastro, C., Crittenden, C., & McGuffee, K. (2020). Freedom to post or invasion of privacy? Analysis of US revenge porn state statutes. *Victims & Offenders, 15*(4), 483–498. https://doi.org/10.1080/15564886.2020.1712567

Connell, N. M., Schell-Busey, N. M., Pearce, A. N., & Negro, P. (2014). Badgrlz? Exploring sex differences in cyberbullying behaviors. *Youth Violence and Juvenile Justice, 12*, 209–228. https://doi.org/10.1177/1541204013503889

Connolly, T. M., Boyle, E. A., MacArthur, E., Hainey, T., & Boyle, J. M. (2012). A systematic literature review of empirical evidence on computer games and serious games. *Computers and Education, 59*, 661–686. https://doi.org/10.1016/j.compedu.2012.03.004

Cuadrado-Gordillo, I. (2012). Repetition, power imbalance, and intentionality: Do these criteria conform to teenagers' perception of bullying? A role-based analysis. *Journal of Interpersonal Violence, 27*(10), 1889–1910. https://doi.org/10.1177/0886260511431436

Dajer, D., & Reilly, P. (2021). *Social media and intergroup contact during contentious episodes in divided societies: Comparative perspectives from Colombia and Northern Ireland. IAMCR (International Association for Media and Communication Research) 2021*, 11–15 July, Nairobi, Kenya. Retrieved from https://eprints.whiterose.ac.uk/176210/

Décieux, J. P., Heinen, A., & Willems, H. (2019). Social media and its role in friendship-driven interactions among young people: A mixed methods study. *Young, 27*(1), 18–31. https://doi.org/10.1177/1103308818755516

Dooley, J. J., Pyżalski, J., & Cross, D. (2009). Cyberbullying versus face-to-face bullying: A theoretical and conceptual review. *Zeitschrift für Psychologie, 217*(4), 182–188. https://doi.org/10.1027/0044-3409.217.4.182

Douglass, M. D., D'Aguanno, S., & Jones, S. (2020). Women as active agents: Female perpetrators of sexual harassment and domestic abuse. *Evolutionary Behavioral Sciences, 14*(1), 32. https://doi.org/10.1037/ebs0000171

Dreßing, H., Bailer, J., Anders, A., Wagner, H., & Gallas, C. (2014). Cyberstalking in a large sample of social network users: Prevalence, characteristics, and impact upon victims. *Cyberpsychology, Behavior, and Social Networking, 17*(2), 61–67. https://doi.org/10.1089/cyber.2012.0231

Drouin, M., Ross, J., & Tobin, E. (2015). Sexting: A new, digital vehicle for intimate partner aggression? *Computers in Human Behavior, 50*, 197–204. https://doi.org/10.1016/j.chb.2015.04.001

Egenfeldt-Nielsen, S. (2011). *Beyond edutainment: Exploring the educational potential of computer games*. Lulu.com.

Eichorn, K. (2013). *Lovers beware: Scorned exes may share intimate data and images online.* McAfee. Retrieved from https://web.archive.org/web/20130729232817/http://www.mcafee.com/us/about/news/2013/q1/20130204-01.aspx

Ellison, N. B., & Vitak, J. (2015). Social network site affordances and their relationship to social capital processes. In S. S. Sundar (Ed.), *The handbook of the psychology of communication technology* (pp. 205–227). Wiley.

Englander, E. K., & McCoy, M. (2017). Pressured sexting and revenge porn in a sample of Massachusetts adolescents. *International Journal of Technoethics, 8*(2), 16–25. https://doi.org/10.4018/IJT.2017070102

Espelage, D. L., & Hong, J. S. (2017). Cyberbullying prevention and intervention efforts: Current knowledge and future directions. *Canadian Journal of Psychiatry*, *62*, 374–380. https://doi.org/10.1177/0706743716684793

Feingold, A. (1992). Gender differences in mate selection preferences: A test of the parental investment model. *Psychological Bulletin*, *112*(1), 125–139. https://doi.org/10.1037/0033-2909.112.1.125

Felmlee, D., McMillan, C., Inara Rodis, P., & Osgood, D. W. (2018). Falling behind: Lingering costs of the high school transition for youth friendships and grades. *Sociology of Education*, *91*(2), 159–182. https://doi.org/10.1177%2F0038040718762136

Festl, R. (2016). Perpetrators on the internet: Analyzing individual and structural explanation factors of cyberbullying in school context. *Computers in Human Behavior*, *59*, 237–248. https://doi.org/10.1016/j.chb.2016.02.017

Fisher, B. S., Coker, A. L., Garcia, L. S., Williams, C. M., Clear, E. R., & Cook-Craig, P. G. (2014). Statewide estimates of stalking among high school students in Kentucky: Demographic profile and sex differences. *Violence Against Women*, *20*(10), 1258–1279. https://doi.org/10.1177%2F1077801214551574

Frampton, J. R., & Fox, J. (2021). Monitoring, creeping, or surveillance? A synthesis of online social information seeking concepts. *Review of Communication Research*, *9*, 1–42. Retrieved from https://rcommunicationr.org/index.php/rcr/article/view/75

Friedlander, L. J., Reid, G. J., Shupak, N., & Cribbie, R. (2007). Social support, self-esteem, and stress as predictors of adjustment to university among first-year undergraduates. *Journal of College Student Development*, *48*(3), 259–274. https://doi.org/10.1353/csd.2007.0024

Galambos, N. L., & Almeida, D. M. (1992). Does parent-adolescent conflict increase in early adolescence? *Journal of Marriage and the Family*, 737–747. https://doi.org/10.2307/353157

Garris, R., Ahlers, R., & Driskell, J. E. (2002). Games, motivation, and learning: A research and practice model. *Simulation and Gaming*, *33*, 441–467. https://doi.org/10.1177/1046878102238607

Geffner, R. (2016). Partner aggression versus partner abuse terminology: Moving the field forward and resolving controversies. *Journal of Family Violence*, *31*(8), 923–925. https://doi.org/10.1007/s10896-016-9898-8

Godwin-Jones, R. (2014). Games in language learning: Opportunities and challenges. *Language Learning and Technology*, *18*, 9–19. Retrieved from https://scholarspace.manoa.hawaii.edu/bitstream/10125/44363/18_02_emerging.pdf

Gordon-Messer, D., Bauermeister, J. A., Grodzinski, A., & Zimmerman, M. (2013). Sexting among young adults. *Journal of Adolescent Health*, *52*(3), 301–306. https://doi.org/10.1016/j.jadohealth.2012.05.013

Goswami, A., & Dutta, S. (2015). Gender differences in technology usage: A literature review. *Open Journal of Business and Management*, *4*(1), 51–59. https://doi.org/10.4236/ojbm.2016.41006

Graham, J. A., Cohen, R., Zbikowski, S. M., & Secrist, M. E. (1998). A longitudinal investigation of race and sex as factors in children's classroom friendship choices. *Child Study Journal*, *28*(4), 245–245.

Granholm, C. (2016). Blended lives: ICT talk among vulnerable young people in Finland. *Young*, *24*(2), 85–101. https://doi.org/10.1177/1103308815613188

Guerra, C., Pinto-Cortez, C., Toro, E., Efthymiadou, E., & Quayle, E. (2021). Online sexual harassment and depression in Chilean adolescents: Variations based on gender and age of the offenders. *Child Abuse & Neglect, 120*, 105219. https://doi.org/10.1016/j.chiabu.2021.105219

Hartup, W. W. (1992). Peer relations in early and middle childhood. In V. B. Van Hessalt & M. Hersen (Eds.), *Handbook of social development* (pp. 257–281). Springer.

Helsper, E. J., & Whitty, M. T. (2010). Netiquette within married couples: Agreement about acceptable online behavior and surveillance between partners. *Computers in Human Behavior, 26*(5), 916–926. https://doi.org/10.1016/j.chb.2010.02.006

Higgins, G. E., & Wolfe, S. E. (2009). Cybercrime. In J. M. Miller (Ed.), *21st century criminology: A reference handbook* (Vol. 2, pp. 466–471). SAGE.

Howes, C. (2009). Friendship in early childhood. In K. H. Rubin, W. M. Bukowski, & B. Laursen (Eds.), *Handbook of peer interactions, relationships, and groups* (pp. 180–194). Guilford Press.

Ingram, G. P. D. (2014). From hitting to tattling to gossip: An evolutionary rationale for the development of indirect aggression. *Evolutionary Psychology, 12*. https://doi.org/10.1177/147470491401200205

Ingram, G. P. D. (2019). Gossip and reputation in childhood. In F. Giardini & R. Wittek (Eds.), *Oxford handbook of gossip and reputation* (pp. 132–151). Oxford University Press.

Ingram, G. P. D., Hondrou, C., Vasalou, A., Joinson, A., Campos, J., & Martinho, C. (2012). Applying evolutionary psychology to a serious game about children's interpersonal conflict. *Evolutionary Psychology, 10*(5), 147470491201000510. https://doi.org/10.1177%2F147470491201000510

James, J. L. (2015). *Mobile dating in the digital age: Computer-mediated communication and relationship building on Tinder*. Unpublished M.A. thesis, Texas State University. https://digital.library.txstate.edu/handle/10877/5529

Jarusriboonchai, P., Malapaschas, A., & Olsson, T. (2016). Design and evaluation of a multi-player mobile game for icebreaking activity. In *Proceedings of the 2016 CHI Conference on Human Factors in Computing Systems* (pp. 4366–4377). https://doi.org/10.1145/2858036.2858298

Johnson, W. L. (2010). Serious use of a serious game for language learning. *International Journal of Artificial Intelligence in Education, 20*, 175–195. https://doi.org/10.3233/JAI-2010-0006

Kabilan, M. K., Ahmad, N., & Abidin, M. J. Z. (2010). Facebook: An online environment for learning of English in institutions of higher education? *The Internet and Higher Education, 13*, 179–187. https://doi.org/10.1016/j.iheduc.2010.07.003

Kandel, D., & Davies, M. (1991). Friendship networks, intimacy, and illicit drug use in young adulthood: A comparison of two competing theories. *Criminology, 29*(3), 441–469.

Khairy, M., Mahmoud, T. M., Abd-El-Hafeez, T., & Mahfouz, A. (2021). User awareness of privacy, reporting system and cyberbullying on Facebook. In A. E. Hassanien, K. C. Chang, & T. Mincong (Eds.), *Advanced machine learning technologies and applications: AMLTA 2021* (pp. 613–625). Springer. https://doi.org/10.1007/978-3-030-69717-4_58

Kiili, K., de Freitas, S., Arnab, S., & Lainema, T. (2012). The design principles for flow experience in educational games. *Procedia Computer Science, 15*, 78–91. https://doi.org/10.1016/j.procs.2012.10.060

Kim, B., & Kim, Y. (2017). College students' social media use and communication network heterogeneity: Implications for social capital and subjective well-being. *Computers in Human Behavior, 73*, 620–628. https://doi.org/10.1016/j.chb.2017.03.033

Kowert, R., Domahidi, E., & Quandt, T. (2014). The relationship between online video game involvement and gaming-related friendships among emotionally sensitive individuals. *Cyberpsychology, Behavior, and Social Networking, 17*(7), 447–453. https://doi.org/10.1089/cyber.2013.0656

Krasnova, H., Veltri, N. F., Eling, N., & Buxmann, P. (2017). Why men and women continue to use social networking sites: The role of gender differences. *Journal of Strategic Information Systems, 26*(4), 261–284. https://doi.org/10.1016/j.jsis.2017.01.004

Kuehner, C., Gass, P., & Dressing, H. (2012). Mediating effects of stalking victimization on gender differences in mental health. *Journal of Interpersonal Violence, 27*(2), 199–221. https://doi.org/10.1177/0886260511416473

Kwan, I., Dickson, K., Richardson, M., MacDowall, W., Burchett, H., Stansfield, C., … & Thomas, J. (2020). Cyberbullying and children and young people's mental health: A systematic map of systematic reviews. *Cyberpsychology, Behavior, and Social Networking, 23*(2), 72–82. https://doi.org/10.1089/cyber.2019.0370

Kwok, I., & Wescott, A. B. (2020). Cyberintimacy: A scoping review of technology-mediated romance in the Digital Age. *Cyberpsychology, Behavior, and Social Networking, 23*(10), 657–666. https://doi.org/10.1089/cyber.2019.0764

Leemis, R. W., Espelage, D. L., Basile, K. C., Mercer Kollar, L. M., & Davis, J. P. (2019). Traditional and cyber bullying and sexual harassment: A longitudinal assessment of risk and protective factors. *Aggressive Behavior, 45*(2), 181–192. https://doi.org/10.1002/ab.21808

LeFebvre, L. E. (2018). Swiping me off my feet: Explicating relationship initiation on Tinder. *Journal of Social and Personal Relationships, 35*(9), 1205–1229. https://doi.org/10.1177/0265407517706419

Lenhart, A. (2015a). Video games are key elements in friendships for many boys. In A. Lenhart, A. Smith, M. Anderson, M. Duggan, & A. Perrin, *Teens, technology and friendships*. Pew Research Center. Retrieved from https://www.pewresearch.org/internet/2015/08/06/chapter-3-video-games-are-key-elements-in-friendships-for-many-boys/

Lenhart, A. (2015b). Social media and friendships. In A. Lenhart, A. Smith, M. Anderson, M. Duggan, & A. Perrin, *Teens, technology and friendships*. Pew Research Center. Retrieved from https://www.pewresearch.org/internet/2015/08/06/chapter-4-social-media-and-friendships/

Levendowski, A. (2013). Using copyright to combat revenge porn. *NYU Journal of Intellectual Property and Entertainment Law, 3*, 422. Retrieved from https://heinonline.org/HOL/LandingPage?handle=hein.journals/nyuinpe3&div=16

Lever, J. (1978). Sex differences in the complexity of children's play and games. *American Sociological Review*, 471–483. https://doi.org/10.2307/2094773

Lewis, R. (2018). Literature review on children and young people demonstrating technology-assisted harmful sexual behavior. *Aggression and Violent Behavior, 40*, 1–11. https://doi.org/10.1016/j.avb.2018.02.011

Liou, H. C. (2012). The roles of *Second Life* in a college computer-assisted language learning (CALL) course in Taiwan, ROC. *Computer Assisted Language Learning, 25*, 365–382. https://doi.org/10.1080/09588221.2011.597766

Maccoby, E. E. (2002). Gender and group process: A developmental perspective. *Current Directions in Psychological Science, 11*(2), 54–58.

Madigan, S., Ly, A., Rash, C. L., Van Ouytsel, J., & Temple, J. R. (2018). Prevalence of multiple forms of sexting behavior among youth: A systematic review and meta-analysis. *JAMA Pediatrics, 172*(4), 327–335. https://doi.org/10.1001/jamapediatrics.2017.5314

March, E., Szymczak, P., Di Rago, M., & Jonason, P. K. (2022). Passive, invasive, and duplicitous: Three forms of intimate partner cyberstalking. *Personality and Individual Differences*, *189*, 111502. https://doi.org/10.1016/j.paid.2022.111502

Markowitz, D. M., & Hancock, J. T. (2018). Deception in mobile dating conversations. *Journal of Communication*, *68*(3), 547–569. https://doi.org/10.1093/joc/jqy019

Mazman, S. G., & Usluel, Y. K. (2011). Gender differences in using social networks. *Turkish Online Journal of Educational Technology*, *10*(2), 133–139.

McAndrew, F. T., & Jeong, H. S. (2012). Who does what on Facebook? Age, sex, and relationship status as predictors of Facebook use. *Computers in Human Behavior*, *28*(6), 2359–2365. https://doi.org/10.1016/j.chb.2012.07.007

McEwan, T. E., Mullen, P. E., & MacKenzie, R. (2009). A study of the predictors of persistence in stalking situations. *Law and Human Behavior*, *33*(2), 149. https://doi.org/10.1007/s10979-008-9141-0

Menesini, E., Calussi, P., & Nocentini, A. (2012). Cyberbullying and traditional bullying: Unique, additive, and synergistic effects on psychological health symptoms. In Q. Li, D. Cross, & P. K. Smith (Eds.), *Cyberbullying in the global playground: Research from international perspectives* (pp. 245–262). Wiley Blackwell. https://doi.org/10.1002/9781119954484.ch12

Menesini, E., & Salmivalli, C. (2017). Bullying in schools: The state of knowledge and effective interventions. *Psychology, Health & Medicine*, *22*, 240–253. https://doi.org/10.1080/13548506.2017.1279740

Mishna, F., Birze, A., Greenblatt, A., & Pepler, D. (2021). Looking beyond assumptions to understand relationship dynamics in bullying. *Frontiers in Psychology*, *12*, 1248. https://doi.org/10.3389/fpsyg.2021.661724

Muscanell, N. L., & Guadagno, R. E. (2012). Make new friends or keep the old: Gender and personality differences in social networking use. *Computers in Human Behavior*, *28*(1), 107–112. https://doi.org/10.1016/j.chb.2011.08.016

Nesi, J., Dredge, R., Maheux, A. J., Roberts, S. R., Fox, K. A., & Choukas-Bradley, S. (in press). Peer experiences via social media. To appear in *The Encyclopedia of Child and Adolescent Health*. Elsevier. Preprint retrieved from https://psyarxiv.com/s8mru/

Olivera-La Rosa, A., Arango-Tobón, O. E., & Ingram, G. P. (2019). Swiping right: Face perception in the age of Tinder. *Heliyon*, *5*(12), e02949. https://doi.org/10.1016/j.heliyon.2019.e02949

Orosz, G., Benyó, M., Berkes, B., Nikoletti, E., Gál, É., Tóth-Király, I., & Bőthe, B. (2018). The personality, motivational, and need-based background of problematic Tinder use. *Journal of Behavioral Addictions*, 7(2), 301–316. https://doi.org/10.1556/2006.7.2018.21

Patchin, J. W., & Hinduja, S. (2020). Sextortion among adolescents: Results from a national survey of US youth. *Sexual Abuse*, *32*(1), 30–54. https://doi.org/10.1177/1079063218800469

Pepler, D. J., Craig, W. M., Connolly, J. A., Yuile, A., McMaster, L., & Jiang, D. (2006). A developmental perspective on bullying. *Aggressive Behavior*, *32*(4), 376–384. https://doi.org/10.1002/ab.20136

Pfaff, N. (2010). Gender segregation in pre-adolescent peer groups as a matter of class: Results from two German studies. *Childhood*, *17*(1), 43–60. https://doi.org/10.1177%2F0907568209351550

Piazza, J. R., & Bering, J. M. (2009). Evolutionary cyber-psychology: Applying an evolutionary framework to Internet behavior. *Computers in Human Behavior*, *25*(6), 1258–1269. https://doi.org/10.1016/j.chb.2009.07.002

Piazza, J. R., & Ingram, G. P. D. (2015). Evolutionary cyberpsychology 2.0: Revisiting some old predictions and posting some new ones in the age of Facebook. In *Evolutionary perspectives on social psychology* (pp. 159–174). Springer. https://doi.org/10.1007/978-3-319-12697-5_13

Popovac, M., Gill, A. S., Austin, L. H., & Maposa, R. (2021). Adults' perceived severity and likelihood of intervening in cyberbullying. *International Journal of Bullying Prevention*, 1–16. https://doi.org/10.1007/s42380-021-00112-8

Pujazon-Zazik, M. A., Manasse, S. M., & Orrell-Valente, J. K. (2012). Adolescents' self-presentation on a teen dating web site: A risk-content analysis. *Journal of Adolescent Health, 50*(5), 517–520. https://doi.org/10.1016/j.jadohealth.2011.11.015

Purcell, R., Pathé, M., & Mullen, P. (2010). Gender differences in stalking behaviour among juveniles. *Journal of Forensic Psychiatry & Psychology, 21*(4), 555–568. https://doi.org/10.1080/14789940903572035

Raacke, J., & Bonds-Raacke, J. (2015). Are students really connected? Predicting college adjustment from social network usage. *Educational Psychology, 35*(7), 819–834. https://doi.org/10.1080/01443410.2013.814195

Rama, P. S., Black, R. W., Van Es, E., & Warschauer, M. (2012). Affordances for second language learning in *World of Warcraft*. *ReCALL, 24*, 322–338. https://doi.org/10.1017/S0958344012000171

Rankin, Y. A., Morrison, D., McNeal, M., Gooch, B., & Shute, M. W. (2009). Time will tell: In-game social interactions that facilitate second language acquisition. In *Proceedings of the 4th international conference on foundations of digital games* (pp. 161–168). ACM. https://doi.org/10.1145/1536513.1536546

Ranzini, G., & Lutz, C. (2017). Love at first swipe? Explaining Tinder self-presentation and motives. *Mobile Media & Communication, 5*(1), 80–101. https://doi.org/10.1177%2F2050157916664559

Reed, E., Salazar, M., Behar, A. I., Agah, N., Silverman, J. G., Minnis, A. M., Rusch, M. L. A., & Raj, A. (2019). Cyber sexual harassment: Prevalence and association with substance use, poor mental health, and STI history among sexually active adolescent girls. *Journal of Adolescence, 75*, 53–62. https://doi.org/10.1016/j.adolescence.2019.07.005

Ringrose, J., Regehr, K., & Whitehead, S. (2021). Teen girls' experiences negotiating the ubiquitous dick pic: Sexual double standards and the normalization of image based sexual harassment. *Sex Roles, 85*(9), 558–576. https://doi.org/10.1007/s11199-021-01236-3

Roberts, L. D., Smith, L. M., & Pollock, C. M. (2000). U ra lot bolder on the net. In W. R. Crozier (Ed.), *Shyness: Development, consolidation and change* (pp. 121–138). Routledge.

Rocha-Silva, T., Nogueira, C., & Rodrigues, L. (2021). Intimate abuse through technology: A systematic review of scientific constructs and behavioral dimensions. *Computers in Human Behavior*, 106861. https://doi.org/10.1016/j.chb.2021.106861

Rodríguez-deArriba, M. L., Nocentini, A., Menesini, E., & Sánchez-Jiménez, V. (2021). Dimensions and measures of cyber dating violence in adolescents: A systematic review. *Aggression and Violent Behavior*, 101613. https://doi.org/10.1016/j.avb.2021.101613

Rodríguez-Domínguez, C., Pérez-Moreno, P. J., & Durán, M. (2020). Ciberviolencia en las relaciones de pareja: Una revisión sobre su metodología de investigación [Cyber dating violence: A review of its research methodology]. *Anales de Psicología, 36*(2), 200–209. https://doi.org/10.6018/analesps.370451

Ruipérez, G., Castrillo, M. D., & García Cabrero, J. C. (2011). El uso de Twitter para mejorar la competencia de la expresión escrita en el aprendizaje de lenguas extranjeras. *Arbor, 187*, 159–163. https://doi.org/10.3989/arbor.2011.Extra-3n3138

Schiappa, E., Gregg, P. B., & Hewes, D. E. (2005). The parasocial contact hypothesis. *Communication Monographs*, *72*, 92–115.

Shane-Simpson, C., Manago, A., Gaggi, N., & Gillespie-Lynch, K. (2018). Why do college students prefer Facebook, Twitter, or Instagram? Site affordances, tensions between privacy and self-expression, and implications for social capital. *Computers in Human Behavior*, *86*, 276–288. https://doi.org/10.1016/j.chb.2018.04.041

Singh, D., Dixson, B. J., Jessop, T. S., Morgan, B., & Dixson, A. F. (2010). Cross-cultural consensus for waist–hip ratio and women's attractiveness. *Evolution and Human Behavior*, *31*, 176–181. https://doi.org/10.1016/j.evolhumbehav.2009.09.001

Smith, P. K., López-Castro, L., Robinson, S., & Görzig, A. (2019). Consistency of gender differences in bullying in cross-cultural surveys. *Aggression and Violent Behavior*, *45*, 33–40. https://doi.org/10.1016/j.avb.2018.04.006

Smoker, M., & March, E. (2017). Predicting perpetration of intimate partner cyberstalking: Gender and the Dark Tetrad. *Computers in Human Behavior*, *72*, 390–396. https://doi.org/10.1016/j.chb.2017.03.012

Spitzberg, B. H., & Cupach, W. R. (2007). The state of the art of stalking: Taking stock of the emerging literature. *Aggression and Violent Behavior*, *12*, 64–86. https://doi.org/10.1016/j.avb.2006.05.001

Ståhl, S., & Dennhag, I. (2021). Online and offline sexual harassment associations of anxiety and depression in an adolescent sample. *Nordic Journal of Psychiatry*, *75*(5), 330–335. https://doi.org/10.1080/08039488.2020.1856924

Standlee, A. (2019). Friendship and online filtering: The use of social media to construct offline social networks. *New Media & Society*, *21*(3), 770–785. https://doi.org/10.1177/1461444818806844

Stoicescu, M. V., Matei, S., & Rughinis, R. (2019). Sharing and privacy in dating apps. In *2019 22nd International Conference on Control Systems and Computer Science (CSCS)* (pp. 432–437). IEEE. https://doi.org/10.1109/CSCS.2019.00079

Stonard, K. E. (2019). Technology-assisted adolescent dating violence and abuse: A factor analysis of the nature of electronic communication technology used across twelve types of abusive and controlling behaviour. *Journal of Child and Family Studies*, *28*(1), 105–115. https://doi.org/10.1007/s10826-018-1255-5

Sumter, S. R., Vandenbosch, L., & Ligtenberg, L. (2017). Love me Tinder: Untangling emerging adults' motivations for using the dating application Tinder. *Telematics and Informatics*, *34*(1), 67–78. https://doi.org/10.1016/j.tele.2016.04.009

Thornburg, H. D. (1971). Peers: Three distinct groups. *Adolescence*, *6*(21), 59.

Thorne, S. L., & Fischer, I. (2012). Online gaming as sociable media. *Apprentissage des Langues et Systèmes d'Information et de Communication*, *15*. https://doi.org/10.4000/alsic.2450

Thulin, E., & Vilhelmson, B. (2009). Mobile phones: Transforming the everyday social communication practice of urban youth. In R. Ling & S. W. Campbell (Eds.), *The reconstruction of space and time: Mobile communication practices* (pp. 137–158). Routledge.

Timmermans, E., & Courtois, C. (2018). From swiping to casual sex and/or committed relationships: Exploring the experiences of Tinder users. *The Information Society*, *34*(2), 59–70. https://doi.org/10.1080/01972243.2017.1414093

Tinder. (2019). About Tinder. Retrieved from https://www.gotinder.com/press. Accessed on September 11, 2019.

Tokunaga, R. S. (2010). Following you home from school: A critical review and synthesis of research on cyberbullying victimization. *Computers in Human Behavior*, *26*(3), 277–287. https://doi.org/10.1016/j.chb.2009.11.014

Tokunaga, R. S. (2016). Interpersonal surveillance over social network sites: Applying a theory of negative relational maintenance and the investment model. *Journal of Social and Personal Relationships*, *33*(2), 171–190. https://doi.org/10.1177/0265407514568749
Trivers, R. L. (1972). Parental investment and sexual selection. In B. G. Campbell (Ed.), *Sexual selection and the descent of Man: The Darwinian pivot* (pp. 136–179). Routledge.
von Ahn, L. (2013). Duolingo: Learn a language for free while helping to translate the web. In *Proceedings of the 2013 International Conference on Intelligent User Interfaces* (pp. 1–2). ACM. https://doi.org/10.1145/2449396.2449398
Waasdorp, T. E., & Bradshaw, C. P. (2015). The overlap between cyberbullying and traditional bullying. *Journal of Adolescent Health*, *56*(5), 483–488. https://doi.org/10.1016/j.jadohealth.2014.12.002
Walther, J. B. (2014). Social information processing theory: Impressions and relationship development online. In D. O. Braithwaite & P. Schrodt (Eds.), *Engaging theories in interpersonal communication: Multiple perspectives* (2nd Ed., pp. 417–453). SAGE.
Wang, C. W., Musumari, P. M., Techasrivichien, T., Suguimoto, S. P., Tateyama, Y., Chan, C. C., … Nakayama, T. (2019). Overlap of traditional bullying and cyberbullying and correlates of bullying among Taiwanese adolescents: A cross-sectional study. *BMC Public Health*, *19*(1), 1–14. https://doi.org/10.1186/s12889-019-8116-z
Wehner, A. K., Gump, A. W., & Downey, S. (2011). The effects of Second Life on the motivation of undergraduate students learning a foreign language. *Computer Assisted Language Learning*, *24*, 277–289. https://doi.org/10.1080/09588221.2010.551757
White, F. A., Maunder, R., & Verrelli, S. (2020). Text-based E-contact: Harnessing cooperative Internet interactions to bridge the social and psychological divide. *European Review of Social Psychology*, *31*(1), 76–119. https://doi.org/10.1080/10463283.2020.1753459
Wollebæk, D., Karlsen, R., Steen-Johnsen, K., & Enjolras, B. (2019). Anger, fear, and echo chambers: The emotional basis for online behavior. *Social Media + Society*, *5*(2), 2056305119829859. https://doi.org/10.1177/2056305119829859
Wouters, P., Van Nimwegen, C., Van Oostendorp, H., & Van Der Spek, E. D. (2013). A meta-analysis of the cognitive and motivational effects of serious games. *Journal of Educational Psychology*, *105*(2), 249–265. https://doi.org/10.1037/a0031311
Wright, M. F. (2018). Cyberstalking victimization, depression, and academic performance: The role of perceived social support from parents. *Cyberpsychology, Behavior, and Social Networking*, *21*(2), 110–116. https://doi.org/10.1089/cyber.2016.0742
Yang, J., Barnidge, M., & Rojas, H. (2017). The politics of "unfriending": User filtration in response to political disagreement on social media. *Computers in Human Behavior*, *70*, 22–29. https://doi.org/10.1016/j.chb.2016.12.079
Zimmer-Gembeck, M. J. (2002). The development of romantic relationships and adaptations in the system of peer relationships. *Journal of Adolescent Health*, *31*(6), 216–225. https://doi.org/10.1016/S1054-139X(02)00504-9

5

CONCLUSION

5.1 Outline of the Argument

I started this book with a consideration of the moral panics that are often claimed to characterize worries about children's and young people's activities online. Cultural evolutionary considerations can potentially explain why moral panics so often focus on young people's activities – especially in relation to new cultural activities, including usage of new technology – since parents feel invested in teaching their children about existing cultural systems and may feel anxiety when faced with the prospect that the latter are spending so much of their time engaged in activities that the former know little about. I also showed that literature on digital moral panics has tended to assume that it is enough to label certain fears as a moral panic in order to dismiss them, without considering the real sources of the fears. Yet logically, the fact that some fears are mostly cultural in origin does not preclude that they may also be justified. In the rest of the book, I described some of the ways in which adolescents may be particularly vulnerable to risks online, as well as emphasizing that the risks of various kinds of new technology are still relatively unknown, and that such technologies may also bring great benefits as well.

As outlined in the introduction, perceived risks about children and young people's online activities can be divided into three main types, which broadly correspond to three interlinked areas of adolescent development. The first risk has to do with the effects of using internet technology in itself (encapsulated in the "screen time" debate), without considering the types of activities that someone is engaging in or who they are interacting with. This type of risk was mostly analyzed in Chapter 2, where I argued that in adolescence, people naturally construct their own independent identities, separate from the identities that they had

DOI: 10.4324/9781003019459-5

as children and which their parents (and other caregivers) are familiar with. This process of "identity separation" can cause parents to feel anxious about the kind of person that their child is becoming, a process exacerbated by the tendency of today's young people to speak a different language online, one in which visual tropes (including emojis and related phenomena, selfies, and memes) are of central importance. But the forging of a new (and newly visual) identity may also be associated with a genuine increase in problems such as depression, loneliness, social anxiety, and body image disorders in adolescents themselves. It is vital to bear in mind that these problems are not *caused* by social media use, but rather that they are/have always been particularly associated with adolescence, and are now being mediated by social media use and possibly exacerbated by them (or not) depending on many different individual and contextual variables. Moreover, as we saw, online modalities can also contribute to helping resolve these problems, since cyberpsychological interventions may be particularly suited to young people's needs, because of their greater anonymity and constant availability, and their audience's very familiarity with internet use.

A key part of adolescents' new identity online is their generation and consumption of new forms of cultural content, which are often poorly understood by their elders. Here the anxiety over separation from children is augmented by fears over the unfamiliar directions in which cultural change is occurring, leading to some particularly powerful moral panics, such as those over violent video games and extreme pornography. We saw that the evidence for the harmful effects of such content is not strong, but that nevertheless, many different studies have found consistent problems. Although we cannot be sure that this effect is not a result of questionable research practices, my personal feeling (along with that of many other researchers) is that it is more likely that there is a small real effect in a few vulnerable people, who may also be more predisposed to consume such material (leading to problems in separating causation from correlation), but that such material does not cause harm to the great majority of the population. Moreover, given the deep psychological roots of the fears over new content, it may be difficult to convince people, especially in older generations, that it is entirely harmless. Thus, rather than arguing endlessly over whether there is a real overall effect or not, it would seem more productive to focus on working out how best to help people who feel that they (or those close to them) have real problems in this area.

As well as constructing their own separate identities and new cultural worlds, young people also learn to form new relationships as they move through adolescence, a process that obviously bears its own risks, including to mental health. The reorganization of social relations in pre-adolescence and early adolescence creates the potential for increased levels of conflict (with peers, siblings, and parents, as well as the wider society), which can have harmful psychological effects. Adolescents may attempt to avoid conflicts with new friends by "vetting" them with an analysis of their social media presence before committing to spend much time offline with them – however, it is important not to overstate the extent to which this results in the development of "echo chambers" in their social groups. A similar (or perhaps even more rigorous) vetting process applies to dating decisions, of course, and we saw that dating and hookup apps such as Tinder blend visual and textual affordances as young people try to use them to attract mates, in ways that recall the hybrid visual/textual modalities of emojis, selfies, and memes described in Chapter 2. Since adolescents are unused to managing sex and romance and the strong emotions that result, new romantic relationships at this age are particularly fraught with risks (particularly for adolescent girls and young women, it must be said), and research in this area would benefit from more mixed-methods studies that include qualitative analysis of victims' and perpetrators' lived experiences alongside quantitative analysis of risk factors, as well as more generally accepted ethical procedures to ensure that such data can safely be gathered from people below the age of sexual consent. Finally, both cyberdating abuse and cyberbullying involve certain factors that may exacerbate the harms done to victims, compared to the equivalent offline behaviors: factors such as the potential to abuse a victim at any time or any place; reduced inhibitions of the abuser/bully due to their perceived anonymity; and the amplification of shame felt by the victim by exposing them to a huge audience online. More systematic quantitative research also needs to be done to isolate the effects of these factors and analyze whether they really make cyberabuse and cyberbullying more harmful than their offline equivalents, given that cyberattacks generally involve less potential for physical harm.

Pending such better-quality qualitative and quantitative data (and perhaps even after we have it), I would suggest that we stop engaging in incessant "Culture Wars"–style arguments about whether there are risks for adolescents of using certain kinds of technology, and how serious they are. We should start by recognizing that adolescents have always been a particularly vulnerable group to many kinds of psychological risks, but also that there have always been unreasonable fears about what "the youth of today" is up to; and that the internet is changing both phenomena in ways that could theoretically make them worse. Dismissing the risks – and adults' real fears – altogether, as "moral panics", does not seem to me to be a sensible way of alleviating them. Rather than leaving adolescents to confront these possible risks alone, we could instead aim to minimize the risks that confront them, today (leaving aside the question of whether they are more serious now than in the past!) while augmenting the possible benefits of online interactions for young people. (One important possible benefit, described at the end of Chapter 4, is the capacity for contact between young people of different ethnic, cultural, demographic, and linguistic backgrounds to take place online: perhaps both technology companies and educational institutions could be more proactive in arranging "online exchange" opportunities for adolescents, taking advantage of the natural flexibility in their identity and the fluidity in their membership of social groups.)

In the next section, I try to build on the above argument by formulating a few basic recommendations for researchers, parents, educators, industry, and government, to try to help them reduce the risks and increase the benefits of online interactions.

5.2 Recommendations

There are many different recommendations that could be made for researchers working in the area of online risks and opportunities for young people. As well as those highlighted in this section, some are mentioned at various points in the three central chapters of the book. I also highly recommend the article of Kaye et al. (2020) – discussed briefly in Chapter 2 – which further elaborates on many of the points that I make here, and makes some additional suggestions for researchers in this area.

One way in which progress has already been made, but much more remains to be made, is in the generation of hypotheses using established theoretical frameworks. In the early days of cyberpsychology, and of various social networks and electronic technologies, hypotheses tended to be rather ad hoc, which may have contributed to a lack of replicability in study findings, and thus a lack of strong effects in meta-analyses (such as we have seen for debates like those around screen time and the link between violent video games and aggression). An example of theoretically driven hypothesis elaboration in my own work is the use of evolutionary psychology to generate hypotheses in a systematic way in Piazza and Ingram (2015; building on earlier ideas in Piazza & Bering, 2009; see also McAndrew & Jeong, 2012, for some exemplary practical testing of similar evolutionary hypotheses). There is no reason why a similar exercise could not take place for other schools of psychological theory. Different psychological theories could also be integrated into process models of young people's online behavior, such as the one set out in Ingram (2020). Instead of simply regressing various sets of predictor variables on a dependent variable in a cross-sectional analysis, the point of such process models is to understand how different moderator variables relate together longitudinally in their effects on a dependent variable, in ways that make theoretical sense. At the moment, it is true that few studies in this area have really produced strong effects even when including moderator variables; but with more high-quality longitudinal or experimental studies and better measures (more observational, less self-reported) of dependent variables, that may change.

Another way in which the quality of studies in this area can be improved is by more targeted sampling of vulnerable populations, since for most of these debates, we do not care so much about effects in the normal range of the outcome variables. In the case of vulnerability to violent video games or pornography, one candidate for such a group would be individuals with callous-unemotional traits, such as those studied by Olivera-La Rosa et al. (2021). In the case of self-esteem and Instagram usage, a candidate group would be individuals with body dysmorphia or other body image issues (Ryding & Kuss, 2020). In all such cases, it is also imperative to conduct more mixed-methods studies to access participants' lived experiences and try to relate these to the quantitative measures used, which otherwise may be of uncertain operational value in terms of relatability to people's lives (Parada & Ingram, 2022, is a simple example of this for loneliness). The goal of cyberpsychological research should be less about demonstrating (or disproving) a general link between internet use and wellbeing-related variables in simple terms, and more about obtaining data that can help people who feel that they or those close to them have problems with internet use. I suggest that the scheme introduced in this book of analyzing risk in terms of identity, content and relationships can have particular value in these kinds of mixed-method studies, by helping researchers to think about the problematic aspects of a young person's identity (e.g., in connection with addiction issues); how these relate to the kinds of content they are consuming online; and, separately, the new social interactions that are taking place at these ages, and the risks inherent in those.

Given the conceptual confusion and lack of strong, replicable effects in the literature, the area of risks and opportunities in adolescents' internet use is a particularly difficult one for which to make clear recommendations to parents. But a good starting point might be the usual guidelines given for authoritative parenting (Klein & Ballantine, 2001), which has been found to be linked to a wide variety of positive outcomes (e.g., on self-esteem) for children in many different study designs over the last 50 years (see, e.g., Pinquart & Gerke, 2019). Authoritative parenting involves two key elements: honestly expressing one's emotions to one's children and allowing them to express theirs; and setting limits on children's behavior that are clearly communicated to them, with the possibility of negotiating changes to these limits if the situation changes. Translated to online contexts, this means setting some sort of limits on adolescent's use of electronic devices, with the actual nature of the limits probably being less important than the simple fact of setting them in the first place (though examples of appropriate limits could be forbidding the use of smartphones during communal mealtimes or before the teenager is ready for school, or of games consoles after bedtime). But it also means communicating honestly and openly about these limits, the reasons for them, how both sides could feel if they are broken, and the circumstances in which exceptions could be negotiated (see Boniel-Nissim et al., 2020, for an example of positive effects of authoritative parenting style in the area of pornography use).

A lot of this communication (and indeed a lot of communication about other matters as well) should take place online, in order to connect with the adolescent's own online world; and while this may not be for all parents, it is probably healthy in many families for parents to engage in game-playing with adolescents as well (Musick et al., 2021). As we saw in Chapter 2, it is also a good idea for parents to focus more on *positively* providing adolescents with plenty of fun, engaging, worthwhile offline activities – in addition to technological resources – than on *negatively* restricting the amount of time they spend online. Finally, bearing in mind the various risk factors identified in the previous three chapters, organized by identity, content, and relationships, parents should watch out for warning signs, such as a particular technological activity totally dominating the identity of an adolescent in problematic ways, to the exclusion of other activities; obsessive use of certain types of problematic content, which may in certain cases require monitoring of their internet usage; and contact with suspicious individuals, which may also require monitoring, or at least asking the adolescent whom they are talking to. In all of these cases, if parents are worried about the identity, content, or relationships of their child online, they are recommended to browse reputable reputable online information services and, if necessary, contact competent counseling services.

As well as parents, educators of course need to share some of the responsibility for protecting adolescents against risks online. Education about online risks should go beyond clichés about "stranger danger", thinking in particular of the risks from online relationships (Dedkova, 2015). We saw in Chapter 4 how problems with online sexual harassment, cyberstalking, revenge porn, and sextortion are more likely to come from individuals (typically ex-partners) known offline, who are usually around the same age or a little older, than from the stereotypical middle-aged, "catfishing" adult male abuser of popular imagination. Yet my impression is that schools often shy away from talking about problems with sexual relationships between adolescents, and even more so when referring to problems that take place online. More work needs to be done by academics and policymakers to help schools educate teens about online relationship risks in more open and evidence-based ways.

As we saw in Chapter 4, this should include pointing out that certain forms of problematic sexual behavior online (e.g., sextortion) are neither very rare nor very widespread: thus, victims should not blame themselves for having suffered from them, nor should potential perpetrators feel that they might be acceptable within their peer group. The same goes for certain dangerous forms of online content and the risks of becoming addicted to them (or dependent on them, if you dislike the word "addicted" in this context). Dealing with online addiction/dependency might require a deep discussion of psychosocial changes in adolescent identity with time, which in my experience is something that almost never takes place in schools, but could potentially be of great value to young people in understanding the changes they are going through and helping them to deal with them. Moving beyond risks, another hugely important way in which schools could help adolescents is by providing them with real opportunities for technology-based learning. Despite all the progress that has been made with integrating computers into the classroom, schools are still somewhat behind the times and need to make strides with incorporating smartphones in general – and social networks such as Instagram and WhatsApp in particular – into the teaching process and the homework that students are assigned.

In terms of setting educational policy, government clearly has a role to play in the above processes as well, by introducing explanations of online risks and exploitation of online opportunities into the official curricula. It also has a vital role in encouraging more joined-up work between academics, private companies, and educational stakeholders (parent groups, schools, and administrative officials) to properly evaluate such programs, and in mandating the collection of open data on adolescents' experiences with technology. Less positively, perhaps, but still importantly, I do think there is room for government regulation to protect minors from certain kinds of extreme content. Back in the pre-internet days, there seemed to be a consensus that age guidelines on movies and video games were a good thing. These have now been rendered obsolete by the ready availability of extreme material on the internet; but it would not be beyond the bounds of possibility for governments to require age-appropriate labeling on websites, apps, streamed videos, and online games, and even require age verification – for example, using a credit card – for content labeled as over-18. (This could be problematic in countries such as the United States that place a high value on freedom of speech – though even there, banning porn for under-18s regularly commands the support of a majority of people surveyed in opinion polls; Lehman, 2019). Governments could and should also enforce tougher criminal sanctions against adult individuals who carry out the sorts of online abuses described in Chapter 4.

These forms of regulatory control are likely to work better than self-regulation by industry; nevertheless, industry still has a role to play in designing automated algorithms to protect minors, by steering them away from extreme content, warning them of dangerous interactions online, and also highlighting tendencies toward obsessive or addictive behavior (perhaps even also warning an adult caregiver about these problems). All of this seems technologically feasible, and there would seem to be little ethical downside, given that parents or guardians in theory should be giving their consent for activities that minors under their protection engage in outside their care. If companies like Google and Meta can use algorithms to sell us products that they think might interest us, they can also use them to protect our children proactively from experiences that might upset or even harm them.

5.3 Complications of COVID-19

Formulating all these recommendations for such varied groups of educational stakeholders, in an area as complex as the risks and opportunities that exist for adolescents online, would be difficult enough without an event from early 2020 onward that shook the world and transformed most people's use of digital technology: the COVID-19 pandemic. Early 2020 was also when I began to write this book. If the restrictions, psychological buffetings, and need to adapt to new virtual working practices hugely complicated the writing process, they also encouraged some reflections about the profound changes the pandemic is likely to have caused (or, in many ways, accelerated) in young people's use of new technology.

One of the most obvious changes is that the notorious "screen time rules", discussed in Chapter 2, have surely gone out the window for most parents. As Nagata et al. put it in 2020, "given current laws and policies during COVID-19, rises in screen time may be inevitable and even beneficial for education and socialization" (p. 1582). They also pointed out that this is particularly true when parents are working from home, since in many cases it is not feasible for them to micromanage children's activities while they are working. Given the realities of COVID-related lockdowns, it is not clear that the use of screens was so negative in its effects compared to alternatives that would still have involved a sedentary lifestyle (such as book-reading); and even obesity could be combated by using smartphones to run fitness apps or watch exercise videos. Nevertheless, while lockdowns are (hopefully) a thing of the past, there remains the slightly worrying possibility that average screen time may have gone up more or less permanently as a result of the pandemic, as people formed new screen-related habits that became hard to change. It will be interesting to look at the results of longitudinal studies on such changes in screen time, and their psychological effects, in the years to come.

One content-related change that is likely to have lasting impact in educational circles is the switch to virtual methods of teaching, especially using video-conferencing. This was ubiquitous during the strictest lockdowns, of course, and could have been used as an opportunity to flexiblize teaching delivery by introducing more blended learning (Hrastinski, 2019; Mali & Lim, 2021). However, the indications are that there has been something of a rush to get "back to normal" by reinstating face-to-face pedagogy, and it is as yet unclear to what extent schools and universities will continue using videoconferencing and related technologies if not required to by legally enforced lockdowns. In this respect, we can see the familiar lag between working environments and educational environments, since many workplaces have adopted more flexible practices regarding remote working even outside official lockdowns (Alexander et al., 2021), and this trend looks set to continue in the short and even medium term. What is certainly lacking is the kind of integrated vision described at the end of Chapter 3, of incorporating teaching into the tools such as Instagram, TikTok, and WhatsApp that adolescents are really spending time on. This is a real pity, since doing so could raise students' academic self-concept (Byrne, 1996), potentially helping to protect their performance in the uncertain post-COVID age (Ramirez et al., 2021).

One final area, relating in particular to social relationships, in which social networks and other online technologies were undoubtedly beneficial during the pandemic, was in helping to combat the intense loneliness and isolation that so many people, especially young people, felt during this time (Bonsaksen et al., 2021; Bu et al., 2020; Lisitsa et al., 2020; Parada & Ingram, 2022). There is a paradox here, however, in that while these technologies may well have diminished levels of loneliness during the pandemic, they also have the potential to increase social isolation after the pandemic if people stick with behavioral patterns that they learned during lockdowns. Again, careful longitudinal analysis will be necessary in order to disentangle these kinds of effects.

5.4 The Future of Online Interactions

What can we say about future changes in online interactions, risks, and opportunities for young people? One thing that seems clear is that the trend toward more and more visual communication, described in Chapter 2, will continue and probably intensify, with increasing use of video-based networks such as TikTok, Instagram Reels, and YouTube Shorts (Shutsko, 2020). While this will not necessarily involve negative effects on mental health – many adolescents will find positive ways of projecting their image via short videos – longitudinal studies should examine whether there are differences in the outcomes of those teenagers who spend a lot of time publishing in the short video form and those who do not, because in theory this activity could have far-reaching effects on the development of self-image in adolescents.

An important content-related change – whether educational institutions like it or not – is likely to be the further integration of social media and video communications into pedagogical practices, partly due to the natural creativity of teachers and partly in order to keep up with the recent move toward much more flexible, partially online working practices. The same will likely be true of online health-seeking behaviors, such as the search for information and support around topics such as diet, exercise, and mental health issues (Popovac & Roomaney, 2021). Hopefully both developments can lead to more positive and educational experiences for adolescents online, balancing out some of the more problematic virtual content that they are frequently exposed to.

Away from educational domains, adolescents' social lives have been transformed by what Nesi et al. (2021) call a "seismic shift" in adolescents' peer relationships: "The advent of social media has profoundly reshaped youths' social worlds, with social media platforms now representing a primary context in which peer experiences occur" (p. 3). As I have done here, these authors argue that existing social experiences that were already quintessentially important to adolescence – such as peer status, peer influence, and peer victimization – have been transformed by the move to largely online forms of interaction. However, an element missing from Nesi et al.'s review is the transformational effect that adolescent adoption of social media (and other forms of new technology) has had on their relationships with older generations in general, and their parents in particular. In contrast to the enabling effect that moving online has had on peer relationships, the effect on parents has been more alienating, as they have to come to terms with their teenage children forming their own identity, speaking their own language, consuming their own content, and engaging in their own relationships online – none of which most parents born before the 1990s can easily understand or relate to.

As we have seen, this sense of alienation probably contributes to a lot of the heat around the "moral panics" that surround the adoption of new technology, while also exacerbating psychosocial risks for adolescents as they become separated from parental protection and begin to make their own way in the online world. However, the pace of technological change is probably slowing (Karpf, 2019), and the alienation between parents and adolescents is likely to diminish as the first generation to grow up with social media raises children in the years to come. This forecast does not absolve us of the responsibility to seriously analyze the risks and work to help people who have issues associated with using new technology in the here and now. But perhaps such problems are less often the causes and more often symptoms of problems with healthy social adjustment in adolescence.

References

Alexander, A., De Smet, A., Langstaff, M., & Ravid, D. (2021). *What employees are saying about the future of remote work*. McKinsey. Retrieved from https://fortcollinschamber.com/wp-content/uploads/2021/04/What-employees-are-saying-about-the-future-of-remote-work-Final.pdf

Boniel-Nissim, M., Efrati, Y., & Dolev-Cohen, M. (2020). Parental mediation regarding children's pornography exposure: The role of parenting style, protection motivation and gender. *Journal of Sex Research*, *57*, 42–51. https://doi.org/10.1080/00224499.2019.1590795

Bonsaksen, T., Ruffolo, M., Leung, J., Price, D., Thygesen, H., Schoultz, M., & Geirdal, A. Ø. (2021). Loneliness and its association with social media use during the COVID-19 outbreak. *Social Media + Society*, 7(3), 20563051211033821. https://doi.org/10.1177/20563051211033821

Bu, F., Steptoe, A., & Fancourt, D. (2020). Who is lonely in lockdown? Cross-cohort analyses of predictors of loneliness before and during the COVID-19 pandemic. *Public Health*, *186*, 31–34. https://doi.org/10.1016/j.puhe.2020.06.036

Byrne, B. M. (1996). Academic self-concept: Its structure, measurement, and relation to academic achievement. In B. A. Bracken (Ed.), *Handbook of self-concept: Developmental, social, and clinical considerations* (pp. 287–316). Wiley.

Dedkova, L. (2015). Stranger is not always danger: The myth and reality of meetings with online strangers. In *Living in the digital age: Self-presentation, networking, playing, and participating in politics* (pp. 78–94). Masaryk Univerzity.

Hrastinski, S. (2019). What do we mean by blended learning? *TechTrends*, *63*(5), 564–569. https://doi.org/10.1007/s11528-019-00375-5

Ingram, G. P. D. (2020). Influence of age, gender and personality on young adolescents' reporting of online risks to third parties. *Computers in Human Behavior Reports*, *2*, 100040. https://doi.org/10.1016/j.chbr.2020.100040

Karpf, D. (2019). Something I no longer believe: Is Internet time slowing down? *Social Media + Society*, *5*(3), 2056305119849492. https://doi.org/10.1177%2F2056305119849492

Kaye, L. K., Orben, A., Ellis, D. A., Hunter, S. C., & Houghton, S. (2020). The conceptual and methodological mayhem of "screen time". *International Journal of Environmental Research and Public Health*, *17*, 3661. https://doi.org/10.3390/ijerph17103661

Klein, H. A., & Ballantine, J. (2001). For parents particularly: Raising competent kids: The authoritative parenting style. *Childhood Education*, *78*, 46–47. https://doi.org/10.1080/00094056.2001.10521689

Lehman, C. F. (2019). *What do Americans think about banning porn?* Institute for Family Studies. https://ifstudies.org/blog/what-do-americans-think-about-banning-porn

Lisitsa, E., Benjamin, K. S., Chun, S. K., Skalisky, J., Hammond, L. E., & Mezulis, A. H. (2020). Loneliness among young adults during covid-19 pandemic: The mediational roles of social media use and social support seeking. *Journal of Social and Clinical Psychology*, *39*(8), 708–726. https://doi.org/10.1521/jscp.2020.39.8.708

Mali, D., & Lim, H. (2021). How do students perceive face-to-face/blended learning as a result of the Covid-19 pandemic? *International Journal of Management Education*, *19*(3), 100552. https://doi.org/10.1016/j.ijme.2021.100552

McAndrew, F. T., & Jeong, H. S. (2012). Who does what on Facebook? Age, sex, and relationship status as predictors of Facebook use. *Computers in Human Behavior*, *28*, 2359–2365. https://doi.org/10.1016/j.chb.2012.07.007

Musick, G., Freeman, G., & McNeese, N. J. (2021). Gaming as family time: Digital game co-play in modern parent-child relationships. *Proceedings of the ACM on Human-Computer Interaction* (*CHI PLAY*), *5*, 1–25. https://doi.org/10.1145/3474678

Nagata, J. M., Magid, H. S. A., & Gabriel, K. P. (2020). Screen time for children and adolescents during the coronavirus disease 2019 pandemic. *Obesity*, *28*(9), 1582–1583. https://doi.org/10.1002/oby.22917

Nesi, J., Dredge, R., Maheux, A. J., Roberts, S. R., Fox, K. A., & Choukas-Bradley, S. (2021). Peer experiences via social media. To appear in *The Encyclopedia of Child and Adolescent Health*. Elsevier. Preprint retrieved from https://psyarxiv.com/s8mru/

Olivera-La Rosa, A., Chuquichambi, E. G., Carmona, C. A., Arango-Tobón, O. E., Amador, O., Rosselló, J., & Ingram, G. P. D. (2021). The "Joker" laugh: Social judgments towards affective deviants in a sample of young offenders with callous unemotional traits. *Personality and Individual Differences*, *183*, 111148. https://doi.org/10.1016/j.paid.2021.111148

Parada, V., & Ingram, G. P. D. (2022). *Instagram and loneliness: Young Colombian adults' uses and perception of Instagram during the COVID-19 pandemic.* Manuscript Under Review.

Piazza, J. R., & Bering, J. M. (2009). Evolutionary cyber-psychology: Applying an evolutionary framework to Internet behavior. *Computers in Human Behavior*, *25*, 1258–1269. https://doi.org/10.1016/j.chb.2009.07.002

Piazza, J. R., & Ingram, G. P. D. (2015). Evolutionary cyberpsychology 2.0: Revisiting some old predictions and posting some new ones in the age of Facebook. In Lisa L. M. Welling, Todd K. Shackelford, & Virgil Zeigler-Hill (Eds.), *Evolutionary perspectives on social psychology* (pp. 159–174). Springer. https://doi.org/10.1007/978-3-319-12697-5_13

Pinquart, M., & Gerke, D. C. (2019). Associations of parenting styles with self-esteem in children and adolescents: A meta-analysis. *Journal of Child and Family Studies*, *28*, 2017–2035. https://doi.org/10.1007/s10826-019-01417-5

Popovac, M., & Roomaney, R. (2021). Measuring online health-seeking behaviour: Construction and initial validation of a new scale. *British Journal of Health Psychology*, *12571*. https://doi.org/10.1111/bjhp.12571

Ramirez, S., Aldunate, M. P., Arriagada, C., Bueno, M., Cuevas, F., González, X., Araya, R., & Gaete, J. (2021). The association between educational experiences and Covid-19 pandemic-related variables, and mental health among children and adolescents. *Frontiers in Psychiatry*, *12*, 647456. https://doi.org/10.3389%2Ffpsyt.2021.647456

Ryding, F. C., & Kuss, D. J. (2020). The use of social networking sites, body image dissatisfaction, and body dysmorphic disorder: A systematic review of psychological research. *Psychology of Popular Media*, *9*, 412–435. https://doi.org/10.1037/ppm0000264

Shutsko, A. (2020). User-generated short video content in social media: A case study of TikTok. In *International Conference on Human-Computer Interaction* (pp. 108–125). Springer.

INDEX

For Product Safety Concerns and Information please contact our EU
representative GPSR@taylorandfrancis.com
Taylor & Francis Verlag GmbH, Kaufingerstraße 24, 80331 München, Germany

www.ingramcontent.com/pod-product-compliance
Ingram Content Group UK Ltd.
Pitfield, Milton Keynes, MK11 3LW, UK
UKHW020135200926
475702UK00005B/764
* 9 7 8 0 3 6 7 8 9 4 8 2 5 *